THE AUTOBIOGRAPHY OF
A HUNTED PRIEST

THE AUTOBIOGRAPHY
OF A HUNTED PRIEST

JOHN GERARD, S.J.

Translated from the Latin by
Philip Caraman, S.J.

IGNATIUS PRESS   SAN FRANCISCO

Cover art:
Edward Oldcorne and Nicholas Owen by Gaspar Bouttats
line engraving, mid-17th century
©National Portrait Gallery, London

Cover design by John Herreid

Published 2012 by Ignatius Press, San Francisco
Introduction by James V. Schall ©2012 by Ignatius Press, San Francisco
All rights reserved
ISBN 978-1-58617-450-7 (PB)
ISBN 978-1-68149-046-5 (eBook)
Library of Congress Control Number 2011940705
Printed in the United States of America ∞

FOR M. C. D'ARCY

CONTENTS

INTRODUCTION

In my early years in the Society of Jesus, I recall that this book, *The Autobiography of a Hunted Priest*, was read at table from the 1950 edition of Father Caraman. At the time, it struck me as an ecclesiastical adventure story with a rather happy ending—that is, John Gerard, its author, finally managed in 1606 to escape from England to Belgium without being, like so many of his Jesuit friends, hung, drawn, and quartered. This was that most brutal way the English Protestant establishment chose to enforce its will. Gerard died a normal death in the English College in Rome in 1637. On first listening to it, the book also struck me as describing a persecution of Catholics that could not happen here. One is no longer quite so sure. It may, in fact, be a very up-to-date book in its own way.

On October 5, 1597, Gerard is famous for having managed to escape from the maximum-security Tower of London prison by lowering himself down its walls with a rope. He eluded capture often enough, though not always. He was tortured brutally. In the England of this period the last quarter of the 1500s, it was against the law to be a priest. The English Jesuits with members of other Orders and diocesan clergy who remained faithful to the Catholic tradition often found refuge with various Catholic families. Indeed, the most moving sections of this account often are those of faithful men and women who tried to protect and hide priests. Many of these good folks quite literally "laid down their lives" for their priest-friends and the truths they stood for.

The effort to provide "hiding holes" in large mansions and houses where priests could be invisible to pursuivants is famous. The ingenious way that these hiding places were constructed so that even the most diligent agents of the police could not find them is part of the drama of this book. When priests were found hiding, often the reason for finding them was not because of faulty construction but because someone betrayed them to the authorities. The Judas theme is also in this book. The subtleties of persecution were such that Catholic families whose houses were investigated had to pay the agents of their enemies for the searching of their own homes.

The *Autobiography* does not spare any sensitivity about the utter brutality of the English Protestants determined to stamp out the traditional faith of the English people. Yet, the acceptance of martyrdom often does reveal a certain almost lightsomeness in serving the Lord in this way. The seminaries on the European continent, where young Englishmen were educated to return home, were filled with men who were under no illusions. They knew what was in store for them if they were captured on their return to their homeland. They knew many were taken by authorities. The list of English martyrs from this period is long and distinguished—Southwell, Campion, Olgive, Fisher, to name but a few.

This noble record, of course, must be understood in the light of the fact that Catholicism was largely eliminated in these and following decades. All the bishops but one went over to the Church of England. The legal penalties against Catholics lasted into the nineteenth century and in some minor form still exist. The visit of Pope Benedict XVI to England in 2010 was a poignant reminder of how difficult reconciliation, forgiveness, acceptance, and truth come together even after so many centuries. The Church of England is but a shadow of its former self.

Still these young priests in Europe did return. They understood that they were to do what they could to serve the Catholics and to convert back those who had lapsed. One cannot but be surprised at the amount of spiritual direction, retreats, and instructions that Gerard gave to all sorts of people in these constrained circumstances. Life under persecution did not interfere with the spiritual life of those persecuted, but in many ways enhanced it.

In the tradition of Thomas More, we also have here a clear carrying out of the Catholic teaching about politics and faith under persecution. The Jesuits were under orders not to involve themselves in politics. They were there to serve God and provide the sacraments. They made this distinction between faith and politics that was not, of course, shared by the Protestants. The Protestant establishment did follow the letter of the common law. If someone was to be tortured, a writ of authority was needed. If evidence could not be provided, the detained were released. Many of the most dramatic passages in Gerard's account have to do with torture, law, and evidence against men and women who would not betray their friends or their faith.

Another striking aspect of this book is how clearly those English Jesuits and other priests drew the line between what was permissible for them and what was not. The famous issue of equivocation comes up here—that is, does one have to tell the literal truth when one is being unjustly questioned. If an ambiguous answer can follow from the question, it is not the fault of the one being persecuted if the authorities misunderstand the answers that the state has no right to ask.

Gerard was finally ordered by his religious superiors to write his memoirs. This is what we read here. Belloc once said that the only way we could save such graphic experiences so that they do not slip away altogether is to write of them. Without this rather charming account of Gerard's experiences during the English persecution of the Catholic Church we would not be able to imagine so well its nature and scope. His Jesuit superiors were prescient in obliging him to tell us what he saw.

We have here the classic case of a government changing the religion of its heritage and people. To do this, it passes laws and sanctions designed to stamp this traditional religion out. The lesson of the English reformation is not that it cannot be done. Its lesson is that it can be in this culture or that. For those who think that governments can do no wrong, this account makes sober reading, unless of course we hold that this religion should be stamped out.

Gerard implies that the one thing the Lord requires of us, even in persecution, is persistence in virtue and faithfulness of belief and sacrament. For this cause, many good priests and laymen gave their lives. They were officially "traitors" to their country even though they stood for what the country traditionally stood for. In fact, they were closer to Socrates and Christ. They gave their lives so that others could believe and live. We are still in their debt. Ultimate sacrifices of life and limb in the name of truth do not always "win" in this world. None of the men depicted here, including John Gerard himself, ever thought that it would.

—Father James V. Schall
Georgetown University
Feast of the Archangels
September 29, 2011

TRANSLATOR'S PREFACE

In his own preface, John Gerard says that he wrote this account of his eighteen years in England at the order of his Superiors. This order was probably given in the spring of 1609, four years after the execution of Henry Garnet, the last event mentioned in the text. At that time Gerard, who had now recovered from the physical and mental strain of his last months in England, was living in Louvain, where he was helping to train the English novices of the Society of Jesus for the mission he had just left. We do not know the origin of the order, but it is probable that in his conversation with his novices Gerard frequently told anecdotes of hunted priests, of torture, and the everyday heroism of his friends among the English laity; and that one of his hearers had the happy idea of suggesting to the General of the Jesuits that he should write an account of his missionary life in England.

It is clear from the text that Gerard was writing a private account of his adventures for his fellow Jesuits and perhaps, in the first place, for the novices under his direction. Consequently, several passages show a complacency and almost a naïve *esprit de corps*, natural enough in the atmosphere of a novitiate, but slightly out of place in a work destined to be read by a wider public. With truthfulness Gerard insists that there were many priests whose achievement in England was more remarkable than his; and on this account he was reluctant to narrate his own experiences. Moreover, he was a man of action; and his early education in letters had been interrupted by sickness, prison, and constant change. Although, as he says himself, he was "ashamed of his Latin"; he wrote in that language in order, perhaps, to make his story available to his foreign friends who had assisted the English community on the Continent. Fortunately for the translator, his Latin is the serviceable and unadorned Latin of ecclesiastical correspondence, and turns readily into the English idiom of an English writer.

At first reading it might seem that Gerard had an undue interest in converts drawn from the noble and wealthy classes; and this charge was, in fact, brought against him in his own lifetime by the apostate priest Watson. No recovery of the open countryside to Catholicism, however, was possible without the technique which Gerard so brilliantly developed. In the counties in which Gerard worked it would have been folly for a stranger with no means of livelihood to have installed himself in a small house or cottage and attempted the work of a priest among people who knew all their neighbors' business. As Gerard and every English priest knew from experience, to lead a simple life among the common people was to invite arrest. It was only the great houses that could provide sheltered accommodation and, with their constant flow of guests, give a safe cover to occasional small gatherings of Catholics and to frequent callers in need of a priest's help. In these circumstances the extent of the priest's activity depended in the main on the willingness of his hosts to face the same risks as himself and to share his work. Their zeal was the measure of his effectiveness. For it was only as a gentleman of fashion in company with other gentlemen that a priest could move about without danger of being questioned; and he consequently depended on his host to ride out with him, to make up hunting parties of likely converts and, after careful enquiry, to introduce him without risk into the society of the neighborhood. In many instances lay-folk subordinated their whole social lives to the priest's activity, sacrificing even the privacy of their homes in order to ensure him a safe hiding [place]. This called for the pursuit of high Christian perfection, and Gerard did not hesitate to demand it of his friends. In their devotion to the work of assisting him, Gerard's friends among the gentry found a substitute for the religious life which was no longer possible for them in their own country.

On the other hand, there were priests, like William Wiseman's first chaplain, who were maintained in a remote corner of the house and scarcely ventured abroad except for a sick call at night. If such a priest was expected to be unobtrusive and take no step which might compromise or inconvenience his host, there was little that he could do, no matter how great his zeal. It was only when the fire of enthusiasm caught the gentry that the priest's work became spectacular. In East Anglia, in Northamptonshire, Oxfordshire, and Buckinghamshire, Gerard with the aid of his lay helpers opened up a great mission field, which was later developed by both Jesuits and secular priests. It is clear that under Garnet's wise direction Gerard made this his special work and was outstandingly successful. It was only after he had lived many months in Norfolk that he seems to have met his first fellow priest, an old man and a survivor from Queen Mary's reign; yet at the time of his leaving England there were at least twelve Jesuits and perhaps more secular priests "doing good work" from stations he had established in East Anglia.

The Latin text of Gerard's *Autobiography* has been used by historians of the Society of Jesus from the early seventeenth century; but it was only eighty years ago that the first English translation was published by Father John Morris. It is an exact translation, but its English is dated, particularly as it attempted to turn Gerard's Latin into Elizabethan English. In making a new translation I have inserted all the passages which Father Morris omitted, either because he considered them indelicate or because they referred to disputes which were still a live issue in his own day. When Gerard describes the Archpriest Controversy, as it is called, as a quarrel between the Jesuits and a "group of restless priests", he is making a distinction between the great body of secular clergy and a mischief-making clique. Though the full story of the controversy has yet to be written, it is now clear that Gerard's distinction is exact. In not a few cases the leaders of this group were men living in comfortable exile, enjoying foreign benefices and never sharing even for a day in the hardships of their brethren on the mission. Others lived in England without molestation under the safe-conduct of a Government which used them to foment dissension in the Catholic body. Inevitably this group favored an understanding with the Government on terms which the recusants were unable to reconcile with their consciences, and which betrayed the position taken up in the first instance by Saint Thomas More and Saint John Fisher. The view of Gerard was the true recusant view: that no discussion was possible until the Government showed evidence of a sincere desire to respect the consciences of Catholics—to dispense them from attendance at Protestant services, to allow them at least limited facilities to attend Mass and educate their children in their own religion. On the assumption that compromise on these points was out of the question, Gerard and the great body of secular clergy exhorted patience and kept out of ecclesiastical politics.

Gerard makes only passing references to the controversy and mentions the factious priest only when he plays a part in his own story. Yet to Gerard, to whom it was a point of honor to suffer any torment rather than reveal the names of his lay friends, it must have seemed an inexcusable betrayal when in the interests of a domestic quarrel a priest like Watson set out in print, at the expense of the Government, a full list of the men and women who had dealings with him and the details of the gifts, real or imaginary, which they had made him. Gerard, however, speaks with moderation when he has occasion to refer to any member of this group, for he knew that their claim to represent the English clergy was fantastic. Nevertheless, in the partial success of their claim lies the true tragedy of the recusant story and the cause of its final collapse. Garnet was one of the first priests to point the distinction. "They are not the clergy of England: seditious men, full of lies and envy. The true clergy of England are the men whose modesty, fine bearing, discretion, learning, and goodness shine out for the whole world to see. In England their number is very great, and they have always shown us the warmest affection." [1] On the side of the secular clergy the same distinction is made by Doctor Bavant, the friend of Cardinal Allen and one of the most respected priests in England. "They name themselves and some others with them", he wrote in November 1608, "the body of the clergy of England: under which name many things may be wrought to the great prejudice of their brethren and many others". [2] It is a vital distinction which has been neglected to the distortion of recusant history by both Catholic and Protestant historians, and resulted in a misunderstanding between secular and regular clergy which persisted to the days of Morris.

[1] Arch. S.J. Rome, *Anglia* 30 (c. March 1598), 2:364.
[2] *C.R.S.*, vol. 41, 83.

Gerard deals no more with this controversy than is necessary for his story; nor does he dwell at unnecessary length on the cases of lapsed priests. The English mission demanded moral as well as physical stamina, and at all times there were priests among every section of the clergy who yielded to persecution or succumbed to moral failings or came to England without guidance or authority in order to escape the regular discipline of ecclesiastical life. In the *Autobiography* such lapses are rightly considered among the inevitable risks of the enterprise; and no narrative dealing firsthand with conditions in England could fail to touch on cases of priests who turned spies and brought their former brethren to the gallows. Every priest in England knew that the lapsed missionary was one of his saddest liabilities and one of the greatest dangers to his security. If Gerard was writing a history of the Church and not his own story he would have doubtless mentioned the case of his fellow Jesuit Father Christopher Perkins, who left the Society and entered the service of the Government abroad.

In translating the *Autobiography* afresh I have therefore omitted none of the passages which deal with the sad or more sordid aspect of a missionary's life in Elizabethan England. The text I have followed is the eighteenth-century manuscript at Stonyhurst. It is the oldest complete text that I have been able to discover, and there is every reason to believe, as the copyist claims, that it is taken from "the authentic version at Sant'Andrea", the novitiate of the Roman Jesuits. When the Society of Jesus was suppressed in 1773, the Archives at Sant'Andrea were scattered and the original of the Stonyhurst text lost. However, the faithfulness of the text can be checked both by a second Stonyhurst transcript of an incomplete seventeenth-century text, which is extant in the Jesuit Archives in Rome, and also by extensive passages from still earlier manuscripts which were incorporated in histories of the Society published in Gerard's own lifetime. It is only in the dating of the events of his boyhood that the Stonyhurst text is difficult to reconcile with sources independent of the biography; but this is probably not the copyist's fault, for the same dating occurs in the very earliest books which drew on Gerard's *Autobiography*.

The manuscript runs from the first page to the last with no chapter divisions. For convenience I have divided the translation into chapters, inserted headings, and formed my own paragraphs. In annotating the text no customary method seemed wholly satisfactory; nor do I think that the system I have devised will please every kind of reader. Since the first translation was made in 1870 a mass of documents has been published—State Papers, the Cecil manuscripts, and a miscellaneous collection gathered in the volumes of the Catholic Record Society—which add color and piquancy to the narrative. To incorporate all this in footnotes would have destroyed the artistic effect of the narrative. On the other hand, it was impossible to relegate everything without discrimination to the back of the book. As a rule I have placed at the foot of the page all certain identifications, explanatory details, and information from other sources which a biographer of Gerard would have incorporated into his text. References, and for the most part longer notes and confirmatory evidence, will be found before the appendices. A dagger in the text marks the phrase annotated at the back; a numeral refers to a footnote.

It was Father Martin D'Arcy who, as Provincial of the English Jesuits, first suggested that I should retranslate and re-edit the *Autobiography*, and to him my thanks are due. Then to many others on whom I have called for guidance: principally to Father Basil FitzGibbon, who has helped me with the annotations of the text to an extent that gives the book whatever value it has for the serious historian; to Father Godfrey Anstruther, O.P., who allowed me to read and use without restriction his most valuable work on the Vaux family, which, I hope, will soon be published; to Father Leo Hicks, who saved me hours of work by putting at my disposal all his transcripts of letters and papers touching on the story of Gerard; to all of them, and to Mr. John Guest of Longmans, the book owes a great deal.

P. C.

ABBREVIATIONS AND SHORTENED REFERENCES USED IN NOTES

C.R.S.	Catholic Record Society
C.S.P.D.	Calendar of State Papers Domestic
D.N.B.	Dictionary of National Biography
Foley	*Records of the English Province of the Society of Jesus*
Hat. Cal.	Calendar of Manuscripts of the Marquess of Salisbury preserved at Hatfield House
Jessop	*One Generation of a Norfolk House* (ed. 1879)
Morris	*John Gerard* (ed. 1881)
Narrative	*Narrative of the Gunpowder Plot* by John Gerard, printed in *The Conditions of Catholics under James I* (1871)
S.P.D.	State Papers Domestic: Elizabeth
Troubles	*Troubles of Our Catholic Forefathers* (ed. John Morris)
†	This sign in the text indicates a note at the back of the book. When the author speaks of "ours" he means "Jesuits".

AUTHOR'S PREFACE

The precepts of Superiors are from God, "from whom all power proceeds". It is at their orders that I am setting down in a simple and faithful narrative all that happened to me, under God's providence, during the eighteen years I worked on the English mission. And it must not, then, be thought an unusual or remarkable thing to do.

What I achieved was insignificant, when it is compared with the work of others, who were fitter instruments of Christ. Besides, it is a "praiseworthy thing to make known the works of God", and, on this account too, I need have no bashfulness in recording the results of my own poor efforts.

With few talents or natural gifts my endowment was slender, and my store of virtue more slender still. My union with God was far from close, and as this is the source of all advancement in spirit and the secret of success in the work of saving souls, it was to be expected that God should work fewer things through me than He did through others. I was lacking in enterprise, I was remiss in responding to the calls of God's grace, and you must not be surprised then that I let slip many opportunities and marred others. What was done, was done by God. And, I believe, He chose to do it through me, because I was a member—an unworthy one, I admit—of that body which has received from Jesus its head a remarkable outpouring of His Spirit for the healing of souls in this last era of a declining and gasping world. This is how I account for anything that God has been pleased to work in and through me.

1. EARLY LIFE

1564–1588

My parents had always been Catholics, and on that account had suffered much at the hands of a heretical Government. I was only a boy of five and my brother not much more when we were taken away from home and placed in a strange house among heretics. It was the time my father and two other gentlemen were imprisoned in the Tower of London because they had plotted to rescue Mary, Queen of Scots, and restore her to her throne. She was then in prison about two miles from us in Derbyshire.† At the end of three years my father paid a sum down for his release; and as soon as he was free he called us home again. Our faith was unaffected, for he had taken good care to put us in charge of a Catholic tutor.

Later, when I was about twelve, I was sent to Oxford, to Exeter College,[1] where my tutor was Mr. Lewknor, a good and learned man and a Catholic in sympathy and conviction. But I stayed less than a year, for at Easter time they tried to force us to go to church and receive the Protestant sacrament. So I went back to my father's house with my brother. Mr. Lewknor followed us; he wanted to become a Catholic and lead a Catholic life, and not just hanker after it as he did before.†

---

[1] J. G. matriculated with his brother, Thomas, on December 3, 1575. See Appendix A, "The Chronology of Gerard's Early Years."

We kept him at home as a Latin tutor for several years. Later he went over to Belgium, where he lived a long time and died holily. For Greek there was a devout priest, Mr. William Sutton, who lived openly in our house under the guise of tutor. Later he entered the Society and was drowned off the coast of Belgium, where he had been sent for by his Superiors.†

At the age of fourteen I got a license to visit France in order to learn French, and I stayed at Rheims[2] for three years. Though I was still a boy and insufficiently grounded in the humanities I started to study Scripture. I consulted the commentaries on the more difficult passages and took down notes at the public lectures given to the theological students in the city. Being my own master I followed my preferences and did not lay a solid foundation as I should have done. But I read the works of Saint Bernard carefully and Saint Bonaventure and other ascetical writers. And it was at this time by God's providence that I met a saintly young man. He had entered the Society at Rome but had left for a time because of his health and was then living at Rheims.† He told me—God reward him—about his former life, how he had been brought up in "the household of God", how good and wholesome a thing it was to have borne His yoke from one's youth. He also taught me to pray, and we used to meet regularly for mental prayer—neither of us lived in the college but in lodgings in the city. And it was here—I was about fifteen at the time—that I first heard God in His infinite mercy and goodness call me from the crooked paths of the world to the straight road and to the perfect following of Christ in the Society.

[2] This was the seminary founded by Cardinal Allen at Douai in 1568. J. G. arrived on August 29, 1577. The following March the College migrated to Rheims. T. F. Knox, *Douai Diaries*, 129.

After three years at Rheims I moved to Cleremont in Paris.[3] My purpose was to see from close at hand what Jesuit life was like and at the same time to get a better grounding in Latin and philosophy. I had only been there a year when I became dangerously ill. While I was convalescing I accompanied Father Thomas Darbyshire† to Rouen to meet Father Persons—he had just arrived from England and was staying secretly in the city in order to complete his *Christian Directory* and see it through the press—a most useful and wonderful book which I believe has converted more souls to God than it contains pages. Even the Protestants appreciated it very much as you can see from the recent edition brought out by one of their clergymen, who tried to steal the credit for it.† To Father Persons, then, I spoke about my vocation and my wish to join the Society. But I was still very weak and could not continue my studies. Also, I had some property in England to dispose of and other arrangements to make. So he suggested that I should return to England and while I was recovering my strength in my native air settle my affairs and free myself to follow my religious vocation. Accordingly, I went home,[4] did the business I had to do, and after about a year started back. This time I did not apply for a license. I had no chance of getting one as I had not dared to inform my parents of my intention.

With some other Catholics I set sail. The wind, however, was against us, and after five days at sea we were forced to put into port at Dover.[5] There we were all arrested by

---

[3] The famous school of the French Jesuits founded in 1564.

[4] He was still in Paris in March 1582, when his father sent him some "relief"—probably some medicines or money for his journey home.†

[5] J. G. embarked at Gravesend. There was a spy on board. Probably he informed on them as soon as they put in to Dover.†

the guards and customs officials and sent to London under custody. The others were imprisoned by warrant of the Queen's Privy Council, but although I confessed myself a Catholic and refused to attend service I was left free thanks to some members of the Council who seemed to be friendly to my family—it was they who got for me my license to travel abroad on the previous occasion.† They had hopes, I think, that it would be merely a matter of time before they won me over, and with a view to perverting me, they sent me to my maternal uncle, a Protestant,† to be kept in custody. At the end of three months he petitioned the Council for my full release and perhaps offered to pay for it. But when he was asked whether I had "gone to church", as they say, he had to admit that all his efforts to make me go had failed.

The Council then sent me with a letter to the Bishop of London,[6] who read the letter and asked me whether I was ready to discuss my religion with him. I told him that I had no doubts about my faith and I did not want to.

"In that case," said the Bishop, "you will at least have to stay a prisoner here."

I pointed out that I had no choice in the matter—I was at the mercy of the magistrates. However, he treated me with nothing but kindness, perhaps hoping to draw me over. Nevertheless, he gave orders that his chaplain's bed should be brought into my room. Time and again I refused to have anything to do with him. I understood my faith and did not want to discuss it, still less to learn from him what I should believe. But as he didn't stop blaspheming and cursing the saints and the Church, I was forced to defend my religion. We spent practically the whole night arguing, and

[6] John Aylmer, Bishop of London, 1577–1594.

to my astonishment I found that he could not put up even a passable defense. It was easy to convince him of his error.

After two days they gave up hope and sent me back to the Council with what they told me was a letter of recommendation. Indeed, the Bishop had assured me that he had done all he could for me and hoped that I would be released. But it turned out to be Uriah's letter that I carried. The Council read it and at once ordered me to be imprisoned until I became a law-abiding subject—to their way of thinking a recalcitrant subject is one who doesn't submit to heresy and attend their services. So I was sent to the Marshalsea[7] and there met a large number of Catholics and several priests who with a light heart were awaiting sentence of death or execution. The place was like a school of Christ.[8] And I was there from the beginning of Lent until the end of Lent in the following year. But I was not in the least downcast, and I had all the opportunity I wanted to carry on my studies.

During this period we were brought before the Assizes on two occasions. We were not tried for our lives but fined according to the statute for refusing to attend church. I was made to pay two thousand florins. On my way back from one of these Assizes, which was held in the country about six miles out of London, I was given permission to visit a friend of mine on condition that I returned to prison before dark. I wanted to see him very much. He was a prisoner in the loathsome Bridewell prison, and I had heard he was sick. He is a man I should tell you about. At one time he had been in attendance on Father Campion, and had been

[7] J. G. was committed to the Marshalsea on March 5, 1584. *C.R.S.*, vol. 2, 233.

[8] "A college of Caitiffs", as Aylmer refers to the forty-seven Catholic prisoners then in the Marshalsea.†

captured and imprisoned for a long time in the same prison as myself. And there I found him chained up because he had let fall some words in praise of the Father. He had fetters on his legs and used to wear a rough hair shirt which he never took off; he was very meek and full of kindness— once I saw a jailer strike him repeatedly in the face without this good man uttering a word. Finally, with three others, he was removed to the Bridewell where one of them died of hunger after a few days.[9] When I visited him (John[10] was his name), he was wasted to a skeleton and in a state of exhaustion from grinding at the treadmill, a most pitiful sight. There was nothing left of him except skin and bones, and I cannot remember having seen anything like it—lice swarmed on him like ants on a mole-hill—but he was patient.

From time to time our cells were entered and a search made for altar plate, *Agnus Deis*,† and relics. Once we were informed on (almost all of us) by a traitor who pretended to be a Catholic.† He disclosed our hiding-holes to the prison authorities, who came and almost filled a cart with the books and altar plate that they took away. In my own cell they discovered all that was needed for saying Mass, since next door there was a good priest imprisoned and we had found a way of opening the door between us, and we had Mass very early every morning. Later we made up our losses, and it was more than the devil could do to deprive us a second time of this great consolation in prison.

In the next year the insistent requests of my friends secured my liberation, but they had to give sureties in cash that I would not attempt to fly the country, while for my part I had to bind myself to report at the prison at the end of

[9] Bartholomew Temple.†
[10] John Jacob, an Oxford musician.†

every three months. Three or four times these sureties had to be renewed before I could go ahead with my plans. At last, however, the chance I had been waiting for occurred. A very dear friend of mine came forward and offered to go bail for me if I should fail to appear at the agreed time.[11] Later, after I had left England, he paid more than the surety; he forfeited his life, being one of the most distinguished in that group of fourteen gentlemen who were executed in the cause of Mary, Queen of Scots.† Their execution was, as it were, the prelude to removing the Queen herself, as later events showed.

Free at last, I made my way to France. In Paris I found Father William Holt,† who had recently arrived from Scotland. He was preparing to go to Rome with the French Provincial, and I attached myself to the party.

At Rome I was advised to finish my studies at the English College and to get ordained before I entered the Society. I took the advice though I very much wanted to enter religion as soon as possible, as I made clear to Father Persons and Father Holt, who was now Rector. But the Roman climate did not agree with me, and I was becoming restive to get back into England. They understood this and I began the year with the course of moral theology and controversy, and I worked through the complete syllabus of positive theology. When I had finished—it was just the time that the Spanish Fleet had set sail and was approaching England—the illustrious Cardinal Allen, for a number of reasons connected with the Catholic cause, petitioned to

[11] Anthony Babington, who evidently went surety at the last renewal, which was due on April 30, 1586. Shortly after visiting his married sister the following Whitsuntide, J. G. escaped to the Continent. J. G. seems to be in error. The third or fourth renewal of a quarterly surety would bring him to Easter 1585, not 1586.†

have me sent to England. But, as I was still some months short of the age for taking priest's orders, a papal dispensation was obtained for me. Still, I was reluctant to leave Rome until I had been admitted to the Society, and here again Father Persons showed me great kindness and arranged for me to begin my noviceship at once, and finish it when I got to England. There were others like myself at the English College who wanted to join the Society, so all of us did our best to follow the life of the noviceship at Sant'Andrea, often giving a hand in the kitchen and visiting the city hospitals. On the feast of the Assumption of Our Blessed Lady, 1588, Father Aquaviva,† the General, admitted dear Father Oldcorne and myself into the Society and gave us his blessing for the English mission.

With Father Oldcorne and two other priests from the English College we set out for home.

2. LANDING

November 1588

Passing through Switzerland, we stayed a night at Basle and decided to see the old Catholic buildings of the town; the Lutherans usually leave them intact but the Calvinists destroy them. We were going round the church when a man joined us and offered to show us all the things we should see. Naturally we were a little taken aback by his unexpected courtesy on the part of a Lutheran toward Catholic priests—we were wearing our soutanes—and as he could speak French I asked him where he came from. It turned out that he was from Lorraine. Then I inquired why he had left his country and his old faith, and he told me he could not live under Catholic rule. I asked him therefore which were the Catholic laws he found particularly hard, for the Catholic Church teaches the gospel of Christ, whose yoke is sweet and burden light. At length I discovered that the man was a priest and had fled to Basle. He was living there with a woman who passed for his wife in the very house where we had lodged the night before, and was supporting himself and her by the practice of usury. Therefore I urged him earnestly to turn from the road to hell and set his feet again on the path to heaven. I begged him to provide for the woman, to lend out no more money at unlawful interest, and to work for his living or to support himself in some other honest way. In the end he promised to do as I advised.

He gave me a letter to his bishop asking to be reconciled. As I passed through Lorraine I delivered the letter, and I can only hope that the poor man did not go back on his good purpose.

As best we could we passed incognito through Rheims—the English seminary was there at the time—and through Paris,[1] and we came to Eu. A school for English boys had been opened there, but later it was given up owing to the wars and a better and flourishing foundation made at Saint Omers. Our Fathers there consulted the priests who had charge of the College,† and all agreed that it would be very unwise to cross to England while things stood as they did at present. The Spanish Fleet had exasperated the people against the Catholics; everywhere a hunt was being organized for Catholics and their houses searched; in every village and along all the roads and lanes very close watches were kept to catch them. The Earl of Leicester, then at the height of his power, had sworn that by the end of the year there would be no Catholics left in the country—but the man had not counted his days, for he was carried off that same year.†

Reluctantly, therefore, we decided to stay here for a time until we received from Rome an answer from Father Persons writing in the name of Father General. The situation, he said, had changed a great deal since we had left Rome, but the work we had in hand was God's undertaking; we were free either to go ahead with the enterprise or stay back until things in England had quieted down. This was the answer we desired. There was a short discussion, and then we found a ship at once to take us across and drop us

[1] However, his passage through Paris was detected and reported to London by one of Walsingham's spies. *S.P.D.*, vol. 219, no. 26.

in the north of England which seemed the quieter part. Two priests from Rheims who were anxious to get a passage joined us, and we took them aboard our ship. Our travelling companions had decided to stay back some time— they did not want to walk straight into such certain danger.

We four priests embarked,[2] a lucky load, if I exclude myself, for my unworthiness robbed me of the crown of martyrdom. The other three all met a martyr's death for the faith. The two priests from Rheims were quickly captured, *consummati in brevi impleverunt tempora multa.* Their names were Christopher Bales and George Beesley.[3] But my companion, Father Oldcorne, worked and toiled for almost eighteen years in the Lord's vineyard before he, too, watered it with his blood.

After crossing the sea we sailed up the English coast. On the third day my companion and I saw what seemed a good place to put ashore in the ship's boat. As we thought it would be dangerous for all of us to land together, we asked God's guidance in prayer. Then we consulted our companions and ordered the ship to cast anchor off the point till nightfall.[4] At the first watch of the night we were taken ashore in the boat and dropped there. The ship spread its canvas and sailed on.

[2] J. G. embarked early November, not as he says later, in October. The "two priests from Rheims" left Rheims on November 2. The names of the two who stayed back were Ralph Buckland and Arthur Stratford. T. F. Knox, *Douai Diaries*, 220–21.

[3] Both were executed in Fleet Street: Christopher Bales on March 4, 1590, and George Beesley on July 2, 1591.

[4] "Seeing a shore where they might set on land, and no town or house near them to see where they landed, they . . . caused the sailors to cast anchor until it was dark, and then in a cock-boat to set them on land." *Narrative*, 280. This was near Happisburgh, roughly halfway between Great Yarmouth and Cromer. Jessop, 134.

For a few moments we prayed and commended ourselves
to the keeping of God, then we looked about for a path to
take us as far inland as possible and put a good distance between
us and the sea before dawn broke. But the night was dark
and overcast, and we could not pick the path we wanted and
get away into the open fields. Every track we took led up to
a house—as we knew at once when the dogs started to bark.
This happened two or three times. Afraid we might wake
the people inside and be set on for attempting to burgle
them, we decided to go off into a nearby wood and rest
there 'til the morning. It was about the end of October,
raining and wet, and we passed a sleepless night.[5] Nor did
we dare to talk, for the wood was close to a house. However, in little more than a whisper we held a conference.
Would it be better to make for London together or separate
so that if one of us was caught the other might get away
safely? We discussed both courses thoroughly. In the end we
decided to part company and each to go his own way.

At the first sight of dawn we cast lots as to who should
leave the wood first. The lot fell on Father Oldcorne, who
was also the first to leave this world for heaven. Then we
shared out our money equally, and embraced and blessed
each other.[6]

The future martyr went off. Walking along the shore to
the nearest town, he fell in with a party of sailors and men
of that sort who were making their way to London.[7] He

---

[5] "[They] got them into a wood, and there stayed all night, whilst it rained
a good pace. But yet they were as merry as might be, and well contented
with their wet lodging." *Narrative*, 280.

[6] "They looked therefore into their provision of money, and he that had
more gave it unto the other to make it equal." *Narrative*, 281.

[7] The town was Mundesley. The sailors had probably been disbanded after
the defeat of the Armada. Jessop, 134.

joined on to them. Being a man of great tact and discretion he succeeded in adapting himself to their ways, when they were talking about nothing that mattered. But two or three times the good Father was forced to reprimand them when they started to blaspheme or drop into filthy conversation. It was a dangerous thing to do, as he told me later. But his zeal in these matters was remarkable. I have heard many instances of it, but one must suffice for all.

Once in London he visited the house of a Catholic who was a close friend of his. In the window of his room he saw a painted pane of glass depicting Mars and Venus. The scene was indecent, and although the house did not belong to his friend—he had merely rented it—Father Oldcorne, unable to endure the sight, struck his fist through the glass and told his friend how unseemly it was to let such things stand. This was typical of his zeal for God's honor and truth.

This good Father, then, attached himself to the sailors. He knew how to combine the prudence of the serpent with the simplicity of the dove, and behaved in a way that made it plain how much he disapproved of their conversation. Yet he won their affection, roughs that they were, and with the protection they unwittingly afforded him he reached London safely. There were watchers in nearly every village he passed, but they took him for one of the party—men whose dress and behavior had nothing in common with people they were on the look-out for.

As soon as my companion had left, I came out of the wood by a different path. I had gone only a short distance when I saw some country folk coming toward me. Walking up to them I asked whether they knew anything about a stray hawk; perhaps they had heard its bell tinkling as it was flying around. I wanted them to believe that I had lost my bird and was wandering about the countryside in search of

it. This is what falconers do. And they would not be surprised because I was a stranger here and unfamiliar with
the lanes and countryside; they would merely think that I
had wandered here in my search. They told me they had
not seen or heard a falcon recently, and they seemed sorry
that they could not put me on its track. So with a disappointed look I went off as if I were going to search for it in
the trees and hedges round about. In this way I got off the
road without stirring their suspicions. In fact, they watched
me sympathetically as I hurried round the hedges and got
farther away from the sea. Whenever I saw anybody in the
fields I went up to him and asked my usual questions about
the falcon, concealing all the time my real purpose, which
was to avoid the villages and public roads and get away from
the coast where I knew watchers guarded the thorough-
fares and kept out strangers.[8] Most of the day went like this
and in all I managed to cover eight or ten miles, not, of
course, walking in a straight line, but diagonally, even turning back now and again the way I had come. At the end of
the day I was soaked with rain and felt hungry. It had been
a rough crossing and I had been able to take practically no
food or sleep on board, so I turned for the night into an
inn in a village I was passing, thinking that they were less
likely to question a man they saw entering an inn.

I got some food and found the people very amiable, especially when I told them I wanted to buy a pony in their
stables. It was a poor man's beast, and I bought it for a

---

[8] On July 27, 1588, an order had been sent from the Privy Council to the
Lords Lieutenant of Norfolk and Suffolk "to see watches kept in every thor-
oughfare town to stay and apprehend all vagabonds and rogues [that] are like
to pass up and down to move disorders; and if any such be found with any
manifest offence tending to stir troubles or rebellion, to cause such to be
executed by martial law". Hist. MSS Commission, *Foljambe MSS*, 53.

small but reasonable price. On horseback I hoped to move more quickly and more safely too—people travelling on foot are often taken for vagrants and liable to arrest, even in quiet times.

The next morning I mounted my horse and started out in the direction of Norwich, the principal town in that county. I had gone barely two miles when I rode straight into a group of watchers at the entrance to a village. They ordered me to dismount, and asked me who I was and where I came from. I told them I was in the service of a certain lord who lived in another county—he did in fact know me well, although these men had not heard of him—and I explained that my falcon had flown away and I had come here to see whether I could recover it.

They could not catch me out in my story. But still they did not let me go. They insisted that I had to come before the Constable and the Officer of the Watch, both of whom happened at that moment to be in church attending their heretical worship.[9]

I saw I could not escape and that it was no good trying to resist. As I could not win them round I submitted and followed them into the cemetery surrounding the church. I told them to go and tell the officer that I was here. One of the watchers went in and came back with the answer that he wanted me to come inside where he would see me at the end of the service.

"If he is unwilling to come out," I said, "I'll wait for him here."

"No, you've got to go into the church."

I tried again.

"I don't want to leave my horse behind, so I'll stay."

---

[9] "It being Sunday morning." *Narrative*, 281.

"In other words, you won't get off and hear God's holy word. I warn you that if you refuse it won't help you. Your horse is nothing to worry about. If it's necessary, I'll get you a better one."

"Go and tell the officer", I said again, "that if he wants to see me, either he must let me wait for him here or come out quickly."

The messenger returned with this answer and the officer came out at once with some attendants and started to examine me. From the expression on his face I could see that he was angry. He asked me first where I came from and I named a number of places which I had learned were not far away. Then he asked me my name, employment, home, and the reason for my coming, and I gave him the answers that I had given before. Finally on asking whether I was carrying any letters, I invited him to search me and satisfy himself, but he did not do it. He insisted, however, that it was his duty to take me before the Justice of the Peace, and I said that if he thought it really necessary I was ready to go, but I was anxious to hurry on for I had been away from my master long enough already. I begged him if he could possibly do it to let me pass on. At first he refused, and it looked as though there would be nothing for it but to go before a higher officer and be sent to prison by him, as certainly would have happened. Then the man looked at me with a milder expression.

"You've got the look of an honest fellow. Go on then in God's name. I won't hold you back any longer."

Nor did God's providence desert me after that. As I was riding along and getting near the city I saw ahead of me a young man on horseback carrying a heavy pack. I wanted to get level with him and find out from him more about the town and, in particular, what was the best place to put up at. He looked the sort of person I could question without raising suspicions, but his horse was better than mine and though I urged on my animal hard I could not make up the distance between us. For two or three miles I followed him. Then providentially he dropped his pack on the road and had to stop and dismount to strap it on again. As I drew level I could see that he was an uneducated youth, just the kind of man I needed. He told me many things which would have been most useful to me if I had gotten into trouble, but though I did not know it, God was guiding me out of further danger through his means. First, I asked him whether he could recommend me a good inn near the city gate to save dragging my horse round the streets looking for one, and he told me that there was an inn at the other end of the town and that I could best get to it by riding round the outskirts. And lastly I got him to show me the road and tell me the sign of the inn. Then I let him ride ahead along the road that led straight into the city—the road I should certainly have taken had I not met him. It would have led me straight into trouble, and none of those things which happened to me later for the greater glory of God and the good of many souls would have fallen to me.

I followed the young man's instructions. Going round the city walls I came to the gate he described. Passing through I saw the inn.†

I was there only a short time when in walked a man who seemed well known to the people of the house. He greeted me courteously and then sat down by the fire to warm himself. He began talking about some Catholic gentlemen imprisoned in the city and mentioned by name a man, one of whose relatives had been with me in the Marshalsea Prison in London seven years before.† I listened carefully but said nothing. After he had gone out I asked the man I had been talking to who he was.

"He is a very good fellow," they said, "except for the fact that he is a Papist."

"How do you know this?" I asked.

"He has spent many years in the city jail." (It was only a stone's throw from the inn.) "There are a lot of Catholic gentlemen there† and this man was released only a short time ago."

"Was he released", I asked, "because he has given up his faith?"

"No, and he never will. He is a most pig-headed man. He is merely out on bail and has to report at the prison whenever he is summoned. There is some business he does for a gentleman in prison which brings him here frequently."

I kept quiet until the man returned and when the others had gone out I told him that I wanted to have a word with him in some safe place. I had heard that he was a Catholic, I said, and was very pleased to hear it because I was one too. Then I explained how I came to be here. I told him that I wanted to get to London and that if he could do me the kindness of introducing me to any people who were known on the road so that I could join on to them and pass as one of their party, he would be doing a good work as a Catholic. I pointed out that I was able to pay my expenses and would not be a burden to them in any way.

However, he knew of no one going to London just then, so I asked him whether he could give me the name of a man whom I might hire as escort. He said that he would make inquiries, but he knew a gentleman who was in town just then who might be able to help me out of my difficulties.

He went out to find him. In a very short time he was back and asked me to follow him into the town. He led me into a busy mart as though he were going to make a purchase. The gentleman he had told me about was waiting there, having selected this place because it gave him a chance to have a good look at me before he made himself known. Eventually he came up to us and told my friend in a whisper that he thought I was a priest. Then he led us out to the cathedral, where he put a lot of questions to me, finally asking me to tell him straight whether or not I was a priest, and if I was, he promised to give me all the help I needed.

For my part, I asked my guide who the gentleman was and when he told me his name[10] and position I realized what a good friend Providence had given me. I admitted at once that I was a Jesuit priest and had recently arrived from Rome. Straightway he got me a change of clothes and a good horse and took me out to the country house of a friend outside the city, leaving a servant to bring my pony after me. The next day we went on to his own house,[11] where he lived with his family and his brother, who was a heretic.

Since these two brothers had a widowed sister who was also a heretic and lived there and kept house for them,† I had to be careful not to give them any ground for suspecting who I really was. On my first arrival the Protestant brother was indeed suspicious—for I was a stranger, I had come here in company with his Catholic brother, and he could think of no reason why his brother treated me so kindly. But after two or three days his suspicions were allayed. When I got the opportunity I spoke about hunting and falconry, a thing no one could do in correct technical language unless he was familiar with the sports. It is an easy thing to trip up in one's terms, as Father Southwell used to complain.† Frequently, as he was travelling about with me later, he would ask me to tell him the correct terms and

[10] Edward Yelverton, one of the wealthiest men in Norfolk. Jessop, 137.
[11] Grimston, six and a half miles north-east of King's Lynn.

worried because he could not remember and use them when need arose—for instance, when he fell in with Protestant gentlemen who had practically no other conversation except, perhaps, obscene subjects or rants against the saints and the Catholic faith. On occasions like this there is often a chance of bringing the talk round to some other topic simply by throwing out a remark about horses or hounds or the like. Thus it often happens, as I experienced now, that an idle interest such as this makes a good mask and protection.

After a few days I suggested to my new friend, the Catholic brother, that I should go to London to meet my Superior. He agreed and gave me horses and a servant. And he begged me to ask my Superior to allow me to return to this county and make my home with him. He was sure it would be possible to bring many people back to the faith if I only talked with them in the way he had seen me do.

I promised to put his request to the Superior and said that for my part I would be delighted to return if he would take me in. I rode off and arrived safely in London. There was no incident on the way.

I have gone into all this detail to show how Providence protected me on my first landing in England. I knew no one at all in the whole of that county. I had never been there before, and it was far away from the places where I had been born and brought up. Yet on the first day I found a friend who drew me out of danger, and afterward, by introducing me to the principal families of the county, made an opening for many conversions. Through my friendship with him many Catholics in those parts came to know of my presence, and this as you shall see later was the beginning of all that God was pleased to do hereafter through His poor servant.

3. GRIMSTON

Christmas 1588–Summer 1589

When I reached London some Catholics helped me to find Father Henry Garnet, who was then Superior. Apart from him the only other Jesuit priests in England at the time were Father Edmund Weston† in Wisbeach Jail (he would have been Superior had he been at large), Father Robert Southwell, and the two of us who had just landed.

My companion, Father Oldcorne, had already arrived. But the Superior had received no news of me and was anxious. On the other hand, for this very reason, they still had hopes that all was well. When I arrived there was great rejoicing all 'round.

I stayed with the Fathers some time, and we had frequent discussions on the methods we should follow in our work. Splendid advice on ways of helping and saving souls was given us by Father Garnet, and also by Father Southwell, who excelled at this work. He was so wise and good, gentle and loveable. But Christmas was drawing near and we had to scatter. The danger of capture was greater at festal times, and besides, the faithful needed our services.

I was sent back, therefore, to the county where I first stepped ashore and to the same gentleman who first helped me and gave me shelter. The Superior provided me with the clothes and other things I needed, for he was anxious that I should not be a burden to my host at the start. Afterward,

however, and throughout my missionary life, Providence provided sufficiently for my needs and others' as well. My dress
was always that of a gentleman of moderate means, and the
wisdom of this was clear and often demonstrated later. It
was thus that I used to go about before I became a Jesuit,
and I was therefore more at ease in these clothes than I would
have been if I had assumed a role that was strange and unfamiliar to me. Besides, I had to move in public and meet many
Protestant gentlemen, and I could never have mixed with
them and brought them slowly back to a love of the faith
and a virtuous life had I dressed in any other way. Apart
from being able to move in their society more freely and
safely now, and with greater authority, I could stay longer
and more securely in any house or noble home where my
host might bring me as his friend or acquaintance.[1]

And that is what happened. Without danger and not without profit I stayed openly six or eight months in the house
of that gentleman who was my first host. During that time
he introduced me to the house and circle of nearly every
gentleman in Norfolk, and before the end of the eight
months I had received many people into the Church, including one of my host's brothers, his two sisters, and later his
brother-in-law. One of his sisters, as I have said, was the
widow who kept house for him. She had been a rabid Calvinist, and one of her brothers, the Judge, is still one of the
leaders of the Calvinist party in England to-day.[2]

---

[1] J. G. was "for the most part attired costly and defencibly in buff leather,
garnished with gold or silver lace, satin doublets, and velvet hose of all colours with clocks correspondent, and rapiers and daggers gilt or silvered".
Description of the spy, Byrd, to Cecil, *Hat. Cal.*, 11:365.

[2] Sir Christopher Yelverton, her half brother. As Queen's Sergeant he took
part in the indictment of the Earl of Essex. In 1601 he was appointed Judge
of the Queen's Bench.

This lady had been brought up in his house and had imbibed the loathsome heresy there. Some time before I met her, a remarkable incident occurred. Being anxious about the state of her soul, she went to consult a Cambridge doctor called Perne.[3] He was known to have changed his religion three or four times to suit the change of ruler, Catholic and Protestant, and still retained a wide reputation for learning. This Doctor Perne was her close friend, and she asked him to tell her honestly and simply which was the holy religion that would see her safe to heaven. The doctor was unused to urgent appeals like this from shrewd women of good sense. He said: "I beg you never to tell anyone what I am going to say. Since, however, you have asked me to answer as if I were responsible for your salvation, I will tell you. If you wish, you can *live* in the religion which the Queen and the whole kingdom profess—you will have a good life, you will have none of the vexations which Catholics have to suffer. But don't *die* in it. Die in faith and communion with the Catholic Church, that is, if you want to save your soul." So the man answered; but what happened to him? The poor fellow had put off his conversion from day to day. Then, when he least expected it, he fell dead just as he got back to his room after dining with the Archbishop of Canterbury in his palace.[4] He had shown no sign of repentance, no sign of a Christian's hope in eternal happiness. He had been only too ready to promise it all round, to himself as well as others, but there was nothing in his life that gave solid hope for it. The lady who had consulted him, however, was more fortunate. At first she

---

[3] Master of Peterhouse, 1554–1589, and perhaps the most notorious turncoat of his day.†

[4] He died at Lambeth on April 26, 1589, and is buried in the parish church there.

would not accept his statement about the truth of the Catholic faith, but later on, when she heard me say time and again that the Catholic faith was the only true and good one, she began to have doubts, and, in this state of mind, she brought me one day an heretical book which more than anything had confirmed her in her heresy. She pointed out to me all the reasons and arguments it contained, and, in answer, I showed her all the dishonest quotations from Scripture and the Fathers, the countless quibbles and misstatements of fact. And in this way, with God's help, I drew out of the scorpion itself a medicine for the scorpion's sting. Since that day she has been constant in her profession of the faith.†

Another remarkable incident I must not pass over: it concerns my host's married sister[5] and illustrates the wonderful efficacy of the sacraments. This lady was married to a man of position and thanks to her brother was well disposed toward the Catholic faith and required little persuasion to become a child of the Church. On her reception she refused to attend Protestant worship and her husband treated her very harshly for it, but her patience won in the end. During the time I am speaking about she was pregnant. She had a very difficult labor; so much so that after she had given birth to a son she became critically ill and her life was despaired of. A very skilled doctor was summoned at once from Cambridge. He saw the sick lady and said that he could prescribe some physic but he could give her no hope of recovery. Then, after ministering the physic, he left.

It happened that I was in the house at the time, for I often went there with her brother. The gentleman was glad

---

[5] Grisell, who married Sir Philip Wodehouse of Kimberley, the ancestor of the present earl.

to see us, although he knew we were Catholics. I had often argued with him about religion and had by now practically convinced him—his mind was made up but his will still clung to the things of earth, for "his possessions were very great." He loved his wife dearly, and now that there was no hope for her life, he was persuaded by her brother to leave her full freedom to prepare herself for the life to come. He made no difficulty therefore in our bringing over to see her the next evening an old priest, one of those ordained before the beginning of Elizabeth's reign.† As such priests do not go about in the same danger and peril of their lives, we made use of him on this occasion to give the lady all the last rites of the Church. After making her confession she was anointed and received Viaticum, and (this is the wonderful thing) within half an hour she had recovered and was out of danger. All she had to do now was to regain her strength—her sickness had completely gone.

When the gentleman saw his wife suddenly snatched from the jaws of death, he wondered how it had happened. We explained to him that one of the effects of the holy sacrament of Extreme Unction was to restore bodily health when God judged it to be for the soul's good. This completed the husband's conversion. Amazed that the sacraments of the true Church had power to effect such changes, he was persuaded at last to seek in the same Church the restoration of his soul's health. As I was anxious to strike while the iron was hot, I began to explain to him how he should prepare for confession—I did not want him to know yet that I was a priest, and therefore I said that I would instruct him just as a priest had instructed me. He made his preparation, then waited for a priest to be brought to him. His brother and I both told him it would have to be done at night, so he sent away the servants who waited on him in his dressing-room and went up into the library. There I left him at his prayers, telling him that I would return almost immediately with a priest. Downstairs I changed into my soutane and returned completely transformed. He was speechless with amazement—no such thing had crossed his mind. His brother and I explained that I had to act in this way both for safety's sake, and still more to trick the devil and snatch souls from his grasp. He surely realized that. It was the only way I could have conversed freely with him and men of his rank, and unless I did this I could never bring them back to the Church, particularly if they were ill-disposed to it. With the same argument I dispelled his anxiety about the ill consequences he feared as a result of my visit. I appealed to his own experience. Though I had been all this time in very close contact with him, never once had he suspected that I might be a priest. So he became a Catholic, and his wife, grateful for this double blessing of God, perseveres still in the faith, though she has had much to suffer for it since.†

Besides these persons, during the time I moved about freely, I reconciled to the Church many fathers and mothers of families, more than twenty in all, of the same or higher social standing,† but it would be wiser not to mention them by name. In addition, I received a large number of servants and poorer people—I forget the precise number—and, through the grace of God, I steadied many tottering souls in their allegiance, and heard numerous general confessions.

There were others, too, in that short period who showed they had a vocation to the religious life, and among them the present Father Edward Walpole. When I was introduced to him I found him leading a holy life and enduring much persecution for the sake of his conscience, and not just from outsiders, "for his enemies were those of his own household." The heir to a large property, he had been disinherited by his father on his deathbed (he was a Calvinist and his mother and brother both Protestants), and the estate was divided between his mother and this Protestant younger brother.[6] All he, the Catholic son, received in his mother's lifetime was an annual allowance of four hundred florins,[7] on which he was then living. His own house had become more a jail than a home, for he saw and spoke to no one save at meal times (the rest of the day he spent in his room). He had studied classics and philosophy at Cambridge, and now he was reading extensively about the Fathers. At this time he began paying me regular visits and came to the sacraments frequently, and God gave him a vocation. The next year he went to Rome and joined the Society. It was due to his influence that his cousin Michael Walpole, who is now a professed Father, went too. Michael at the time was my attendant, and used to travel round with me as my confidential servant whenever I went to a house where my assumed status made it necessary for me to have one. Both are now doing fine work on the mission and with their zeal and greater gifts are making good what was lost through my lack of enterprise and ability.†

After six or seven months here a Catholic gentleman from another county came to see me.[8] He was related to one of my flock and was anxious to meet a Jesuit. He was a devout

---

[6] Callibut Walpole, through whom the estates descended to Sir Robert Walpole, the Minister of the first two Hanoverian kings, who was born at the family home at Houghton, W. Norfolk, in 1676.

[7] By "florin" J. G. means the Flemish silver gulden or florin, which was worth about two shillings in English money at the time.

[8] Henry Drury of Lawshall, six miles south-east of Bury Saint Edmunds, Suffolk.

young man and heir to a fairly big estate, half of which he inherited when his brother died, while the other half went to his mother for life. This lady, a widow, was a good Catholic also, and she lived in her son's house, where they supported a priest. After I had been with him a few days, I noticed that his only desire was to lead a more perfect life, and I told him of certain spiritual exercises which could lead a generous soul on that way by holding out before him all that was good and thus help him to make the best choice of life.[9] He at once begged me earnestly to let him make them. I agreed, and he got so much profit from them that he decided to do what he thought was the best thing, namely, to join the Society with as little delay as possible and in the interval, while he was settling his affairs, to take care that he lost none of his fervor.

When the retreat was over, he implored me to come and live at his house, and he gave me no peace until I promised to put the proposal to the Superior. I reflected on his offer. The way I had gone about in public had advantages in the beginning, but it could not continue for ever, since the danger of recognition grew as I came to know more people. I had less security now and more cause to worry, and I realized that this opportunity was providential. As Father Garnet approved when I consulted him, I went to this gentleman's house in the next county, but I first said goodbye to all my friends and stationed a priest where he would be in the best position to help the Catholics in the county. He is there to this day, doing great work and enduring much.

[9] The Spiritual Exercises of Saint Ignatius of Loyola. J. G. makes frequent mention of them later. They are a systematic course of meditations on spiritual subjects designed to help persons to a right choice of life.

4. LAWSHALL

Summer 1589–Winter 1591

In this new place my life was much more quiet and congenial. Almost everyone in the house was a Catholic, and it was easier to live the life of a Jesuit, even in the external details of dress and arrangement of time. I was also able to do much reading.

However, there were a number of things in the house that needed attention. For one the altar furnishings were old and worn and anything but helpful to devotion. But here I had to be careful. The chaplain had been with the family some time, and he might easily take offense if I started to make a lot of changes, especially if he realized that the master of the house followed the smallest suggestion I might make. But, thank God, everything went well. I saw to it that all the changes I thought urgent were proposed and carried out by the master of the house himself. Then I brought out some fine vestments, which were a gift to me, and in this way encouraged the good widow to make others like them. As for the priest, he asked to make the Exercises—he had heard my host praise them so much— and went through them with great profit. In fact, he said afterward in the hearing of others, that he had never before realized the full obligations of his priesthood. Afterward he always showed great affection for me, and he gave proof of it later when I was in prison, bringing me alms and doing me other kindnesses. He used to consult me in his affairs, and he won three times as many souls to God and His Church as he had done before, and he was held in much greater esteem by everyone. In the year that the appointment of the Archpriest was made, he was nominated one of his assistants. He still holds the office.†

During my stay here—it lasted almost two years—I gave much time to study. But I also travelled about. As well as reconciling some heretics and schismatics, I was able to strengthen several Catholic families in their faith and to place two priests in places where they could do good work. I heard a number of general confessions; one penitent, a widowed lady of high position, devoted the rest of her life to pious works, and not to mention her other gifts, she made the Society an annual donation of a thousand florins;[1] another widow[2] gave four hundred.

In this period also I gave the Spiritual Exercises to a number of persons with good effect. The first to make them were two men related to one another; both decided to join the Society and settled their affairs and went to France. At the end of their studies one entered the Society and is now a zealous priest on the English mission. He is Father Thomas Everett. The other was ordained, but he was pusillanimous: he wanted at first to return to England, but he didn't turn out well in the end.[3]

Two others who made a retreat under me at the same time were fine young men.[4] They were brothers and both

[1] Mary Lady Lovel, who later founded at Antwerp the first convent of English Carmelites.†
[2] Isabel, widow of Edmund Fortescue of Sawston. She was a sister-in-law of Thomas Wiseman. Jessop, 220.
[3] Father Anthony Rowse, the apostate priest.†
[4] Thomas and John Wiseman.

decided to become Jesuits. The elder had read classics and philosophy at Cambridge and for the last nine years had been studying law in London. Exceptionally talented and industrious, he had made such a mark for himself that I heard men of balanced judgment say that they ranked an opinion of his on a level with those of the leading lawyers of the past. He was a prudent and serious man as well, and even before he thought of joining the Society, Father South-well had remarked to me, that if he ever came to that decision he would be the finest Superior we could possibly wish to have.

So at the suggestion of my host, who knew them very well, this man and his brother started a retreat under me. With the younger one there was no difficulty, but the other, during the whole of the first "week",† found it hard going. Then he discovered the reason and put things right.

What happened was this. I had advised him to do certain penances, slight in themselves, which for reasons of health he begged to be excused. As the reasons he gave were good, I agreed. Later, however, he realized that his lack of good will even in such an unimportant matter as this might be the cause of his dryness, and when one day I came to his room to comfort him, he fell down at my feet and begged my pardon, saying that he would not get up until, as an assurance that I had forgiven him, I allowed him to kiss my feet. After that he was filled with great consolation of soul and the light of God's grace shone so clearly there that no shadow of doubt was left about his vocation. He had much to do to settle his own affairs and others' also before he could leave England—he had decided to sell his estate lest he should ever think of returning to it—but he dispatched everything very quickly and within five or six weeks set out with his brother for Rome. Before he left, not to mention other gifts and good works, he gave the Society between eleven and twelve thousand florins.

Providentially this happened at the time the Society was beginning to grow in England,† and shortly after Father Southwell's capture. Father Southwell had lived in London, and when he was taken, Father Garnet had to move there so that he could keep in touch with us all, scattered as we were up and down the country, and, in this central position, be more accessible when we wanted to see him. But this meant a heavy expenditure. The persecution was most severe in London, and Father Garnet had to keep up two or three houses there at the same time out of his own small funds. We then had few friends in a position to help us. Father Southwell alone had a great benefactress,[5] and while we had him with us, he was able with her help to maintain himself and some other priests as well as keep a private house where he usually received the Superior on his visits to London.

It was there that I first met them both; there, too, that Father Southwell had his printing press, where his own admirable books were produced.† But after we had lost Father Southwell we should have been very hard pressed indeed had not these two men, I mean the gentleman I have just mentioned and my host, come to our help. The latter gave nearly half his property to the Society.[6]

Immediately on their arrival at Rome the two brothers entered the noviceship at Sant'Andrea under the names of Starkie and Standish. These were the two names I had used in the two counties I had been working in; and they assumed

---

[5] Anne, Countess of Arundel.

[6] Father Garnet divided this money "among the clergymen in prison, or otherwise in want, and among other poor Catholics labouring under persecution".†

them as *aliases* in gratitude to me. The younger brother (I am told) died a holy death at Sant'Andrea; the other was rather indiscreet in his application to study at the Roman College and became a consumptive. He was sent to Belgium, but it was too late. His death took place at Saint Omers, and it was felt as a great loss by all who knew him.†

Apart from these two I gave the Exercises to others during my stay here, and all drew much profit from them. Two of these gentlemen were the leading Catholics of the county. One of them got as far as the last day but one in the second "week" without any spiritual emotion; then suddenly the south wind (so to speak) blew over the garden of his soul and brought down such copious showers of tears that he went on weeping for three or four days without stopping. Even when business forced him to go out, he could speak only in a voice broken with sobs. He followed me everywhere like a one-year-old, and the chaplain, to whom I referred above, used to call him "the weeping-one" and write in letters to me, "John, the weeping-one, wants this or that" or "presents you with such and such a thing". But henceforth his life was one full of good works, and he died a happy death.

About the same time I persuaded another Walpole, Christopher by name, to come from Cambridge and see me. Then I received him into the Church, and, giving him the money for the journey, sent him to Rome. At the end of his studies there he entered the Society and was ordained. He was then sent to Spain and died there. His death caused us all great sorrow, and it was a heavy loss to his country.†

I mentioned two brothers just above. The older one, before he left England, was able to persuade his eldest brother,[7]

---

[7] William Wiseman.

who had a great respect for him, to try the Spiritual Exercises. He was indeed a Catholic, but his thoughts were very far from Christian perfection. Lately his father had died and he had succeeded to the family estate and its fine mansion.[8] There he lived with his wife and children to whom he was deeply devoted. He had laid out a deer park or enclosure and enjoyed all the independence of a little prince. As he kept at a distance from the seminary priests he was not disturbed by the authorities and he felt none of the "heat and burden of the day". The persecution at that time was directed chiefly against the seminary priests and on the whole was unconcerned with the old men ordained before Elizabeth came to the throne. It was a distinction similar to that now made between secular priests and Jesuits, for to-day the persecution is much fiercer against us and our friends, as you can judge from the way they treat the good people who shelter us. The reason, I presume, is that our numbers have grown so much. Also it has something to do with the quarrels that have broken out between us and a section of the secular clergy (first in the seminaries and then in England) which makes the Government anxious to crush the more uncompromising party first by imposing fearful penalties on the people who house and protect us. But the Israelites increased in spite of the rage of Pharaoh, who sought their lives.†

As I was saying, this gentleman lived peacefully with his family on his estate and carefully avoided the attentions of the Government. His eyes were blind to the snares of Satan—he did not even fear them. But, in spite of this, he found himself ensnared in the toils of grace. He walked straight into the net, was trapped, and showed no wish to escape.

[8] Braddocks, between Thaxted and Saffron Walden, Essex.†

It was after the first or second day. He had thoroughly turned over in his mind God's purpose in creating him and all things else, when he began to feel the stirrings of the waters and went down into the pool and was healed. From that time he made all the meditations with great care, as you could see from the benefit he derived from them. He resolved henceforth to devote the whole of his life to furthering God's greater glory. All the good things that God had given him, he would use as a treasure committed to his keeping, and not treat them as though he owned them, and he would regard his family as a trust from Him. Moreover, he decided to take in two more priests, and insisted that one of them must be a Jesuit who would have the direction of him and his household. If he had any time over from the administration of his estate, he would devote it to reading and translating ascetical books. He was a scholar, and he did in fact translate many useful works, including the life of our blessed Father,[9] the *Dialogues* of Saint Gregory, Jerome Platus' *De Bono Statu Religiosi*,† and others as well. He also drew up some rules for his own guidance in his dealings with others, with the object of helping and encouraging them to lead a good life.

These were his resolutions and he kept them. He had to overcome many difficulties which he foresaw clearly from the beginning. For one thing most of his servants were Protestants. Then there was his wife, who could not be expected to fall in with his plans, and his chaplain, one of those old priests who were always at odds with the young men, especially the Jesuits whom they looked on as meddlesome innovators. It was no easy matter, as he fully realized; but he was determined all the same, come what might, to replace

---

[9] Saint Ignatius, founder of the Society of Jesus.

his Protestant servants by carefully chosen Catholics (but in a kindly and generous way), and to win over his wife and chaplain, if he could, by gentle persuasion, and if that failed, by using his authority as master of the house.

When all this was done, he begged me very earnestly to move to his house. The reasons he gave were convincing. I had come here for the sake of my host. Now he was on the point of leaving, for Father Garnet had decided that he should live with him until he could cross to the Continent. Also, the good priest who was here when I came was remaining behind and would be able to take care of the gentleman's mother. And there was this advantage in the change. I would be nearer London and be able to do more good there than if I stayed on where I was after my host had left. All these reasons I put to the Superior, when I went up to introduce my host and leave him at his house.†

Father Garnet urged me to take the opportunity while it offered itself. But I was careful to see that all the readjustments in the new house were made, as far as could be done, before I arrived. I had no wish to become a source of contention, and I waited a full two months before I moved in. A good and capable staff of servants was assembled, chiefly men I had known in other places and whom I knew could be trusted. Nor was it anything like as difficult as I had feared to bring the mistress of the house and the old priest to agree to the changes; they even lent a hand in them, particularly the wife who surpassed everyone in the care she lavished on the chapel and in her attention to all my wants. She was rather quick-tempered and found it hard to keep her patience with servants and others. However, I always checked her and pulled her up every time—usually, of course, when we were alone—but sometimes, too, before others when the occasion called for it. I did this all the time I was with the family. She took it very well and tried hard to keep her temper in control. Every day she seemed to give me some new proof of her affection and respect, as you shall see later.

As for the chaplain, he became very friendly to me when he saw that his status had improved as a result of my coming, and he often showed his satisfaction by the things he said and did. It was, of course, only to be expected that reverence for him should grow with the increased devotion and piety of the household. In actual fact he was much better off now than he had been before, and although he soon realized that it was I who was really behind the changes, he found that he himself counted for much more than before.

My host's mother lived here, a widowed lady and a wonderfully good person. Her children were a constant comfort to her—she had four sons and four daughters. All the daughters became nuns: two had already joined the Bridgettine Order, before I came,[10] and one of them is now Abbess at Lisbon. The other two I helped on their way to Flanders, where they entered the Augustinian convent at Louvain.[11] The sons also were all fine young men. Two of them, as I said above, died in the Society. A third[12] found his career in soldiering. He distinguished himself in battle against the heretics in the Low Countries and was killed there a short time ago fighting hard to the end when all around him had surrendered. The fourth was the master of the house and to his mother's intense joy devoted himself to good works of every kind. This lady was such a holy soul that she felt that the world had nothing more to give her. On the day I

---

[10] Anne and Barbara Wiseman.
[11] Jane and Bridget Wiseman.†
[12] Robert Wiseman.

came to the house she asked her son to bring me up to her room. As I entered she threw herself down at my feet and begged me to let her kiss them—she said I was the first member of the Society she had seen. I refused, and she then kissed the floor where I was standing. That day she was filled with a wonderful consolation of soul that has never left her. Now she is living away from her son and keeps two Jesuit priests in her house, but what she had to endure meanwhile will be told in another place.

5. BRADDOCKS

Winter 1591–Spring 1594

When the family had settled down to this new life, I was able to find time for study,[1] and for some missionary journeys. My first concern, however, was to see that the whole house came to the sacraments frequently. With the exception of the widow they had been used to coming perhaps four times a year at most; now it was every week. On feast days and usually on Sundays I preached in the chapel, and instructed all how to examine their conscience, and taught those who had the leisure for it the way to meditate. Another practice I started was that of reading ascetical books, which we did even at table, when there were no guests or visitors present. Those were the days when priests used to take their meals with the family, often in clerical dress. I had, of course, a soutane and biretta with me, but Father Garnet had forbidden us to wear them except in the chapel.

In nearly every journey I managed to bring some people into the Church. But there is a great difference between these counties, where I was now working, and other parts of England. In other places, where a large number of the people are Catholics and nearly all have leanings toward

[1] Probably at this time J. G. was working on his translation of *The Exhortation of Jesus Christ to the Faithful Soul*, by the Carthusian monk Lanspergius (John of Landsberg). It was published secretly in London in 1598. Nathaniel Southwell, *Bibl. Scriptorum Soc. Jesu*, 452.

Catholicism, it is easy to make many converts and to have large congregations at sermons. For instance, in Lancashire, I have seen myself more than two hundred present at Mass and sermon. People of this kind come into the Church without difficulty, but they fall away the moment persecution blows up. When the alarm is over, they come back again. By contrast, in the districts I was living in now Catholics were very few. They were mostly from the better classes, none, or hardly any, from the ordinary people, for they are unable to live in peace, surrounded as they are by most fierce Protestants. The way, I think, to go about making converts in these parts is to bring the gentry over first, and then their servants, for Catholic gentle folk must have Catholic servants.

At this time I received into the Church my hostess' brother.[2] He was the only son of a knight, and he proved himself one of my most steadfast friends at all times. Later he married a cousin of the most illustrious Duke of Feria, and both are most devoted to our Fathers. They always have one of them in their house, sometimes two or three, quite regardless of the danger of the times.

It was in the same year too that I saw safely across to France the daughter and three sons of a Catholic gentleman.[3] The girl[4] entered the Augustinian convent at Louvain and became the talk of the place for her holiness. Even now, after her death, they speak of her with veneration and always refer to her as "the saint". Her esteem and love for the religious life was very great indeed, and she was embarrassingly thankful to me for the little part I played in her vocation; she would sing my praises to the community, and so extravagantly that when I came on a visit to Louvain

[2] Henry Huddlestone of Sawston, near Cambridge.†
[3] Richard Rookwood of Coldham, near Bury Saint Edmunds.†
[4] Dorothy Rookwood.

crowds pressed to see me. I even found that one of the Flemish Sisters, who was very fond of her while she was alive, had taken the trouble to learn English merely to make her confession to me. Others were doing the same. That Providence was at work here I am sure from this, that it proved the salvation of some souls who otherwise would never have confided in me.†

Her three brothers were among the first set of pupils at Saint Omers. One of them died in Spain soon after he left school; the second, the heir to the estate, was executed on a charge of treason, but really died a martyr for the faith;[5] the third is living and working in England to-day, a good priest and a great friend of our Fathers.†

I said something above about my host's two sisters. It took some time to arrange for them to go abroad. Before they left I had persuaded their mother that it would be a good thing if she returned to her own house[6] and maintained there a priest I had recommended to her. I felt that such a noble and generous soul should be a support to many, as in fact she became. Her house was a shelter and sure stronghold for Jesuits and all priests, and when I or others visited her she welcomed us with great joy. Sometimes she would clap her hands or give some other sign of her pleasure. Indeed she was a true widow, given up to all good works and full of zeal.

Not to mention many persons of less standing she brought to me to be reconciled, there was one great lady whom she all but won over. This lady[7] was her neighbor. She was sister to the Earl of Essex (then at the height of his favor

---

[5] Ambrose Rookwood.†
[6] At Northend, in the parish of Great Waltham, Essex.
[7] Penelope Rich, the most celebrated beauty of her day.†

with the Queen) and was married to the wealthiest lord in the whole country. Though she led a life of frivolity, she was brought to the point where she was ready to see a priest provided he could come without anyone knowing. The good widow told me this. So I went to the house openly and, according to an arrangement we had made, addressed her as though I were bringing her a message from another great lady, a relative of hers. I dined at her table with all the gentlefolk in the house and afterward talked to her for a good three hours in private. First, I set at rest all the doubts she raised about the faith; then I tried to stir her will. Before I left she asked me to instruct her how to prepare for confession, and we fixed a day for making it. Then she wrote to me protesting earnestly that there was nothing in the world she wanted more than to lay bare to me what was deepest in her heart.

But God's judgments are unfathomable, and it is a dread thing to expose oneself to the temptation of sin. There was a nobleman in London,[8] who loved her with a deep and enduring love. To him she wrote to announce the step she proposed to take, intending perhaps to break with him. But she roused a sleeping viper. At once he rushed down to see her and began to talk her out of her resolve for all he was able. He was a Protestant and was well read and cleverly persuaded her to ask her "guide" the answers to certain doubts he himself had about the faith.[9] He assured her that if he was convinced, he too would become a

---

[8] Charles Blount, eighth Lord Mountjoy.†

[9] "His chief delight was in the study of Divinity and more especially in reading of the Fathers and Schoolmen . . . and I will be bold to say that of a Lay-man he was (in my judgement) the best Divine I ever heard argue, especially for disputing against the Papists." Fynes Moryson, *History of Ireland* (ed. 1735), vol. I, 110.

Catholic. Meanwhile, he begged her to take no irrevocable step—unless she wanted him to commit suicide. He filled two whole sheets of paper about the Pope, the worship of saints, and that kind of thing. With his letter the lady enclosed a note of her own, begging me to do her the kindness of answering, for it would be a great gain if we could convert him. But the man had no intention whatever of learning the truth; he merely wanted to delay her own conversion. He received all his answers, and long ones at that, but he did not reply. In the interval he tried to bring her to London. He succeeded first in persuading her to postpone her reconciliation, and then to drop the idea altogether.

But all this time he was working his own destruction. Later, he returned from Ireland in triumph. He had administered the country well and defeated the Spanish forces that landed there (this was the occasion that he brought back the Earl of Tyrone, the stoutest opponent of heresy in the island and the firmest support of the old faith), and for his services he was created an earl by his present Majesty. But the poor man who had conquered others failed to conquer himself! His love of this lady held him a helpless captive. His madness drove him to excesses; he became notorious at court and was publicly disgraced. This was more than he could bear. Incapable of shaking himself free from his infatuation, he died of a broken heart. With his last breath he invoked, not God, but his goddess, his "angel", as he called her, and left her his sole heir. A miserable end indeed with his good name ruined.

Though the lady was now wealthier than ever, her thoughts often turned to her forgotten purpose. Frequently she would talk about me to one of her maids of honor who was a Catholic. And when about three years ago this girl crossed to Belgium to become a nun,[10] she told me this and suggested that I should write and see whether I could fan these embers into a flame. I was, in fact, composing a letter, when I got word that she had died of fever. Happily she had been reconciled to the Church on her deathbed by one of our Fathers.

I know I have spent a long time on this story, but I wanted to show the providence of God in regard to her and His Judgment on her lover, who had delayed her conversion.

[10] Among the ladies professed at the English convent at Brussels was "Mistress Deacon that heretofore attended on the Lady Riche". Edmondes to Salisbury, April 15, 1607. *S. P. Flanders*, vol. 8, 274.

6. SEARCH AT
BADDESLEY CLINTON

October 1591

During my stay here I made occasional long journeys to counties in the north. The route I followed passed through my own home and many places belonging to relatives and people I knew well. Yet I could do little there, though many folk professed a warm friendship for me. In fact, I experienced for myself the truth of the saying of Our Lord that "no man is a prophet in his own country"; and I was never anxious to stay with them very long.[1]

On one of these journeys I happened once to turn off my route and visit a Catholic relative. I came upon him just as he was going off to join a grand hunt for which all his friends had gathered. He invited me to come with him; he was anxious for me to win over a gentleman who had recently married a cousin of ours. I answered that it would be better to leave it to another day. He persisted, however, saying that unless I took my chance now I might never be able to get at him again. So I decided to go and join the gentleman, and all day I rode alongside him—the huntsman whom I was hunting down myself. Whenever the pack was at fault and stopped giving tongue, I used the pause to

[1] J. G., in company with William Wiseman and his servant Richard Fulwood, was at Lady Gerard's house at Bryn, Lancashire, sometime before Michaelmas, 1592. *S.P.D.*, vol. 248, no. 103.

follow up my own little chase and gave tongue myself in real earnest. From talk about the trouble we were taking in pursuing a poor animal I brought the conversation round to the need of seeking an eternal prize and the way to lay hold of it, and all the toil and pains that were required. The devil, I said, never rested but was always trying like a hound to bring us to bay—the man, you see, was more of a schismatic than a heretic and little controversy was needed. But it was only after much talking that I made any impression on his will. All that day and the next I worked on him. On the fourth day he gave in and became a Catholic. He is practicing his religion still and often keeps priests in his house and introduces them to other families.

Before I go on I must tell another story about the same man. It is an astonishing tale. He happened once to go and see a friend of his who was laid up in bed. Knowing well that the gentleman was no hard-headed heretic, but a good man who had been led astray, he began to instruct him in the faith. He persuaded him that, as he was dangerously ill, it was time that he began to think about his eternal salvation. His words went home, and the sick man begged him to find a priest to hear his confession. Meanwhile his friend instructed him how to stir up sorrow for his sins and prepare for a general confession. Then he left. At that time he had no priest staying with him and he could not find one quickly. Meanwhile the man died, evidently with a great desire to confess, for he was constantly asking when his friend was coming who had promised to bring a doctor back with him. (Priests usually pass as doctors when they visit houses of the sick.)

These holy desires seem to have stood the dying man in good stead. Every night after his death his wife saw a kind of light flicker through the air in her room and enter past the bed-curtains. In her fright she ordered her maidservants to bring their own beds into her room and stay with her during the night. But they saw nothing at all. Only the mistress saw it still every night and was very disturbed. In the end she sent for her husband's Catholic friend, told him all that had happened, and asked him to see some learned man to get his opinion. He in turn asked a priest who advised him to tell the lady that the strange light probably meant that she should come to the light of the faith. Her friend returned with this answer, and she became a Catholic. After her reception she had Mass said in that room for a long time. Yet the light still appeared every night. The widow was more worried than ever. The priest now consulted other priests. The answer they gave was this: probably her husband was on his way to heaven (he had been a Catholic at heart and had wanted to receive the sacraments) but he still needed prayers for the purgation of his soul. He suggested, therefore, that Mass should be offered for him for thirty days according to the old custom of the country. The lady arranged for this and went to Communion herself several times with the same intention. The night after the last Mass had been offered in the room, three lights appeared instead of the customary one, the outside two seeming to support the third between them. All three entered past the bed-curtains and after staying a few moments they mounted heavenward through the top coverings, leaving her in great comfort of soul. Nothing of the kind appeared again, and she interpreted it all as a sign that her husband's soul had been freed from suffering and carried up by the angels to heaven.

This happened in the county of Stafford.

The object of these journeys farther north was always to visit and encourage certain persons who gave great support to our common cause.

Among the people I used to visit were two sisters. They were the daughters of one of the oldest earls in the country, who had died a martyr for the faith.[2] At the time the two ladies lived in the same house, and they wanted to have me to stay with them altogether, and not merely visit them occasionally. This was impossible, but they placed themselves under my direction in spiritual matters. The elder sister was the mother of a family and she became, as it were, a pillar supporting the afflicted Church in those parts.[3] She kept two priests in her house and received with great kindness any others who happened to be passing (and there were many, for that part of the country was well provided with priests, and the Catholics were numerous, though they belonged mostly to the lower classes). Actually I was hardly ever in her house without meeting six or seven priests before I left. The help she gave extended over the whole district—at least up to the time I was captured and put in prison. After that her husband persuaded her to live in London. Neither benefited from the move, and the poor Catholics of the district suffered a heavy loss.

The other sister God kept for Himself. She was unmarried, self-effacing, and modest, with a disposition well-suited to higher things. Much of her time she gave to prayer, and the world seemed to lose its luster and heaven to dazzle her. Later I sent her over to Father Holt in Belgium and he wrote to me about her in these words: "No person who has ever come here from our country has given more edification or done more to raise the good name of England." She was the principal founder of the English Benedictine

[2] Thomas Percy, Earl of Northumberland, beheaded at York in 1572.

[3] Lady Elizabeth Percy, wife of Richard Woodroff of Wooley, Royston, in the West Riding. She is noted as an obstinate recusant in the returns for 1592–1593. *C.R.S.*, vol. 18, 79.

convent at Brussels, where she is living now.† She has attained great sanctity and self-denial, and it is her constant wish to lead a more secluded life. Often she asks her director for permission to become a recluse; but he is not in favor of it, and she has submitted to his advice.

At first I used to take round with me my own Mass equipment. It was simple but fitting and specially made so that it could be carried easily, with the other things I needed, by the man who acted as my servant. In this way I was able to say Mass in the morning wherever I happened to lodge, but I was always careful to examine every corner of the room first to make sure that there was no one peering in at me through the cracks. I should explain. My hosts could seldom provide the essentials for Mass and I had therefore to bring them myself. But after a few years there was no need to do this. In nearly every house I visited later I would find vestments and everything else laid out ready for me. Moreover, before very long I had so many friends on my route and so close to one another that I hardly ever had to put up at a tavern in a journey of a hundred and fifty miles. In my last two years I don't think I slept in one a single night.

I used to see my Superior several times in the course of the year. Often I had some important question to discuss with him. And regularly twice every year all of us came to give him our six-monthly account of conscience and offer Our Lord Jesus the renewal of our vows. As I can bear witness, this good custom of the Society was a great help to the others,† and, to speak for myself only (I will tell you my feelings simply) I never found anything that did me more good. It braced my soul to meet all the obligations of my life as a Jesuit and meet all the demands made of a priest on the mission. Apart from the consolation I got from renewing my vows, I experienced—after renewing them—a new strength and an ardent and freshened zeal. If I failed, then, in my work it was through no fault of the Society, which provided me with means such as this and gave me assistance in striving for the perfection that is its aim.

On one occasion we were all together in the house where Father Garnet was living[4]—it was the time he was still in the country. We had held several conferences and the Superior had seen each of us for a talk in private. Suddenly one of us raised the question: what would we do if the priest-hunters broke in without warning? (There were many of us there and an insufficient number of hiding places for all; we were nine or ten Jesuits and some other priests, besides a few laymen who were forced to live in hiding.) "Yes," said Father Garnet, "we ought not to meet all at the same time now that our numbers are growing every day. But we are gathered for God's glory. Until we have renewed our vows the responsibility is mine; after that it is yours." Up to the day we renewed our vows he gave no sign of being worried; but on the day itself he warned us all to look to ourselves and not to stay on without very good reason. "I won't guarantee your safety any longer", he told us. A number of the party, when they heard this, got on their horses immediately after dinner and rode off. Five Jesuits and two secular priests stayed behind.[5]

---

[4] "We had fixed on the same house which we had nearly always used previously for the purpose, belonging to two sisters, a widow [Mrs. Eleanor Brooksby] and a maiden lady [Miss Anne Vaux]" for it had a "very safe refuge in a well-hidden cave". The meeting lasted from October 14 to 19, 1591. Garnet to Aquaviva, March 17, 1594. Stonyhurst MSS, *Anglia*, vol. 1, no. 73.

[5] "At table on the feast of Saint Luke", says Father Garnet, "I know not what inspiration made me address them as follows: saying that, though up to now I had taken on myself all responsibility, I was no longer willing to guarantee them their safety, when dinner was over." Stonyhurst MSS, ibid.

It was about five o'clock the following morning. I was making my meditation, Father Southwell was beginning Mass, and the rest were at prayer, when suddenly I heard a great uproar outside the main door. Then I heard a voice shouting and swearing at a servant who was refusing them entrance. It was the priest-hunters, or pursuivants, as they are called. There were four of them altogether, with swords drawn, and they were battering at the door to force an entrance. But a faithful servant held them back, otherwise we should have all been caught.

Father Southwell heard the din. He guessed what it was all about, and slipped off his vestments and stripped the altar bare. While he was doing this, we laid hold of all our personal belongings—nothing was left to betray the presence of a priest. Even our boots and swords were hidden away—they would have roused suspicions if none of the people they belonged to were to be found. Our beds presented a problem: as they were still warm and merely covered in the usual way preparatory to being made, some of us went off and turned the beds and put the cold side up to delude anyone who put his hand in to feel them.

Outside the ruffians were bawling and yelling, but the servants held the door fast. They said the mistress of the house, a widow, was not yet up, but was coming down at once to answer them. This gave us enough time to stow ourselves and all our belongings into a very cleverly built sort of cave.

At last these leopards were let in. They tore madly through the whole house, searched everywhere, pried with candles into the darkest corners. They took four hours over the work but fortunately they chanced on nothing. All they did was to show how dogged and spiteful they could be, and how forbearing Catholics were. In the end they made off, but only after they had gotten paid for their trouble. Yes, that is the pitiful lot of Catholics—when men come with a warrant to upset their homes in this or any other way, it is they, the Catholics, not the authorities who send them, who have to pay. As if it were not enough to suffer, they are charged for suffering.

When they had gone, and gone a good way, so that there was no danger of their turning back suddenly, as they sometimes do, a lady came and called us out of our den, not one but several Daniels. The hiding-place was below ground level; the floor was covered with water and I was standing with my feet in it all the time. Father Garnet was there, also Father Southwell and Father Oldcorne (three future martyrs), Father Stanney and myself, two secular priests, and two or three laymen.

So we were all saved that day.

The next day Father Southwell and I rode off, as we had come, in company. But Father Oldcorne stayed on, as the place where he lived was not far away.[6]

---

[6] A description of the underground hiding-place is given in Appendix B. In a letter to the General written the following March Garnet gives a much longer account of this search.†

7. FATHER OLDCORNE

Now that I have mentioned Father Oldcorne I shall explain briefly how he came to be living there. On his first arrival in England he stayed with the Superior, as he had no home of his own to go to. Only a short way from this place there was a very fine mansion belonging to a Catholic gentleman.[1] At the time this man was held a prisoner for the faith in the Tower of London. His sister[2] was a Protestant. She had been brought up at the Queen's court and there had drunk in heresy so deeply that no one could be found to cure her. Many indeed had tried, for she liked talking about religion, not that she had the intention of learning anything, it was just that she enjoyed a good argument. Through her obstinacy a good Catholic house was lost to us as long as she was mistress in her brother's absence; and there was not a finer house in the whole county. Beautifully built and in most pleasant surroundings, it was perfect as a Catholic center.†

After a number of priests had tried to win over the lady and failed, Father Garnet thought of Father Oldcorne and wanted him to make one further attempt. The Father went; he found her as obdurate as ever; he tried arguments from Scripture, reason, and authority, but he got nowhere. However, his persistence was more than a match for the woman's

---

[1] Thomas Habington of Hinlip House, Worcestershire.†
[2] Dorothy Habington, whose father had been the Queen's cofferer.

obstinacy, for turning to God he tried whether he could not cast out the dumb devil by prayer and fasting. The lady noticed that the Father ate nothing for a whole day, and then another. This made her wonder, but she kept up her show of obstinacy. "Perhaps he is an angel and not a man", she said to herself. And then with a woman's curiosity: "I'll see whether he can live as the angels do. If he can't, then he won't convert me." For four whole days the priest kept up his fast. In the end he put her devil to flight, and the lady "was healed from that hour". Father Oldcorne had truly obtained for her "ears to hear": the headstrong and petulant woman became most humble and pliable in his hands.

Looking back over this I think it was all part of God's providence to allow the other priests to fail; He seems to have kept her specially for this Father, and not just her, but nearly the whole county which followed her over. For sixteen years Father Oldcorne lived in her house. It was his work to bring many to the faith in this and neighboring counties, to support the wavering and lift up the fallen, and to station priests in many places. Many therefore who knew him speak of him in the words Saint Jerome uses of Saint John—"he founded and governed all the churches in those parts." Everyone indeed looked on him as his father. He was prudent and gave more than satisfaction to all, hardworking and long-suffering and never failing anyone that needed his ministrations. Countless poor Catholics relied on him for alms. And the place where he lived was every bit like one of our houses in some foreign country—so many Catholics flocked there to receive the sacraments, or to hear him preach or to get his advice. Father Thomas Lister,† a very learned and remarkable man, was his fellow-worker.

The servant of others, Father Oldcorne dealt very harshly with himself. His heavy work and this "care of all the churches in those parts"—they seemed in fact to depend on him for almost everything—did not satisfy him. When he was at home he studied hard and, at the same time, did much corporal penance. His fasts I have mentioned already. Also, he used to wear a haircloth, and scourge himself often and very hard. Though, of course, he meant merely to "chastise the enemy and bring it into subjection", he nearly made himself an "unprofitable servant". First of all he burst a blood vessel and began to vomit great quantities of blood. He got over this, but almost every year he became so anemic that he looked as if he would never get his strength back. In this weak condition he developed a growth in his mouth— the English word for it is a "canker"—which developed so much that it seemed incurable. As he told me afterward, the doctors declared that they would have to cut out some bones which were beginning to decay. The good Father, afraid that the operation would prevent him from ever preaching again—he was a talented preacher[3]—decided first to go on pilgrimage to Saint Winefrid's well, a famous shrine and, as it were, a standing miracle.[4]

Saint Winefrid was a saintly and very beautiful girl in North Wales, and her faith and love of chastity made her more beautiful still. The son of a chieftain fell in love with her and sought her in marriage. But she rejected his suit, for he was a heathen, and she had, besides, made a vow of virginity before the bishop of the place, and was unwilling to yield it to any man. Her suitor's love then turned to wrath and he cut off the girl's head with his sword. He did this on the slope of a hill, and the head rolled down to the

[3] In the *Narrative* (284) J. G. speaks of his "earnest manner of preaching in which he had good talent, though his voice were somewhat hoarse and painful unto himself, yet audible unto his hearers".

[4] Cf. Appendix C.

foot where a powerful spring instantly burst forth. Since that day the valley, which had been known as "the arid valley", has been made fertile by the stream which rises at the spring and flows down into the sea, and the power of the water that gushes out every minute is sufficient to turn a mill about fifty yards away. In the well itself there are some very large stones, all red as if covered with fresh blood. When pieces are chipped off—the people of the place try their best to prevent pilgrims doing this—the fragments are the same shade of red, and the place they are chipped from turns in time from white to red. Also lying on the bed of the stream can be found stones covered or at least sprinkled with blood. These the Catholics gather out of devotion and preserve reverently; as they do also with a tufty weed (the English word is "moss") which clings to the stones and gives a sweet smell when it is plucked.† The water from the spring is extremely cold, but no one ever came to any harm by drinking it or bathing in it. I took several gulps of it myself on an empty stomach and nothing happened to me.

Once I was there on the third of November, Saint Winefrid's feast, and saw the change that takes place in the well that day. (The water rises a good foot above its ordinary level, and turns red as it rises, but the next day it is clearer than ever.) I myself watched the water moving and turning a reddish color, water (mind you) that on any other day is so remarkably clear that you can pick out a pin lying on the bottom. It was winter. There was a hard frost at the time, and though the ice in the stream had been broken by people crossing it the previous night, I still found it very difficult to ford on my horse the next morning. But frost or no frost, I went down into the well like a good pilgrim. For a quarter of an hour I lay down in the water and prayed. When I came out my shirt was dripping. But I kept it on and I pulled all my clothes over it, and I was none the worse for my bathe.

These are true facts. Also, there are frequently great and manifest miracles at the well. For instance, there is the story of the Protestant visitor who was watching some Catholics bathe and stood mocking their devotion. "What are they up to, washing here in the water? I'll show them. I'll clean my boots in it." So in he jumped, boots, sword, and all. Scarcely had he touched the water than he felt its supernatural powers which he had refused to believe in. There and then he was struck with paralysis: he lost the use of his limbs; his sword could hardly be pulled out of his grip. For several years afterwards he was wheeled around in a push-cart like a cripple.

Thus was he punished, and others confirmed in their belief.

I have myself spoken to a number of people who saw the lame man and heard the story both from his own lips and from men who knew him. It was they who told me the sequel: how the man repented and recovered the use of his limbs in the very well where he had been struck down. This is just one of many stories of the kind.

As I was saying, Father Oldcorne had his heart set on visiting the holy well; but Saint Winefrid forestalled him. On his way he stopped at the dwelling of two maiden sisters. They were poor people, but rich in other ways, for they feared God, living and serving Him together, and keeping in their house a priest whom they looked up to as their father. This good priest had taken from the stream one of those stones sprinkled with blood that I have just described. At the time of Mass he used to place it on the altar with the other relics. When Father Oldcorne noticed it he took it in his hands and kissed it very reverently. Then going aside by himself, he went down on his knees and began to lick the stone and hold part of it to his mouth. He prayed silently all the time. After half an hour he got up—all his pain was gone and the cancer cured. But he finished his pilgrimage to the well—not to beg a cure from Saint Winefrid, but to make his thanksgiving for it. While he was there he recovered also from that anemia which was thought to be the cause of his cancer, and he came back stronger and healthier than he had been for many years.

I have told the story in the words that Father Oldcorne told it to me. The priest, in whose house Father Oldcorne found the stone, confirmed the facts when I met him at Saint Omers. He told me, too, of the wonderful things that had occurred after Father Oldcorne's death. About these later. This will do now for Father Oldcorne; I must get back to my own miserable story.

In the course of my stay in this third residence I gave the Spiritual Exercises to several people—and, among others, to two gentlemen who to this day both stand loyally by the resolutions they then made and are both firm friends of the Jesuits, each in his district. The first, Mr. John Lee,† only quite recently defended some thesis in philosophy at Rome. He is now back in England and is always ready to shelter ours and to supply their financial needs. The other is a man who has proved himself utterly trustworthy in one difficult business after another. Five or perhaps six years later both made a second retreat, and it was most consoling to see how well they made it.

I must not forget to mention a certain lady and her husband (they were gentlefolk) who made a vow of chastity. They had often proposed it to me, but I knew the dangers of an undertaking such as this and would not hear of it. However, they persisted; I compromised and let them try it for a year. They did, and at the end of the year they were more eager than ever to make the vow. So I let them. Of course, they took all the obvious precautions regarding separation *quoad torum* though they still lived under the same roof. Indeed, the affection they showed one another and the real love that existed between them seemed to grow. I kept in touch with them for many years afterward and I can say that during all that time they remained faithful to their vow.

I also sent abroad for study a number of young men who aspired to the priestly life. One of them died at Douai. During his studies he had done very well and gained the reputation of being a very holy young man. He had worked with the Blessed Father Francis Page, the Jesuit martyr, when they were together in a London office; and it was he who introduced me to the good Father. You will see later what resulted from this introduction. Others are now Jesuit priests. Father Silvester and Father Clare are at present, I think, at Valladolid; some also are serving God in their own different spheres, for example, Father John Bolt.† His musical talent was outstanding and won him the affection of a very powerful patron. But he laid this aside and with it all his hopes of fame, in order to attach himself to me and to follow the counsels of Our Lord explained in the Spiritual Exercises.[5]

At this time I was given some very remarkable relics, and my friends had them finely set for me. They included a complete thorn of the holy crown of Our Lord which Mary, Queen of Scots, had brought with her from France (where

[5] J. G. probably also knew William Byrd, the madrigalist who was a close friend of Father Garnet and at a later period used to play "the organs and other instruments" at the meetings of the Jesuits in Anne Vaux's house at Erith, Kent. *Hat. Cal.*, 17:611.

the whole crown is kept) and had given to the Earl of Northumberland, who was later martyred. While he lived, the earl used to carry it round his neck in a golden cross, and when he came to execution he gave it to his daughter, who gave it to me. It was enclosed in a gilt case set with pearls. With three other silver reliquaries it is in the Superior's keeping.

Two of these relics are old ones and were rescued from the pillage of a monastery. They came to me through a trustworthy source. The third is a forefinger of the martyr Father Robert Sutton, the brother of the priest I mentioned on the first page of this book. By a wonderful providence of God this finger, together with the thumb, was preserved from decay, although the whole arm had been pinned up to be eaten by birds. When some Catholics came to remove it secretly (it had been exposed for a whole year) they found nothing but bones. The only parts still covered with flesh and skin were the thumb and finger which had been anointed with sacred oil at ordination and had been sanctified by the touch of the Blessed Sacrament. His brother, another good priest, kept the thumb in his possession and presented me with the forefinger.†

About the same time, also, I was given a silver head of Saint Thomas of Canterbury, and his miter studded with precious stones. The head is small and of no great value in itself, but it is quite a treasure because it contains a piece of the saint's skull. It is the breadth of a gold double crown, and it is thought to be the piece that was chipped off when he was so wickedly slain. The silver head was old and had lost some stones, but the gentleman in whose house I was staying had it repaired and finely ornamented. For this reason the Superior afterward let him keep it in trust for the Society in his private chapel. Another gift was a large piece of Saint Vita's arm. It is now in the keeping of another Catholic gentleman in the same county.

The virgin Vita was the daughter of a West of England King, and many churches were dedicated to her under the name of Witchurch. The relic came to me in this way. The parson of the place where the whole body (or at least a great part of it) was preserved and venerated in the old days found that he was always restive at night and could get no sleep. This went on for a long time. Then one day the thought struck him that this trouble came from his not paying proper and due respect to the bones which he had in his keeping. He felt he ought to give them to Catholics who were their rightful owners. This he did, and he slept well ever afterward. A good priest told me this story, and he gave me a large bone, which a devout Catholic is keeping on behalf of the Society.

There were many other beautiful things which were given me for the Order. The Catholics of the house and visitors got great comfort and devotion when they were used.

8. "PEINE FORTE ET DURE"

But there is a time for gathering stones and a time for scattering them. The moment had come for the testing of God's servants—I mean my hosts and myself with them.

In order to make them more like the Master for whom they suffered, God allowed them to be betrayed by one of their own household,† a man they all loved. He was not a Catholic; nor was he a servant of the house, but had been employed once by the second brother who had recommended him to his mother and elder brother before he went abroad. His home was in London but he often visited the family and knew almost everything that happened in both their houses. I must confess myself that I saw no reason for distrusting a person whom everybody else trusted, but I was careful all the same not to let him see me acting as a priest or even dressed in a way that would give him grounds for saying that I was one. But he guessed it, as he admitted to me later, when he saw the respect with which the master of the house treated me: how he nearly always accompanied me on the first two or three miles of my journeys, and often went the whole way to London with me. It was at his house† that we used to lodge on our visits to town. I had still to learn from experience that the safest course was to have a house of my own.

These small things gave rise to suspicions in the traitor's mind, as he himself told me afterward. Certain as he was of more than thirty pieces of silver for the sale of his master, he went to the magistrates and bargained with them for his betrayal. Meanwhile—I think this is what happened—they sent him to keep a close watch on the two houses, the widow's and her son's, to note the priests who came there and to count their number.

The widow's house was the first to be searched. The priest who usually lived there[1] was at home but he got away into a hiding-place and was not found that time. But they forced the good widow to go to London† and appear before the officials who acted as judges in cases concerning Catholics. She appeared, and answered very boldly, more like a free woman than a wronged and persecuted lady. She was sent back to jail and showed very great patience and piety, attending to her own wants like a servant girl, cooking her own food, and doing her own washing. She desired this humiliating work for its own sake—she knew it was the only way to true humility—and also because it kept down her expenses. With the money she saved she supported poor Catholics.

While she was in prison she always sent me half her annual income—six hundred florins. The other half she spent on the support of a priest to bring her Holy Communion on fixed days and to attend her fellow-prisoners, and also on other good works. She devoted all her time to prayer or needlework—she made vestments and other things for the altar and sent them to different people. For two whole years this was her life until God asked an even greater sacrifice of the holy lady.

---

[1] This was a Father Brewster, probably an old Marian priest, who is described as "a tall man with a waxen beard". *S.P.D.*, vol. 148, no. 103.

It happened this way. God allowed it to come to the knowledge of the authorities that she received visits from a priest. If I remember right, he was Father Jones, a Franciscan Recollect who was later martyred.[2] They decided therefore to invoke the law against her, and she was brought up for trial. The usual false witnesses were produced and she was charged with being privy to the maintenance of priests contrary to the laws of the land. The judges empanelled a jury to declare her guilty or innocent. But in order to save the jury staining their consciences with her blood by returning a verdict of guilty, this good woman decided to hold her tongue and to make no reply when the judge ordered her to plead guilty or not guilty. She did this knowing full well the provision of the law—I mean that far more severe and cruel sentence reserved for men and women who refuse to plead in a matter of life and death. They are laid on their backs on a sharp stone and a heavy weight placed on their chests until life is crushed out of them.

Up to the time I am writing about we had had only two women martyrs (not including Mary, Queen of Scots). One of them, Clitherow, chose the same death and martyr's crown at York for the same reasons.† She knew that the jury were certain to declare her guilty in order to please the judge, and she wanted to spare their consciences. She knew they would be fully aware of the injustice. It was her example

[2] It appears to have been a single visit and arranged by Topcliffe with the purpose of framing an indictment against Mrs. Wiseman. Nicholas Blackwall, a hanger-on at the Gatehouse, acting in collusion with Topcliffe, asked Mrs. Wiseman, who used to make poultices for the poor, whether she would attend to the leg of a friend of his. She agreed; Father Jones was brought in, and Mrs. Wiseman applied a cerecloth to his leg. This was the "receiving, comforting, helping and maintaining priests" for which she was indicted. *C.R.S.*, vol. 5, 363.

that this good widow had in mind. She chose the same course and the same penalty. She was silent and she received the sentence—to be pressed to death.[3]

She left the court rejoicing that she had not been thought unworthy to suffer for Jesus' sake the form of death she had hoped would be hers. But her position and her good name gave the Queen's councillors second thoughts. They did not want to shock London by their barbarity, so after her condemnation they had her removed to another and worse prison and kept her there. What they were after was her property for the Queen. And had she been executed, this would have gone, not to the Queen, but to her son, my host.[4] So the good widow lived on in this prison, deprived of all she possessed except her life, which was the one thing she hoped they would take from her.†

There in a filthy cell she lingered on until the accession of King James when she received the pardon usually granted at the coronation of a new king. On her return home she continued to serve God's servants as she had done before and still kept two of ours in her house.

So much for this good widow. Now to get back to the rest of my own story.

[3] "The sentence is that the said Jane Wiseman shall be led to the prison of the Marshalsea of the Queen's Bench, and there naked, except for a linen cloth about the lower part of her body, be laid upon the ground, lying directly on her back: and a hollow shall be made under her head and her head placed in the same; and upon her body in every part let there be placed as much of stones and iron as she can bear and more; and as long as she shall live, she shall have of the worst bread and water of the prison next her; and on the day she eats, she shall not drink, and on the day she drinks she shall not eat, so living until she die." Indictment of Jane Wiseman, June 30, 1598. *C.R.S.*, vol. 5, 367.

[4] A person dying under *peine forte et dure*, as this penalty was called, could transmit his estates to his children, whereas, if he were found guilty, they went to the Crown. This form of death was abolished in 1772.

The traitor did not reveal himself and he was still unsuspected by his master and he was looking now for an opportunity to betray us without giving himself away. His first plan was to seize me in the London house which I had recently rented for my own and my friends' use.[5] As his master employed him in a great deal of his business, he could not help knowing the place which his master had rented for my benefit. So he promised the magistrates that he would give them word when I next came there and they could call out the officers, surround the house at night, and cut off my escape. This is exactly what would have happened had not God intervened through an order of my Superior.

The Superior had come to live in a house four or five miles from London,† and I had gone over to see him. But as I had business to do in town, I wrote after a day or two and informed the people who kept the house to expect me on such and such a night, and to ask in a number of friends whom I wanted to see. The traitor learnt the time (he was often in the house, which ostensibly belonged to the master) and arranged for the pursuivants and their men to surround the place at midnight.

Just before I mounted my horse I went to say good-bye to the Superior. He urged me to stay the night with him, but I said that I had business in town and explained what it was, and that I had certain appointments to keep. But the blessed Father would not hear of my going, though, as he told me later, he had no idea why he had acted in such a peculiar way. It certainly was not his usual manner and I have no doubt at all that he was guided by the Holy Spirit.

[5] At the upper end of Golding Lane, Holborn.†

Early next morning rumors reached us that papists had been seized in the house.[6] It was said that a priest had been found among them—actually it was my servant, Richard Fulwood. The place was without hiding-holes, though I had planned to build some, and he was hiding in a dark corner of the house. Since he cut a good figure he was taken for a priest—neither the traitor nor anyone else who knew him was there.

Three Catholics and one schismatic were taken and put in prison. (By "schismatic" I mean a person who is a Catholic by conviction but attends the Protestant church.) In this case he was a trustworthy person whom I had employed as housekeeper and as a sort of agent in the district.

When these men came up for examination they stood firm and true;[7] none of their answers gave the slightest clue as to who was the real owner of the house, namely, myself, not my host. This was a good thing because had it been known that the house belonged to me, my host would have received even worse handling. As things turned out he got a special summons; they were still hoping to capture me and so make out a stronger case against him. As soon as my host got to town in answer to the summons, he went straight to the house. Knowing nothing of what had happened, he was anxious to find out whether I could tell him anything about the summons and advise him how to answer it. He came to the door and knocked; but he fell—the poor sheep of Christ—into the clutches of wolves, not into the hands of his shepherd and friend. It was only the night before

---

[6] The raid was on March 15, 1594.†

[7] With Fulwood were captured John Bolt, the musician; John Tarbuck, a Lancashire Catholic; and William Suffield, the "schismatic", a Norfolk weaver in William Wiseman's service. Their examination is extant, confirming J. G.'s tribute to their constancy. *S.P.D.*, vol. 248, nos. 37–40.

that the house had been broken into, and some of the rascals were still hanging about the place on the look-out for any Catholics who might visit it before they got the scent of danger.

Out they came and fell on him and led him off in custody to the magistrates. "How many priests visit your house? How many do you keep there? What are their names?"—he was asked innumerable questions, but in his reply he made the point that the harboring of priests was a capital offense and he had taken good care not to run such a risk. But they pressed him, and he answered that he was prepared to meet any charge brought against him on this head. However, they insinuated nothing about me. Disappointed as they were this time, they still had hopes of catching me for they knew the traitor was still unsuspected.

At the time of his arrest my host was working on a translation of Father Jerome Platus' *On the Happiness of the Religious State*. Recently he had completed the second part and had brought it up with him so that he could discuss it with me. When he was taken these manuscripts were found on him, and on being asked what they were he replied that they were just a book of devotion—the Protestants are afraid of anything being published against them or their false doctrines, and they scrutinize carefully all papers that fall into their hands. As they had no time to go into his whole case there and then they pressed him merely on the point of these papers. Again he insisted that they contained nothing whatever against the State or against sound doctrine, and offered to vindicate on the spot the propriety of the book. While he was doing this, as he told me later, he felt great consolation of soul at being answerable for such a fine work.†

However, he was imprisoned, and his confinement was so strict that only one of his servants, and the traitor at that, was allowed to visit him.[8] They knew his master still had no suspicion of his bad faith and they hoped this way to find out where I was hiding and seize me sooner than they could have done otherwise.

Actually, when I heard that our London house had been taken and my host imprisoned, I went to his country place, being anxious to confer with his wife and friends on what we had better do. I also wanted to get everything hidden neatly away. We needed of course most of the altar things for Easter, which was very close now, so only a few of them were packed off to friends. It was really impossible for me to desert the family now, for they were going through such an anxious and difficult time.

Holy Week came. The traitor turned up from London with a letter from his master. It gave an account of all that had happened to him, the questions he had been asked, and his answers.[9]

The letter of course had been seen by the authorities, but they let it through in order to give the traitor credit and provide him with an excuse for finding out whether I was in the house during Holy Week. He carried also a second letter. This was from my servant, whose capture at the house I have just described. They had put him in solitary confinement in the most loathsome of all the prisons, the Bridewell. They knew he was my servant, because the traitor had told them, and they confined him in that prison in the hope that he would give away the names of his friends and accomplices. In this letter he said that he had answered

---

[8] He was imprisoned in the Counter in Wood Street. *Hat. Cal.*, 5:25.

[9] It was very important for friends of a prisoner to know, if possible, what answers he had made, both to take steps to ensure their own safety, if necessary, and to know how far to go in their own answers if they were caught and examined.

firmly "No" to all their questions, and went on to describe the threats they had made and the treatment he was receiving. He said that he was given barely sufficient bread to keep body and soul together. His cell was narrow; it had thick walls; it had no bed in it, and he had to sleep in a sitting posture perched on the window-ledge. For months he had not taken his clothes off. There was only a little straw in the place and it had been trodden flat, and now it was crawling with vermin and quite impossible to lie on. Worst of all, they left his excrement in an uncovered pail in that tiny cell, and the stink was suffocating. In these conditions he was waiting to be called out and examined under torture.

I read out the letter to my hostess—the traitor was standing by—and as I came to the last passage I murmured: "Would to God I could suffer some of this myself so that he might suffer less!" It was this remark that made it possible for me later to identify the traitor who had caused all this trouble. When I was captured and questioned and stated that I had not known any of the family, the examiners forgot their secret and called out: "Lies! Lies! You said this and that in this lady's presence, when you were reading out your servant's letter." But I continued to deny it all the same and gave them good reasons why I could and should do so even if it were true. But to resume my story.

9. SEARCH AT BRADDOCKS

April 1, 1594

The traitor returned to London and made a full report. Straightaway a couple of messengers (or pursuivants, as they are called) were sent to two gentlemen of the county, Justices of the Peace, carrying an authorization for their men to search the house carefully.

On Easter Sunday the traitor came again from London with a fresh letter. That was the pretext; his real motive was to be present on the spot to help the searchers and keep them informed of our movements.

On Easter Monday[1] we rose earlier than usual for Mass, for we felt there was danger about. As we were preparing everything for Mass before daybreak we heard, suddenly, a great noise of galloping hooves. The next moment, to prevent any attempt at escape, the house was encircled by a whole troop of men. At once we realized what was afoot. We barred the doors; the altar was stripped, the hiding-places opened, and all my books and papers thrown in. It was most important to pack me away first with all my belongings. I was for using the hiding-place near the dining-room—it was farther away from the chapel (the most suspected part of the house) and it had a supply of provisions—a bottle of wine and some light sustaining biscuits and other

[1] April 1, 1594.

food that would keep. Also there was more chance there of overhearing the searchers' conversation and picking up some information that might prove helpful to us. This is why I preferred it, and it was also a well-built and safe place. However, the mistress of the house (it turned out to be providential) was opposed to it. She wanted me to use the place near the chapel; I could get into it more quickly and hide all the altar things away with me. As she was very insistent, I agreed, although I knew I would have nothing to eat if the search was a long one. We hid away everything that needed hiding and I went in.

I was hardly tucked away when the pursuivants broke down the door and burst in. They fanned out through the house, making a great racket. The first thing they did was to shut up the mistress of the house in her own room with her daughters;[2] then they locked up the Catholic servants in different places in the same part of the house. This done, they took possession of the place (it was a large house) and began to search everywhere, even lifting up the tiles of the roof to examine underneath them and using candles in the dark corners. When they found nothing, they started knocking down suspicious-looking places. They measured the walls with long rods and if the measurements did not tally they pulled down the section that they could not account for. They tapped every wall and floor for hollow spots; and on sounding anything hollow they smashed it in.

Two days of this revealed nothing. On the second day the justices went off thinking that I must have left the house on Easter Sunday. Some pursuivants remained behind to take the mistress of the house and the Catholic servants,

---

[2] Dorothy and Winifred Wiseman, the younger of whom was ten years old.

men and women, up to London to be examined and imprisoned.[3] They were going to leave the other servants—I mean
the non-Catholics—to watch the house. The traitor was
one of them.

This pleased the lady and she hoped with his help to
save me from dying of slow starvation, for she knew I had
made up my mind to die in this way between the two walls
rather than come out and save my life at the sacrifice of
others. Indeed, during those four days of hiding all I had to
eat was a biscuit or two and a little quince jelly which my
hostess happened to have by her and had handed to me as
I was going in. As she had not expected the search to last
more than a day she had looked for nothing else.

But now two days had passed and she was to be taken off
next morning with all the servants she could trust. Afraid I
might die of starvation she called up the traitor. She had
heard he was to be left behind and had noticed that, when
the searchers first broke in, he had made a great show of
resisting them. Certainly she would never have given away
my hiding-place to him had I not been in such straits, but
she thought it better to save me from certain death, even
though she was taking a risk. So she instructed him after
she had been taken away, when there was no one about, to
go into a certain room and to call out my name; he was to
say that everyone else had been taken off, he alone was left
and would set me free. She told me that I would answer
from my hiding-place behind the paneling and plaster.

The traitor promised to carry out these instructions faithfully; yes, he was faithful but only to men who did not
know the meaning of faith. Of course he reported everything

---

[3] Presumably, from what follows, they were taken for temporary confinement in a neighboring house. When nothing could be proved against them
they were allowed to return.

to the party who had been left behind, and they at once sent a call for the magistrates who had already left. First thing in the morning they were back and the search was resumed. Much more thoroughly than before they measured up and sounded every place for a hollow spot, particularly in that room, but during the whole of the third day they found nothing at all. They decided, therefore, to spend the next day tearing off the plaster.

Meanwhile they set guards that night in every room round it to watch any attempt I might make to escape. From where I was hidden I heard the password which the head of the party gave his men, and if I could have come out of my hiding-place without being seen I would have used it and tried to get away. But there were two men watching in the chapel where the entrance to my hiding-place was, and there were several others in the plastered room, which they had been told about.

But an amazing Providence protected me. Here I was in my hiding-place. I had gotten into it by raising part of the floor under the grate. It was made of wood and brick and constructed in such a way that a fire could not be lit in it without damaging the house. But wood was kept there as though it were meant for a fire.[4]

That night the men on guard decided to light a fire in the grate and they sat down by it for a gossip. In a few moments the bricks, which were not laid on other bricks but on wood, came loose and almost fell out of position as the woodwork subsided. The men noticed this and poked the hearth with a stick and found the bottom made of wood. I heard them remark what a curious thing it was and thought

[4] As J. G. states later, this hiding-place was constructed by Nicholas Owen. A plan of it is given in Appendix D.

that there and then they would smash open the hiding-place and peer in. However, they decided to put off their investigations until the next day.

Escape was out of the question now. I began to pray earnestly that, if it was for God's greater glory, I might not be captured in that house and bring retribution on my host, nor in any other house whatsoever where others would suffer for it. My prayer was heard and in a most wonderful manner. God kept me safe in that house. A few days later, when I was captured, no one suffered for it, as you shall see in a moment.

The next day the search was resumed with great thoroughness. But they left alone the top room which had served as a chapel and in which the two guards had made the fire above my head, and had commented on the strange structure of the grate. God had wiped all memory of it from their minds. During all that day not a single pursuivant entered the room, and it was, not without reason, the most suspected room in the house. If they had entered they would have found me without any search at all; rather, they would have seen me, for the fire had burned a hole in my hiding-place, and I had to move a little to one side to avoid the hot embers falling on my head. The pursuivants seemed to have forgotten all about this room; at any rate they seemed not to care about it. Instead they concentrated on the rooms below, in one of which they had been told I was hiding, and did in fact discover the other hiding-place which I had wanted to use (as I said above). It was quite near to where I was and I heard their yelps of joy when they came on it, and then their consternation when they found it empty. All they discovered was an untouched store of provisions laid up against a long search like this. Possibly they concluded it was the place that the mistress of the house meant, it would certainly have been easy to answer from there any call made by a person in the room she had mentioned.

But they kept to their plan of stripping off all the plaster from the other large room and with the help of a carpenter they began their work close to the ceiling not far from where I was. (The lower parts of the walls were covered with tapestries.) Going right round the room they ripped off the plaster until they were in front of the exact spot where I was hiding. There, despairing of finding me, they gave up. My hiding-place was in a thick wall of the chimney behind a finely inlaid and carved mantelshelf, which they could not remove without risk of breaking. Yet if they had had the slightest suspicion that I was behind it they would have smashed it to pieces. They knew that there were two flues and thought it would be impossible for a man to hide there.

Earlier, on the second day of the search, they had been in the room above and had examined the fireplace through which I had gotten into my hole. With the help of a ladder they had climbed into the flue and sounded it with a hammer, and I had heard one of them saying to another: "There might conceivably be room for a person to get down here into the wall of the chimney below if this grate were raised." "Hardly", said the other, whose voice I recognized, "there is no entrance down that way into the other chimney. But there might easily be an entrance at the back of the chimney."

As soon as he had said this he gave the place a kick. I was afraid he would notice the hollow sound of the hole in which I was hiding. But God, who sets limits to the sea, said to these determined men: "You have come as far as this, but you go no farther", and He spared his sorely stricken children and would not give them up into the hands of their persecutors. Nor would He allow anything worse to come upon them for their great charity to me.

As their search was a failure they thought that I had managed to escape somehow or other, and they went off at the end of the fourth day. The mistress of the house was set free and her servants also; the traitor, however, still undiscovered, stayed behind after the searchers had left.

The doors of the house were then barred, and the mistress came to call me out. Like Lazarus, who was buried four days, I came forth from what would indeed have been my tomb if the search had continued a little longer. I was very wasted and weak with hunger and lack of sleep. All that time I had been squatting in a very confined space. While the search was on, the mistress of the house had eaten nothing whatsoever, partly because she wanted to share my discomfort and find out by testing herself how long I could live without food, but chiefly to draw down God's mercy upon me and upon herself and her whole family by fasting and prayer. When I came out I found her face so changed that she looked a different person; and had it not been for her voice and her dress I doubt whether I would have recognized her.

The traitor met me after I had come out. We still had no suspicion of his treachery. He did nothing then; he did not even call the pursuivants back for he knew well that I meant to be off before they could be recalled.

10. ARREST

Spring 1594

I took a little refreshment and after a short rest set out for a friend's house not very far away. There I lay low for a fortnight. However, I felt very uneasy over the situation in which I had left my friends and went to London to see whether I could help or comfort them in any way. On this occasion I stayed with a person of high rank[1] and was completely safe. It was at this house that Father Southwell had lived until, a year before, he was captured and imprisoned in the Tower of London.

In the meantime, however, I looked about for a lodging where I could be safe and unobserved and be free to do all the business I had to do with my friends—this was difficult in somebody else's house and, particularly, in the one where I was staying. With the help of that excellent man who was so experienced in transactions of this sort, I mean Father Garnet's servant, "Little John", as he was called, I found a very suitable place, and we came to an agreement with the landlord about the rent.

(It was "Little John" who made our hiding-places and, in fact, had made the one to which I owed my escape a short time before.)

[1] Anne, Countess of Arundel, who was then living at Arundel house in the Strand.

While this house was being gotten ready I lodged in an apartment in my landlord's own house,† intending to spend two or three nights there preparing to move. I also wanted to receive letters from my friends whom I had just left and to write and console them. But this was my undoing, for they used the traitor as a messenger. Only a few friends knew about the place, but God decreed that my hour had come.

One night, when "Little John" and I were together in our bedroom, the traitor had to bring us a letter that required an immediate answer, and he left with it about ten o'clock. I had only returned from the other house about nine o'clock, very much against the wishes of the lady, my hostess, who had urged me with unusual insistence not to leave it that night. At once the traitor went off and told the pursuivants where and when he had left us. They got together a gang and arrived at the house at midnight. I had just fallen asleep when John and I were woken up together by the sudden uproar outside. I guessed at once what it meant, and I ordered John to hide away the letter we had received that evening in the ashes of the fire. He did this and got back into bed; then we seemed to hear the noise travelling up toward our room. There were sharp raps on the door—it was clear the men intended to break it down if we did not open quickly. There was no escape. That door was the only way out of the room and the men were barring it, so I told John to get up and open to them. The next moment men "armed with swords and staves" burst in and filled the room, while many more stood outside, unable to get in. Among them I noticed two pursuivants, as they are called, one of whom knew me well.† That meant that I had no chance of passing unknown.

They ordered me to get up and dress, which I did. Everything I possessed was examined, but they found nothing that could compromise my friends. Then they took me off in custody with my companion; but God blessed us, for neither of us was distressed or showed any fear.[2] But I was very concerned about the lady's house, which I had left that night to return to my apartment—they might have seen me come out and shadowed my steps, and I was afraid that very illustrious family might suffer for my sake. But my fears were ungrounded. I learned later that the traitor had told them merely where he had left me, and it was there that they found me.

For two nights the pursuivant (I mean the one who knew me) kept me in his own house. Either the examiners were not free to deal with me the first day or, as I reflected later, they wanted to question my companion, "Little John", first.

The first night I noticed that the room in which I was locked up was not far from the ground, and that it would be possible to lower myself through the window by tearing up the bedclothes and knotting them together into a rope. And I would have done this the same night, but I heard someone stirring in the room next to mine. I suspected he had been put there to spy on my movements; and so it turned out. Consequently I decided to put off my escape 'til the following night, provided the watchman was not there. The chance never came. To save himself the expense of paying for a guard, my captor manacled my arms and did it in such a way that I could not bring my hands together or even move them farther apart.

[2] J. G. was arrested on Saint George's Day, April 23, by the two pursuivants Newell and Worsley. *Hat. Cal.*, 6:311.

Though I was more uncomfortable now, my mind was more at rest. All idea of escape had gone, and in its place I felt great happiness that I had been allowed to suffer this much for Christ's sake, and I thanked Our Lord for it as well as I could.

The next day I was brought before the commissioners. Presiding over them was a gentleman who is now the Chancellor of the Realm. He had been a Catholic once, but he was a worldly person and had gone over to the other side.[3]

They first asked me my name and my station in life. When I gave them the name I was using, one of them called out my true name, and said that I was a Jesuit. Realizing at once that the pursuivant had given me away, I said that I would be quite frank and give straight answers to all questions concerning myself, but added I would say nothing which would involve others. I told them my name and profession, saying I was a Jesuit priest, though I did not deserve to be one.

"Who sent you over here?" they asked.

"The Superiors of the Society."

"Why?"

"To bring back wandering souls to their Maker."

"No, you were sent to seduce people from the Queen's allegiance to the Pope's, and to meddle in State business." "Regarding things of State," I answered, "they are no concern of ours and we are forbidden to have anything to do with them. This prohibition is general to all Jesuits; and there is, besides, a special prohibition included in the

---

[3] This was Sir Thomas Egerton, who was appointed Chancellor in 1609. He was returned as a recusant in 1577, but later lapsed and as Attorney-General took part in the prosecution of Campion, the Earl of Arundel, and many other Catholics. *C.R.S.*, vol. 22, 101.

instructions given to the Fathers sent on this mission.† As for the allegiance due to the Queen and the Pope, each has our allegiance and the allegiances do not clash. The history of England and of all other Christian states shows this."

They went on:

"How long have you been acting as a priest in this country?"

"About six years."

"How did you land? And where? Whom have you lived with since then?"

I answered that I could not reply to these questions with a good conscience, particularly the last one.

"It would involve others," I pointed out, "so I pray you will excuse me for not doing as you wish."

However, they urged that it was precisely on these points that they wanted to satisfy themselves, and they ordered me to answer in the Queen's name.

I answered:

"I honor the Queen, and I will obey her and you in all that is lawful. But on this point you must hold me excused. If I name any person who has harbored me or mention any house where I have found shelter, innocent people will suffer for the kindness they have done me. Such is your law, but for my part I would be acting against charity and justice, which you will never persuade me to do."

"If you won't answer," they retorted, "then we will have to force you to answer."

"By God's grace I hope this will never happen. I ask you again to accept what I say. I will not answer your questions, neither now nor at any other time."

They then made out a warrant for my imprisonment and handed it to the pursuivants, ordering them to take me to prison. As they were leading me off, the present Chancellor called after them.

"See that he is put in close confinement." (This is what they do with traitors.) "But tell the jailers to treat him well—he is a gentleman."

These were his humane instructions. But possibly the head jailer gave other orders, for they put me in a most uncomfortable cell.[4] It was a small garret which had only a bed in it and such a low ceiling that I could not stand upright except near the bed. It had one window, which was always open and let in the foulest air, and whenever it rained the bed was soaked. The doorway was so low that I could not enter the room on my feet, and even when I crawled down on my knees I had to stoop to get through. But this proved an advantage, since it helped to keep out the smell of the privy next door, which was not slight. It was the only one that the prisoners in that part of the building had for their use, and the stench from it often kept me awake at night or even woke me up.

In this tiny place I had two or three quiet days. I felt no pain, my mind was at rest, and by God's blessing, I enjoyed that peace of soul which the world does not and cannot give.

On the third or perhaps it was the fourth day I was taken out to my second examination, this time to the house of a magistrate called Young. He was, so to speak, the chief inquisitor of Catholics living in the neighborhood of London and was in charge of searches and prosecutions; and it was he who had brought all this trouble on my host and had received the traitor's reports. With him there was another man who for many years now had conducted examinations

---

[4] J. G. was confined in the Counter in the Poultry.†

under torture. His name was Topcliffe. He was a cruel creature and thirsted for the blood of Catholics.† He had an
uncommon cunning and slyness and in his presence the other
man, deceitful and crafty fellow though he was, seemed
silenced. In fact he said only a few words during the
examination.

I found the pair of them alone. Young was wearing ordinary clothes, Topcliffe had on his court dress with a sword
hanging at his side. He was old and hoary and a veteran in
evil. Young opened with a question about the places where
I had lived and the Catholics I knew, and I answered that I
could and would not mention names for the reasons I had
already given. I had no intention of bringing trouble down
on other people. Then he turned to Topcliffe.

"I told you so", he said. "I knew you would find him
like this."

Topcliffe looked up at me and glared.

"You know who I am? I am Topcliffe. No doubt you
have often heard people talk about me?"

He said this to scare me. And to heighten the effect he
slapped his sword on the table close to his hand as though
he intended to use it, if occasion arose. But his acting was
lost on me. I was not in the least frightened.

Now at times like this I always answered with defer-
ence, but when I saw that he was trying to frighten me I
was deliberately rude to him.† He realized that he was
going to get nothing more out of me, so he took his pen
and wrote out a most clever and mendacious report on
the examination.

"Here, look at this paper", he said. "I am placing it before
the Privy Council. It shows you up as a traitor, and on
many counts."

This is what he had written:

"The examinee was sent to England by the Pope and by the Jesuit, Persons, on a political mission to pervert the Queen's loyal subjects and to seduce them from the Queen's allegiance. He came by way of Belgium where he had interviews with the Jesuit, Holt, and with Mr. William Stanley. If, therefore, he refuses to disclose the places where he has stayed and the persons with whom he has been in contact the presumption is that he has done much mischief to the State."

And so it went on. I read through the paper and saw at once that I could never meet all these lies with a single denial. As I wanted him to let the Council see my answer, I told him that I would reply in writing. Topcliffe was delighted.

"Oh, you are showing some sense now."

However, he was disappointed. He was hoping to trip me up in what I wrote, or at least to get a sample of my handwriting. If he had this he could prove that certain papers found in the search of the houses belonged to me. I saw the trap and wrote in a feigned hand:

"I was sent to England by my Superiors. I never set foot in Belgium nor have I seen Father Holt since I left Rome. I have not seen Mr. Stanley since he left England with the Earl of Leicester. I am forbidden to meddle in State affairs and I have never done and never will. My endeavor has been to bring back souls to the knowledge and love of their Creator, to make them live in due obedience to God's laws and man's, and I hold this last to be a matter of conscience. I humbly beg that my unreadiness to reply to questions concerning persons now may not be put down to contempt of authority. I am forced to act thus by God's commandments. To do otherwise would be a sin against justice and charity."

While I was writing, the old man became more and more angry. He shook with passion and wanted to tear me away from the paper.

"I'll write the truth or nothing", I said.

"No," he snarled, "write such and such, and I will make a fresh copy of what you write."

"I shall write what *I* want and not what *you* want. If you like, you can show what I've written to the Council. All I am going to add is my signature."

Then I signed very close up to the line so that he had no space to add anything. He saw he was beaten and in his frustration he blurted out threats and blasphemies.

"I will see that you are brought to me and placed in my power. I will hang you up in the air and will have no pity on you; and then I shall watch and see whether God will snatch you from my grasp." He spoke from the cesspool of his heart. But his effect on me was the opposite of what he wanted: he raised my hopes. Then and always I have despised blasphemers, and I have learned from experience that God puts hope in the hearts of His servants the moment He lets a storm burst about them. I answered in a few words:

"You can do nothing unless God allows it. He never abandons those who trust in Him. God's will be done!"

Young then told the jailer who had brought me to take me back to my prison. As he was leading me away, Topcliffe called him back and ordered him to see that my legs were placed in irons. The pair of them then fell to upbraiding the jailer for bringing me along by himself—they were afraid I might escape.

So I crept back into my little room and my legs were adorned according to instructions. The man who chained me up seemed sorry he had to do it, but I did not feel the least bit sorry for myself. Quite the contrary. I became very happy—so good is God to the least of His servants. To recompense the man for his good turn I gave him a little money and told him that it was no punishment to suffer in such a good and noble cause.[5]

---

[5] J. G. did not make much of his physical sufferings. In a letter to the General of the Society (May 7, 1597) Father Garnet, describing J. G.'s fortitude in prison, gives some information which J. G. modestly withheld: "When he was first taken and the gaoler put very heavy irons on his legs, he [J. G.] gave him some money. The following day the gaoler, thinking that if he took off the irons, he would doubtless give him more, took them off but got nothing. After some days he came to put them on again and received a reward; and then taking them off did not get a farthing. They went on playing thus with one another several times, but at last the gaoler, seeing that he did not give him anything for taking off his irons, left him for a long time in confinement, so that the great toe of one foot was for almost two years in great danger of mortification." Stonyhurst MSS *Anglia A*, vol. 2, no. 27.

11. THE COUNTER IN THE POULTRY

Spring–Summer 1594

I stayed chained up for three months or a little more. The first month I spent making the Spiritual Exercises as well as I could from memory, devoting four and sometimes five hours a day to meditation. During all this time I felt the great goodness of God, and I realized how lavishly He treats His suffering servants when He deprives them of every kind of earthly comfort.

Several days passed before they brought me out and examined me again. But while I was lying here quietly they examined and questioned Richard Fulwood (the traitor had told them he was my servant) and "Little John", who was captured with me. They tried to coax and bribe them but they could not get out of them a word that would injure others. Then they resorted to threats and force. But the force of the Holy Spirit working in them was too great to be overcome by men. For three hours on end (I think) both were hung up with their arms pinned in iron rings and their bodies suspended in the air—an excruciating pain that distends the limbs unbearably. But it was to no purpose—neither of them spoke a syllable that could be used in evidence against any one of us. Blandishments and threats and tortures failed equally to extract from them the name of a single place where any of ours had lodged or the name of a single person who had met or protected us.†

And this is the place to mention God's great goodness and mercy to me, the least deserving of all His servants. I refer to this, that there was not a single traitor among the men who were taken at my house or at the house of that good gentleman, my host—nor among those who were later imprisoned, tortured, and maltreated in persecutions that God allowed me to suffer. Not one, I say, failed me. All, by God's grace, were steadfast throughout. Nor did any of those who were my companions in my work and used to go as my servants to do business with countless gentlemen—they knew all my friends and could have done untold harm and got rich overnight at their expense—not one ever gave away information or was guilty of betrayal, or through malice or indiscretion ever did or said anything which brought suffering on others, or so much as gave cause for correction. On the contrary God in His goodness gave many of them His good and best Spirit.†

My first servant was John Lasnet, who died in Spain as a Jesuit Brother. The second was Michael Walpole; he was with me a short time and is now working in England as a priest.† The third was Ralph Willis. He had a vocation to the Society and I sent him to Rheims to study in the seminary there. He did his philosophy very creditably, but later in the Roman College he joined a rebellious faction—an ungracious act. He was the only one of all my companions who went a little wrong, but nevertheless he was ordained priest and sent to England. There he was captured and condemned to death for the faith and he answered his charges unflinchingly, but instead of being executed he was kept in prison and later managed to escape. He is still working in England.

After him I had John Sutton, a devout man who had three priest brothers, one of them a martyr and another a

Jesuit. For many years, in fact up to the time of his arrest, Father Garnet kept him in his house.

The next was Richard Fulwood, the man I have just spoken about. He made good his escape and during the period of my imprisonment Father Garnet took him also into his service and retained him right up to the day of the Father's blessed death. The Government knew he was his agent in nearly all his business and offered a large sum for his capture, both before and especially after they had seized Father Garnet. In fact, they gave him no rest and eventually he had to fly the country. He is in exile now and still doing very valuable work in support of the mission.

After him came John Lillie, who is well known in Rome, for he became a Brother and died in England a short time ago. Following him were two good men whom I did not take into regular service, but merely retained temporarily while I looked round for a good religious person who was suited to my needs in every way.

In the end I found the man; and when I left England I took him with me and left him at Saint Omers. There he was well grounded in Greek and Latin and was liked very much by all the Fathers who later sent him to Spain for his higher studies. He is there now gathering learning and virtue; and as I heard a short time ago in a letter from the Prefect of Studies, he is the best man in the course.†

These were the men God in His mercy gave me, and I did nothing to deserve them. It was an answer to my constant prayer. The defection of any of those we had to work with would have damaged and set back our cause more than anything else. If any one of them had chosen to betray us he would have worked havoc among Catholics. Many gentlefolk trusted them in the same way that they trusted priests; they confided in them, told them our whereabouts, even our hiding-places. And if just one servant and a man who was neither a Catholic nor a member of the household (I am speaking of the traitor) was able to cause such an upheaval in his master's family, just imagine what a priest's servant could have done to all the people of high rank who had given him and his master shelter. But to this day God has spared me such a misfortune.

To get back to my story.

They could extract nothing from the two men, "Little John" and Richard Fulwood, nor from any of my host's Catholic servants—not even an admission that they knew me. And so it happened that through the lack of witnesses they gradually gave up hope of seizing all my host's goods and revenue.

Every now and again, when they had anything new to bring against me, they summoned me for examination. On one occasion they brought me out to try on a suit of clothes that had been discovered in my host's house.[1] The traitor had told them that it was mine and when I put it on it was an exact fit (actually, it had been made for me), but I refused to admit that it was mine. Young then flew into a rage and said that I was being stubborn and stupid.

"How much more sensible Father Southwell is", he said. "Like yourself he was obstinate at the beginning. Now he is ready to conform and wants to talk with some learned man."

I answered: "I don't believe for a moment that Father Southwell wishes to treat with anyone, I mean from any faltering on his part or from any wish to learn from a heretic what he should believe. He may well have challenged some divine to a debate. Father Campion did it and many

---

[1] By proving that the suit belonged to J. G., Young would be able to indict William Wiseman for harboring priests.†

others would have done so too, if you had allowed it and appointed impartial judges."

Young took his Bible and kissed it.

"I swear on this book that Southwell has offered to treat with a view to accepting our religion."

"I don't believe he has done any such thing", I said.

"What!" answered one of his men. "You don't believe Young when he swears that what he says is true?"

"I do not believe him and I will not believe him", I answered. "I put more faith in Father Southwell's steadfastness than in any words of Young. No doubt he thinks he is quite justified in making statements like this in order to deceive me."

"Nothing of the kind", said Young.

"But you are ready to conform if Southwell has?"

By "conform" they mean embrace their deformed religion.

"Of course not", I answered. "I don't keep out of heresy and avoid heretical gatherings because he or any other person does so, but because I would be denying Christ by denying His faith. And this can be done by action as well as by words. It is something which Our Lord forbade us to do under penalties much worse than any man can inflict. He said, did He not: 'He that shall deny me before men, him will I deny before the Father who is in heaven'?"

The heretic held his tongue after this and merely said I was stubborn—the very thing he was himself—and ordered me back to prison.

On another occasion I was sent for and confronted by three witnesses. They were servants of a nobleman, Lord Henry Seymour, the son of the Duke of Somerset. They were not Catholics and they stated that on a certain day they had seen me dine with their mistress and her sister. They had been waiting at table with some other servants.

These two sisters were daughters of the Earl of Northumberland. One of them was a devout Catholic[2] and she had come up to London a short time before my imprisonment to ask my help in getting her over to Belgium. She was on her way to join a convent there and she was staying with her sister, the earl's wife. After her saintly father's death her sister had given up the faith, and she was anxious to bring her back. It was Lent when I visited them, and these two servants declared that the mistress of the house ate meat, while the Lady Mary and I took only fish.

Young threw this charge at me. He looked exultant as though he had something at last which I could not deny without giving away the names of my friends. But I answered that I did not know the men he had brought as witnesses.

"But we know you", they said. "You are the same person who was at such and such a place on such and such a day."

"Now," I said, "to talk like this will do your mistress great harm. You cannot expect me to harm her."

"What impudence", said Young.

"Quite so," I answered, "presuming, of course, that what these men say is true. But I am not in a position to give you a definite answer for the reasons which I have stated time and again. It's their own business to see whether what they say is true, and whether they should say it."

In a rage Young ordered me back to prison.

---

[2] The Lady Mary Percy was the "devout Catholic". The other sister was Jane, married to Lord Henry Seymour, the son of the Protector Somerset.

12. THE CLINK

Summer 1594–Spring 1597

As only my priesthood could be proved against me, some of my friends (it was about three months later) tried to get me moved to a better prison; and they achieved this by bribing no less person than Young himself.

Therefore they sent to my prison, called the Counter, and took off my chains. When I first had them on, they were rusty, but I had made them bright and shining by wearing them every day and moving about in them. Though my cell was narrow and I could have walked across in three paces if my legs had been free, I used to shuffle from side to side with short steps. In this way I got some exercise. Also, and this mattered more, when the prisoners below started singing lewd songs and Geneva psalms, I was able to drown their noise with the less unpleasant sound of my clanking chains.

My chains, then, were taken off and I paid my expenses, which did not amount to much since all I had had was a little butter and cheese with my bread. Then I was brought before Young, who made a pretense of being angry. He began to abuse and insult me with a violence he had never shown before. Again he demanded whether I would confess where and with what people I had lived, and again I replied that I could not tell him with a safe conscience, and therefore I would not.

"In that case," he said, "I will have to confine you more closely. You will be locked away more securely, and your window will be barred."

Then he wrote out a warrant and sent me off to the Clink.[1] All this was just a show he put up in order to cover himself for receiving the bribe. In point of fact my new prison was much better than the old one. All the prisoners found it so, and I, in particular, for there were more Catholics confined there.† No longer now could they prevent me receiving the sacraments and, as what follows will show, deprive me of many other consolations.

There, then, I was taken. And after a few months we had, by God's grace, everything so arranged that I was able to perform there all the tasks of a Jesuit priest, and provided only I could have stayed on in this prison, I should never have wanted to have my liberty again in England.

Though I was locked up, I looked on this change to the Clink as a translation from Purgatory to Paradise. I no longer heard obscene and bawdy songs, but, instead, I had Catholics praying in the next cell. They came to my door and comforted me; then they showed me how I could have freer dealings with them through a hole made in the wall, which they had covered over and concealed with a picture. Through this hole they handed me, the next day, letters from some of my friends, and at the same time gave me paper, pen, and ink, so that I could write back. In this way I was able to send a letter to Father Garnet and tell him the true story of all that had happened to me, detailing my answers under examination, just as I have written above.†

---

[1] On the south bank of the river a short distance below the present Blackfriars Bridge. J. G. was transferred there on July 6, 1594. *Hat. Cal.*, 6:311.

Through this same hole I also made my confession and received the Blessed Sacrament. But there was no need to carry on like this for long, for some Catholics in the prison contrived to make a key that would open my door. Then every morning before the warder came round, in fact before he was out of bed, they came and took me to another part of the prison, where I said Mass and gave the sacraments to the Catholics confined in that section. All of them had keys of their own doors.

Had I been given a choice I would have chosen just the neighbors I had. Next door to me was Ralph Emerson, the Brother who was referred to by Father Campion in a letter to Father General as "my little man and I". He was a very little man in build, but in endurance and sturdiness of spirit he was as great as you could wish anybody to be. Through many long years of imprisonment he was always the same devout and good man, a true son of the Society. He stayed on in the Clink six or seven years after my arrival there, and was finally taken off to Wisbeach Castle with other confessors. There he was attacked by paralysis, losing control of half of his body, and he could not move about or do the smallest thing to help himself. But he lived on and heaped up great merit by his patience. Eventually, with the same priest companions, confessors of Christ, he was sent into exile and came to Saint Omers, where he died a holy death, edifying all those who stood by him.†

This good Brother, then, was my neighbor on one side, and above me I had John Lillie, whom Providence had placed there to the advantage of both of us. Also around me were other good and holy men. As they had the freedom of the prison and anyone could visit them without risk, I was able to arrange that my friends, on coming to the door of the prison, should ask for them and thus come along and speak to me without attracting attention. However, I did not yet allow them to enter my cell, but I talked to them through the opening I just mentioned.

And so for a while I had a quiet and pleasant time, and I tried to make it a helpful time for others, by writing letters to friends outside and talking inside with visitors. The first jailer had a fierce temper and took good care to see that all the regulations were observed. While he was in charge, I had to be very careful to avoid discovery. But God took him from the custody of the prison and from the prison of his body at the same time.

His successor was a young man and much more pleasant. With bribes and a little coaxing I induced him not to pry too closely into our doings, and to come to me only when I called him, except for certain regular times when he always found me ready to receive him.

With this concession of liberty I was able to take up my apostolic work again. I soon heard a large number of confessions and I reconciled many people to the Church; some were heretics, but the greater number schismatics, for it was much easier to approach them than the others. I had to know heretics for a long time and get reports on them from friends I could trust before I dared let them into the secret of my freedom. In fact, I cannot remember more than eight or perhaps ten converts from heresy. However, four of them entered religious Orders, two the Society, and two other Orders. But the converts among the schismatics were numerous. Some of these, too, became religious; others devoted their lives to good works in England during the persecution. Mr. John Rigby was one of them. This is his story.

On one occasion he appeared on behalf of a certain Catholic lady who was up before the courts.[2] As the judges were unwilling to allow a Catholic party any advantage at law, they asked him what his religious profession was, that he pleaded so boldly for his client.

"Are you a priest?" they inquired.

"No", he answered.

"A papist?"

"I am a Catholic."

"Really? And how long have you been one?"

He told them.

"And who made you a Catholic?" they asked.

He did not want to implicate me, so he mentioned the name of a priest who had been martyred a short time before.[3]

"Then you have been reconciled to the Church of Rome?"

The present iniquitous laws make reconciliation to the Church high treason: but he did not see the trap. He had been told that it was always sinful not to confess his Catholic faith, and he may not have known that it was lawful to throw the burden of proof on the prosecution, as Catholics who are wise to it do. So bravely and magnanimously this God-fearing and forthright man readily admitted that he had been reconciled. He was bound there and then and thrown into prison and, when later he was brought out to trial, he repeated his fine confession and said that it was his greatest pride to be a Catholic.

---

[2] This was Mrs. Wiseman's sister, Mrs. Fortescue. She had been summoned to the sessions at Newgate "for causes of religion", and being sick at the time, she had asked Rigby, who was in the service of her father, to testify this in court. Dr. Worthington's *Life of John Rigby* (ed. Newdigate), 6.

[3] The Franciscan Father Jones, who was executed on July 12, 1598.

He heard the sentence with great joy, and while it was being pronounced, the chains in which he stood bound before the court came loose and fell from his legs. The jailer replaced them, but (I think I am right) they fell a second time. He was taken back to prison and from there he sent me, a short time before his martyrdom, a letter full of thanks for my making him a Catholic and helping him (it was ever so slightly) to that state of soul which he hoped would soon be made perfect by God. He sent me also his purse which I still have and use to this day in the martyr's honor—I carry my reliquary in it.

As the martyr was being drawn to execution on the hurdle he happened to pass an earl and a group of other noblemen in the street. The earl,[4] seeing him dragged along, inquired what was his offense. The martyr overheard the question.

"I am guilty of no offense whatever against my Queen and country," he said, "but I am dying for the Catholic faith."

The earl saw what a well-built and handsome man he was.

"You were made for a wife and children, not to die for your faith", he said.

"As for a wife, I ask God to bear me out that never in my life have I had intercourse with a woman." (I can confirm this statement myself.)

The earl was very moved and from that time held Catholics and their faith in greater esteem, as he showed afterward in many ways.

---

[4] The Earl of Rutland. A good deal about his youngest brother, Sir Oliver Manners, occurs later in the narrative.

Thus this holy man went to heaven, where I trust he intercedes for his unworthy Father in Christ.[5]

While I stayed in this prison, I found it possible to give the Spiritual Exercises, for the jailer did as I wanted and came to me only when I called him, and he never came near my neighbors' cells. We were able then to set up a chapel in a room upstairs, and there six or seven men went through the Exercises. All decided to follow the counsels of Christ Our Lord and they were all faithful to their resolve.

At that time also many priests of my acquaintance used to come to London. As they had no place where they could lodge in safety, they put up at taverns while they were doing their business. Also, the majority of priests coming from the seminaries over here were instructed to get in touch with me, so that I could introduce them to their Superior and give them other help they might need. My whereabouts were known and never changed, and I could be found without difficulty. On the other hand I had not always got lodgings ready for them and I could not always find a Catholic home to send them to. So I rented a house with a garden of its own in a suitable district and, with the help of friends, I bought the necessary furniture for it. There I sent all the men who came over with letters of commendation from our Fathers abroad and other good people whom I thought would be useful to our cause. And I maintained them there until, with the help of my friends, I was able to get them suitable clothing and other things they needed, or find them a residence or buy them a horse so that they could visit their friends and relatives in the country. All these expenses and those of the house I paid out of the

[5] John Rigby was executed with great barbarity on June 21, 1600, at Saint Thomas Waterings, then a marsh about two miles outside London at the present junction of the Old Kent and Peckham Park Roads.†

alms given to me. It was not that I got alms from a large number of people, much less begged them from everybody who visited me in prison. In point of fact I did not accept alms from all who offered them. Both in prison and out of prison I had no wish to do this for I might have gotten the reputation of receiving alms promiscuously and so kept from seeing the men who were anxious to consult me in their spiritual difficulties; or I might have taken money from those who could ill afford it and would have regretted afterward that they had given it to me. So I made it my rule to accept money only from a few persons whom I knew very well. Actually, by far the greater part of the alms I received were from a few devoted friends who first offered me their services and later gave me money without my asking and looked on it as a favor to themselves when I accepted it.

In charge of this house I put a very good and prudent widowed lady, who was later to receive the honor of martyrdom. She was from a distinguished family; her maiden name was Heigham and her husband's name Line. She and her husband were both blessed by God and had much to suffer for His sake. When her father, a Protestant, heard that his daughter was becoming a Catholic, he refused to give her the dowry which he had promised her. For the same reason, too, he deprived one of his sons of his inheritance; but this man, William Heigham, became a Brother and he is now working in Spain. It is twenty-six years since I first met him, a well-spoken and well-dressed young man, like other gentle-born Londoners of his day. At that time he kept a priest in his house, a Father Thomson, whose martyrdom I witnessed later.[6]

---

[6] Father William Thomson was executed at Tyburn on April 20, 1586, before J. G. left England for Rome.

When his father learned that he, too, had become a Catholic, he sold the estates that formed his patrimony, in order to keep him out of them. Their yearly income was reckoned at six thousand florins. The young man himself was later arrested for his faith and, I think, was put in Bridewell with the priest who lodged with him.† This is the prison which they use for vagabonds, making them do hard labor under the lash. There I visited him and found him working the great tread-mill, dripping with perspiration. After his liberation he took up service with a gentleman whose Catholic wife I knew well. She entrusted him with her son's education, and besides the rudiments of Latin he taught the boy the harp, an instrument which he himself played with great skill.

While he was there I went to call on him and had a long talk with him about his vocation.

His sister, Mistress Line, married a very good gentleman and a staunch Catholic, and was heir to a large estate. At the time his father, or perhaps his uncle (he was heir to both), lay on his deathbed and sent him a message in prison. In it he begged him to conform and attend church at least once, for otherwise his patrimony would go to his younger brother. The good man replied firmly, "If I must desert either the world or God, then I desert the world, for it is good to cleave to God." So both his father's and his uncle's estates went to his younger brother.† I met him once in his elder brother's room. He was dressed in silk and finery, while his brother wore plain and cheap clothes. This good soul afterward went to Belgium, and the King of Spain gave him a pension, part of which he sent to his wife. Theirs was indeed a life of poverty and holiness.

When her husband died in Belgium, Mistress Line was without friends in this world and was entirely dependent on God's providence. Therefore, before my imprisonment, I introduced her to the house where I was staying, and the family gave her board and lodging while I provided her with whatever else she needed.[7]

When I decided to establish the house I mentioned above I could think of no better person than her to put in charge of it. She was able to manage the finances, do all the housekeeping, look after the guests, and deal with the inquiries of strangers. She was full of kindness, very discreet, and possessed her soul in great peace. She was, however, a chronic invalid—she was always suffering from one ailment or another. Often she would say to me: "I naturally want more than anything to die for Christ, but it is too much to hope that it will be by the executioner's hand.[8] Possibly Our Lord will let me be taken one day with a priest and be put in some cold and filthy dungeon where I won't be able to live very long in this wretched life." So she said, and indeed her delight was in the Lord, "and the Lord granted the petitions of her heart."

After my escape from prison she gave up managing the house. By then she was known to so many people that it was unsafe for me to frequent any house she occupied. Instead, she hired apartments in another building and continued to shelter priests there. One day, however (it was the Purification of Our Blessed Lady), she allowed in an unusually large number of Catholics to hear Mass—a thing which

[7] Roger Line died in banishment for the faith in 1594, and it is evident that the widow found shelter with the Wisemans through J. G.'s introduction.

[8] "She told her confessor some years before her death, that Mr. Thomson, a former confessor of hers, who ended his days by martyrdom in 1586, had promised that if God should make him worthy of that glorious end, he would pray for her that she might obtain the like happiness." Challoner, *Memoirs*, 258.

she would never have done in my house, because she was more anxious about my safety than her own. Some neighbors noticed the crowd, and the constables were at the house at once. They rushed upstairs and found a room full of people. The celebrant was Father Francis Page, the martyr and Jesuit. He had pulled off his vestments before the pursuivants broke in, so it was difficult for them to pick out the priest. But the Father's tranquil and modest look gave him away, and they seized him on suspicion and began to search him and a number of others present. No one, however, admitted that there was a priest in the room; though, as the altar was prepared for Mass, they did say that they had been waiting for a priest to come. The pursuivants would not accept the story and while an altercation was going on Father Page, seeing someone open the door, took his chance, slipped the grasp of the men who were holding him, and dashed out, shutting the door behind him. He rushed upstairs to a room where he knew Mistress Line had prepared a hiding-place and got safely into it. The whole house was searched but they did not find him.

Mistress Line and the well-to-do people in the party were taken off to prison, while the others were released on bail. God prolonged the martyr's life beyond what she dared hope, and after some months she was brought up for trial on the charge of harboring priests. Asked by the judges whether this was true or not, she neither denied nor admitted it, but said in a loud voice so that the whole court could hear:

"My Lords, nothing grieves me more but that I could not receive a thousand more." [9]

She received the sentence of death with manifest joy and thankfulness. At the time she was so weak that she had to

[9] These words are in English in the MS.

be carried to the court in a chair and had to sit down during the whole trial. Back in prison she sent, a short time before her execution, a letter to Father Page, the priest who had escaped at the time she was caught. I have the letter with me now. In it she disposed of her few possessions and left me a large, finely wrought cross of gold which had belonged to her husband. Three times she mentioned me in the letter, referring to me as her Father. She left also some few debts which she begged me to pay off. Later, by word of mouth, she bequeathed me her bed, but when I came to buy it back from the jailers who had ransacked her cell after her death, all that I could get was her coverlet, which I used afterward whenever I was in London and felt safer under its protection. When she reached the place of execution she found the ministers there ready to pester her with exhortations to abandon her errors. But she would have none of it.

"Away, I have nothing in common with any of you", she said shortly.

Then, in her exaltation, she kissed the gallows and kneeling down began to pray. She went on praying until the hangman had done his work.

So she gave up her soul to God in company with the Jesuit martyr Father Filcock,[10] who had often been her confessor and had always been her friend. But her martyrdom took place six or seven years after the time about which I am writing. For three years she kept my house for me and

---

[10] She was executed at Tyburn on February 27, 1601. "She behaved herself most meekely, patiently and vertuously to her last breath. She kissed the gallowes and before and after her private prayers blessinge herself, the carte was drawne awaye, and she made the signe of the crosse uppon her, and after that never moved." From an account of her execution written the same day. Hist. MSS Commission, *Rutland* MSS, 1, 370.

attended to many holy priests there. At this time she made
a vow of chastity, a virtue she practised even in her married
life.

In this house there was always a priest who would make
visits of mercy to my friends, as I could not go myself. The
first of these priests was the Franciscan Recollect and martyr Father Jones. He was a recent arrival in England and I
was particularly glad to give him the hospitality of my house
in order to foster good relations between his Order and
ours. But after a few months he found friends of his own
and, being anxious to help them, he thanked me for my
hospitality and went to stay with them. A short time afterward he was captured and showed great fortitude when he
came to be martyred.†

After his departure I received into the house a priest who
had lately come from Spain and whom I had met before. He
was well-born and well-educated (his name was Robert Drury)
and he could move about in the best society without suspicion. I gave him an introduction to my friends among the
gentry, and he was of great assistance to them for the two
years and more during which he occupied the house.

This priest was chosen by God to be His witness and
martyr.[11] After my leaving England he was captured, just
two years ago now, and condemned on a charge of high
treason and punished accordingly. But they could bring nothing against him except the fact that he was a priest and had
refused the new oath which is offered to everybody to-day.
At his execution a remarkable scene occurred. Some of the
important officials who were present begged him to take
pity on himself and conform to the King's laws. He only

---

[11] Father Drury was the first martyr of the seminary at Valladolid. He left from
England in 1595 and was executed on February 26 1607. *C.R.S.*, vol. 30, 9.

had to go to church, they said, and he would save himself from death.

"Well, sirs," the martyr answered, "is it really in your power to save me from death here and now, if I am willing to go to your church?"

"Of course", they said, "we promise you in the King's name, you shall not die."

Then the martyr turned to the people and spoke:

"Now you can see what sort of treason I am condemned for. It is merely for our religion that I and other priests die."

In their rage the officers cruelly cut him down when he was half-dead. In the end they killed him, but there was nothing more that they could do.

During the time that I was in prison, one of our Fathers, Father Curry,† who had been an invalid for some time, lived in my house. There he died a holy death and was buried in a secret place, for all priests who live in hiding on the mission are also buried in hiding.[12]

Meanwhile my former host,[13] who had been arrested shortly before me, was kept locked up. For three or four months neither his wife nor any friends were allowed near him. Later, however, they gave up hope of producing evidence against him, for none of his Catholic servants would confess anything† and the traitor, who was the single witness, had never seen me performing any priestly act. So

[12] In the worst days of the persecution priests who lived in towns were often buried in the houses in which they died, since it was dangerous to bring out for burial a corpse that could not be accounted for. In country places, it was usual to bury them in places that had sacred associations, near an abandoned chapel or monastery. Father Curry died on August 31, 1596. Arch. S.J. Rome, *Fondo Gesuitico* 651, Garnet to Aquaviva, January 18, 1597.

[13] William Wiseman.

gradually they allowed in his friends to attend to his wants, but they still kept him in close confinement.

While he was in prison he wrote a notable work which he divided into three parts, calling it *A Triple Farewell to the World* or *Three Deaths in Different States of Soul*.

In the first book he described a man of good moral character and, in men's opinion, a virtuous man; but he had acted as his own guide in everything. He fell mortally ill, but before he died all he had done wrong came clearly before his eyes and he confessed to those who stood about him that he would be rightly damned, especially because he had been unwilling to lay open his soul to a spiritual father and be governed and ruled by him for God's sake.

The second part was devoted to the story of a good and devout lady who was willing at first to submit completely to direction but was later deceived by the devil and decided to become her own director in certain matters. Then she was taken very ill. When her death was near she repented and saved her soul by contrition and alms-giving. But in the moment of her particular judgment she was greatly afraid, and she suffered a long Purgatory because she had always loved her own opinion and will. His account of her contained many pathetic passages, and he described the deceits and wiles of the devil with such true discernment that some good and holy priests were amazed that a layman could know and analyze them so well.

In the third part he pictured the holy death of a good religious man. He had lived in the world and was well-off and had always sought and followed the guidance of his spiritual father and manifested his soul to him for the glory of God. In this section he laid it down that the surest way of knowing both oneself and the will of God was to take up the practice of meditation on spiritual things under a good director. Then he went on to exhort everyone to choose a guide in their spiritual lives, to obey him, which, of course, they were not bound to do, and to seek his confirmation of their own judgment.

This was the aim of the third part—in fact of all three—and he described the ideal spiritual guide in such detail that no doubt was left in the reader's mind that he meant a Jesuit, or, failing a Jesuit, a priest who was friendly to the Jesuits and sought their advice in his own difficulties.

Later some copies of the book were made by friends and caused a stir when they fell into the hands of a group of priests who were not well disposed to the Society. They complained that the effect of the book would be to exclude them from the direction of souls. One of their number went so far as to send the author a long epistle damning the book,† and then he circulated tracts damning the author. He presumed that I had written the book myself, using the author's name. This simply was not true. Since he had been closely confined and had been deprived of ink, he had scribbled most of the book in pencil on loose scraps of paper, and as he completed each part he sent it to me to look over and correct any mistakes in doctrine. What inspired him to write it, he said, was the immense benefit which he thought he himself had gotten from placing himself under a spiritual director, and, resulting from it, the great peace of soul which he enjoyed even when the threat of death hung daily over him. It was his desire that others should share this blessing which prompted him to write. But he made it clear that the books were not for the general public: he had in mind first his own household, his wife, and his children, and, in the second place, his friends and relatives, and wished to put down in writing the safest and most meritorious path to perfection in their state; and as he was not allowed to meet them and talk to them he had written out his advice. He tried also to show that perfection was more necessary to lay-folk than to religious.†

So much for what this good man wrote. And he was far from regretting that for four years he had placed himself in my hands, although he found himself now in such straits, and saw himself and his whole family bitterly persecuted for the reception they had given me. But he never lost his patience and, what is more, he reckoned all these tribulations the height of blessedness. He was wonderfully happy.

Although his wife loved him very dearly and was very sensitive to his plight, she bore her sorrow with patience and resignation. And when I was moved to this prison where she had hopes of seeing me, she took a house nearby so that she could talk and write to me frequently, give me little things I needed, and ask my advice and direction in all her affairs.

Later, her husband purchased his release, and the two lived there together all the time I was in prison and helped me in my escape from the Tower. But soon after my escape they returned to their country house because they wanted to have me there again with the family.

13. THE DEAN'S SYLLOGISM

Meanwhile my time was fully taken up in prison. So many Catholics came to visit me that there were often as many as six or eight people at a time waiting their turn to see me in Brother Emerson's room next door. Some of my closest and dearest friends often had to wait many hours on an afternoon and even then I sometimes had to tell them to come another day.

In this way I was able to hear a large number of general confessions. Among others there was a wealthy gentleman who had been a Catholic for a long time, but had lived cautiously and quietly, avoiding anything that might bring him into conflict with the authorities. However, in the end he found himself thrown into our prison. It was the last thing he expected, but it was providential. He was surprised that he was arrested on such slight and trivial grounds, but when he told me his story I pointed out that everything happened by God's decree and providence, and especially things like this.

"Our Lord and Judge", I said, "frequently chooses to admonish us in this way. He wants us, while we still have the chance in life, to 'agree quickly with the adversary'. And this is not just my counsel, but Our Lord's too, who prefers the part of Father to Judge."

I urged him to take the chance he had been given and to reflect on his life, examining his state of soul and seeing what his obligations to God were. And I told him that he could not be sure that this would not be his last chance; perhaps it was given him as a kind of last summons. He did what I told him and as he could not meditate, he read a book called the *Memoriale* by Father Granada,† and prepared himself for confession. He made it with great exactness and we were both very satisfied after it. During all this time he was in good and even robust health, but a few days after his release from prison he fell ill. Less than two months later he was dead.†

During this period God used me as His instrument to turn many hearts from worldly ambitions to the love of God and the following of Christ's counsels. Among others were two young clerks who worked together at a considerable salary in the same office in London. The name of one of them is now inscribed in the roll of the martyrs. He was Father Francis Page. The other, his companion, was a good man and he later studied theology with a view to becoming a priest. He wanted also to enter the Society, but he died a holy death before the end of his studies. I have heard people who were with him say that he was a model for his virtue and modesty.

Mr. Francis Page was the son of well-to-do parents. He had a very handsome appearance and polished manners and was deeply loved by a lady, the daughter of rich and influential people who owned the office. Intending to marry him, the lady very praiseworthily persuaded him to become a Catholic. She was good and devout and often came to see me. Then one day she brought with her her friend Mr. Page, who was now a Catholic.

His thoughts were on marriage. But I saw at once that he was a very modest and open young man, the sort of person who could easily be kept from doing any wrong, and inspired by an ideal. I came to like him very much and began to talk to him on serious topics, pointing out that perhaps the girl's parents would not give their consent, as she would be marrying below her station. I also talked about wealth and the illusiveness of worldly happiness. Finally, I gave him some meditations to take away with him and drew up in writing some rules for the conduct of his spiritual life. And God gradually drew his soul from the things of this world to the things of eternity; and in the end he decided to leave his friend and the position he had in the office. In order to be closer to me he wanted to live in my hostess' house near the prison, and accordingly he took service with her, though this was far humbler than his former employment. He had higher aspirations and this was his preparation of soul. Father Coffin† was living in my hostess' house and was able to give much friendly help. This Father often visited me in prison and comforted me in more ways than I can tell. You will hear more about Father Francis Page later.

Working from this prison I was able to send many young men and boys to the seminaries. Some of them are now Jesuits and are working in England; others remain in the seminaries training more laborers for the mission.

Once I sent over two boys. They were to go to Saint Omers and I gave them letters of commendation. I had written in lemon juice, so that no writing should appear on the paper, and then I wrapped the paper round one or two collars to make it look as if it were being used to keep the collars clean.

The boys were captured. Under examination they confessed that I had sent them and given them these letters and had instructed them, when they came to a certain Jesuit College which they would pass on their way to Saint Omers—they had to cross by Ostend, not the usual route, and that was why they were caught†—to tell the Fathers there to wet the paper and then read what I had written. The boys revealed this, and the two letters, written on a single sheet of paper, were read not by a friend of the Society but by an enemy. The first letter was in Latin, and as it was addressed to our Flemish Fathers I had signed it with my proper name. The second was to our English Fathers at Saint Omers. So the letters were read and I was summoned for examination.

This time Young was not there. He had died in his sins, and died as he had lived—miserably. In his life he was the devil's confessor and in his death the devil's martyr. Not merely did he die in the devil's service, but it was the actual cause of his death. Day and night he toiled to bring more and more pressure on Catholics, drawing up lists of names, giving instructions, listening to reports. Then one rainy night, at two or three o'clock, he got up to make a search of some Catholic houses. The effort left him exhausted; he became ill, contracted consumption, and died.†

He left only debts behind him, as though he had renounced all to serve the devil. His position was well-paid and he got much booty from poor Catholics, and, what's more, received heavy bribes from them to stave off a threat of prosecution. Yet it was said that his debts amounted to one hundred thousand florins, and I have heard it put at far more. Possibly he thought that the Queen would pay them off, but nothing of the sort. All she did was to send one of her courtiers to visit him when he lay sick and dying. He was so pleased at this favor that he was ready to sing his *Nunc Dimittis*. But it was a false sense of peace that came over him, the exaltation of a soul that rides for a fall. Like another Aman he was bidden not to a banquet but to an eternal doom. With the Queen's praises on his lips and singing his own indebtedness to Her Majesty he died miserably, and his joy passed into anguish. "The joy of a hypocrite lasts but an instant." [1]

It is the way of the Council always to have an agent and put down to his machinations any hateful orders they give. It was his office to harass and hunt down the servants of God, and he was succeeded by William Wade, the present Governor of the Tower, who was then Secretary to the Lords of the Queen's Council. It was this man who summoned me now. He showed me the piece of white paper which I had given to the boys and asked me whether I recognized it.

"No", I answered.

It was true, for I had no idea then that the boys had been captured. Then he put the paper into a basin of water and the writing appeared on it with my full signature at the bottom. When I saw it I said,

"I don't admit that the writing is mine. My hand is an easy one to forge and my signature may well be faked; and in their fright the boys you speak of might say exactly what their examiners wanted and thus might harm themselves as well as their friends. You cannot expect me to act like them. However, I don't deny that it is a good thing to send boys abroad to give them a better education. Certainly I would willingly do it if I had the chance, but no

---

[1] Young wrote to the Queen on November 30, 1594: "I think no subject in the world more infinitely beholden unto his Sovereign, in that in these my aged and extreme or last days it pleaseth you so favourably to respect the weak estate of so poor a vassal, weakened in body with infirmities, but so much revived in heart with your gracious remembrance of me"; and with this letter he sent the Queen all the papers concerning the case of the Wisemans and J. G. "as the last fruits of all my endeavours". (*Hat. Cal.*, 5:24–25) From a report on Young's estate it is clear that J. G. did not overstate the amount of his debts. *C.S.P.D.* (1595–1597), 103.

matter how much I wanted to, how could I, being shut up closely in prison?"

Wade cursed me heartily because I refused to confess to my signature and handwriting.

"The fact is," he said, "you have got far too much liberty. You won't have it any longer."

Then he turned on the jailer, rating him for giving me so much freedom of movement.

On two or three other occasions I was summoned for examination. Whenever I came out of this prison I put on my Jesuit gown and cloak, which had been made for me as soon as I came to live with my fellow Catholic prisoners. In the street the boys laughed when they saw me, but my enemies were wild with rage. The first time I wore my gown they called me a hypocrite.

"When I was arrested you called me a courtier", I said, "because I dressed like one to disguise myself and in order to move at my ease among people of rank, without being recognized. Then I told you that I did not like wearing lay clothes, that I would have much preferred my proper dress. I have it on now, and you are angry with me. Whether I pipe to you or whether I mourn I cannot please you. You must find some complaint against me."

"Why didn't you go about in these clothes before?" they said. "Instead, you had a disguise and assumed a false name. No decent person behaves like that."

"I know why you don't like it", I said. "You want to catch us quickly and put an end to our work for the salvation of souls. Don't you know that Saint Raphael did just what I'm doing? He took a disguise and a false name, and his incognito helped him to do the work which God entrusted to him."

Another time I was examined before the Dean of West-minster,[2] the substitute for the abbot of that great royal mon-astery. Topcliffe was there too, and some other commissioners. They wanted to confront me with the good widow, my host's mother, who was then confined in a prison near the Abbey.[3] Sentence of death had not yet been passed on her, though it was later. They wanted to see whether she would recognize me.

So I came to the place and found her waiting there. When she saw me enter with the warders she almost gesticulated for joy. But she held herself back and asked them:

"Is this the man you told me about? I don't know him, but he looks to me like a priest."

Then she made a deep reverence toward me. I bowed to her in acknowledgement. Then they asked me if I recognized her.

"I don't recognize her", I said, "and you know how I always answer questions like this, how I never mention by name any place or any person whom (unlike this lady) I may happen to know. As I have told you before, if I were to do so, I would be acting against charity and justice."[4]

Then Topcliffe said:

"Speak the truth. Have you or have you not reconciled people to the Church of Rome?"

I saw his bloody purpose clearly, for this was expressly forbidden under penalty of high treason, as I mentioned before in the case of Mr. Rigby. But I knew that I was

---

[2] Gabriel Goodman, Dean of Westminster, 1561–1601.†
[3] The Gatehouse.
[4] It seems to have been J. G.'s regular practice, which he taught his friends, to add to the denial some remark which made it clear that he regarded the occasion as a privileged one and was making his answer in the sense allowed by modern law and practice.

already compromised because of my priesthood, so I answered forthrightly:

"Yes, I have reconciled people to the Church and I am sorry I have not brought this blessing to more."

"Well", said Topcliffe. "And how many would you wish to have reconciled if you had had the chance? A thousand, say?"

"Yes, certainly", I answered. "A hundred thousand. And more than that, if I could."

"It would be enough to raise an army against the Queen", said Topcliffe.

"The men I should reconcile", I said, "would be the Queen's men. They would not be against her. We hold that obedience is due to those in authority."

"All the same", answered Topcliffe, "you teach rebellion. Look, I have a Bull of the Pope here. It was made out to Sanders when he went to Ireland to raise rebellion among the Queen's subjects. Here it is, read it for yourself." [5]

"There is no need to read it", I answered. "It is probable enough that if the Pope sent him he had authority. But I have none. We are expressly forbidden to meddle in politics. I have never done so and I never will."

"Take it", he said. "Read it. I want you to read it."

So I took it. Seeing the name Jesus stamped at the top I kissed it reverently.

"What!" cried Topcliffe. "You kiss the Pope's Bull?"

"I kissed the name Jesus to which all honor and love is due. But if, as you say, it is really a Bull of the Pope, then I reverence it on that account too."

---

[5] It is unlikely that the Government went to the trouble of forging a Brief, though no Brief or Bull giving Sanders faculties for his mission to Ireland in 1579 has yet been found. *The Month* (January 1903), 80.

As I said this, I kissed the embossed paper a second time. Topcliffe flew into a rage, cursing and abusing me.

"You do this here, but in other places you go kissing women."

"God forbid!" I said. "It's a thing that's never been said of me before. A thing you cannot say."

"It was you, wasn't it," he went on, "who on such and such a day stayed in such and such a house with Lady so-and-so, the Earl of Northumberland's daughter? No doubt you lay in bed together."

To tell you the truth, this impudence made me shake with anger, though I knew he was speaking without what even he considered the slightest evidence.[6]

"By the goodness of Almighty God," I said, "I swear that all your insinuations are untrue", and as I spoke I put my hand on a book that lay open on a table beside me. It happened to be a copy of the Sacred Bible done into English by the Protestant reformers.

Topcliffe said nothing more, but the old Dean broke in. "So you are ready", he said, "to swear on our Bible?"

Now Catholics who know enough to show up the mistakes of the translation do not use it. But I answered:

"I didn't look carefully to see what version it was. I was only anxious to rebut his false charges. But there are certain truths in this book, for instance, the Incarnation and the Passion of Christ, which are not vitiated by the bad

---

[6] Father Garnet recounts a similar accusation made against himself by Salisbury. "I never had discourteous words of the Commissioners", he writes, "but only once, when they having taken a letter of Mrs. Vaux to me, subscribed, Your loving sister A. G., my Lord of Salisbury said, What, you are married to Mrs. Vaux: she calls herself Garnett. What! *Senex fornicarius!* But the next time he asked me forgiveness, and said he spoke in jest, and held his arm long on my shoulders; and all the rest said, that I was held for exemplar in those matters." *Hat. Cal.*, 18:111.

translation, and on these I invoke God's testimony. But there are many other passages, badly turned, which contain heresies. These I detest and abominate."

And then with greater emphasis than before I placed my hand on the Bible a second time.

The old man was irritated.

"I will prove that you are a heretic", he said.

"You won't be able to prove that", I retorted.

"I can prove it", he said. "Whoever denies the Sacred Scriptures is a heretic. You deny this is the Sacred Scriptures. Ergo."

"That's no syllogism", I answered. "It descends from the general to the particular and it contains four terms."

"I could make syllogisms before you were born", the old man answered.

"I am prepared to admit that", I said, "but the one you have just made isn't a syllogism at all."

But other people present broke in; they had no intention of beginning a disputation. They just threw questions at me in the hope that I would say something I did not want to say. Eventually, they sent me back to prison.

14. THE BLOODY QUESTION

Another time they had me up for examination with all the other Catholics in our prison in the public place called the Guildhall. Topcliffe was there with many other commissioners; and after they had run through the usual questions and I had given the answers I always gave they came to the point: they wanted, as far as I could see, to find out how we were all disposed toward the Government. They hoped to trip us up in the way we spoke about the Queen and then frame a charge against us. Turning to me they asked:

"Do you recognize the Queen as the true and lawful Queen of England?"

"I do", I answered.

"And in spite of the fact that she has been excommunicated by Pius V", said Topcliffe.

"I recognize that she is Queen," I replied, "though I know too that there has been an excommunication."

I was aware, of course, the Pope had stated that the excommunication had not yet come into force in England; its application had been withheld until it could be made effective.

Then Topcliffe asked:

"What would you do if the Pope were to send over an army and declare that his only object was to bring the kingdom back to its Catholic allegiance? And if he stated at the same time that there was no other way of re-establishing the Catholic faith, and commanded everyone by his apostolic authority to support him? Whose side would you be on then—the Pope's or the Queen's?" [1]

Then I saw the man's subtlety and wicked cunning. He had so framed his question that whatever I answered I would be sure to suffer for it, either in body or in soul.

I picked the words of my reply.

"I am a loyal Catholic and I am a loyal subject of the Queen. If this were to happen, and I do not think it at all likely, I would behave as a loyal Catholic and as a loyal subject."

"Oh, no", he said. "I want a plain and straight answer. What would you do?"

I answered:

"I have told you what I think and I will not give you any other answer."

Then he flew into a most violent rage and spat a torrent of oaths at me. Finally he said:

"You fancy that this year you will be creeping to adore the cross. But before that time comes round I will make quite sure that you will not." [2]

In his great kindness the man wanted to insinuate that he would make sure I went to heaven with a halter before that time. But he had not seen into the sanctuary of God and he knew nothing of my great unworthiness. God indeed permitted him to do his worst on those whom His divine wisdom judged fit and worthy—on Father Southwell, for instance, and on others whom he persecuted to their death—yet his wrath worked no such mercy in me.† Nor was it in the power of this angry man to obtain for me this heavenly

---

[1] This was the famous "bloody question" devised by Burghley in 1583 with the object of trapping Catholics into a statement which could be construed as disloyalty to the Crown.†

[2] The reference, of course, is to the liturgy of the Church on Good Friday.

blessing, although through his means Our Lord Jesus had taken to heaven others for whom a Kingdom had been prepared by the Father. However, to some extent he was a prophet in his words, but the sense in which they were fulfilled was very different from the sense he intended.

This happened about Christmas time.[3]

The following Lent, Topcliffe himself was in prison. He had in some way insulted members of the Council, while (if I am not mistaken) he was pleading before them in a most brazen way on behalf of his son, who had struck a man dead with his sword in the forecourt of the great hall where the Queen's Bench was sitting.† It was about Passion Sunday, and Catholics like myself who were in prison for the faith began to hold up our heads when we saw our arch-enemy Aman about to be hanged on his own gibbet.† We became more carefree in the way we made use of our liberty, and many more people came to the sacraments and to the ceremonies of the Church.

On Good Friday there was a large crowd in the room above mine, including every Catholic in the prison and many others from outside. I had been through all the ceremonies and read the prayers proper to the day up to the point where the priest takes off his shoes. I had just taken off mine and had moved a couple of paces to start creeping to the cross, making the three genuflections as I approached, when the head jailer of the prison came to the door of my cell below. He knocked, got no answer from inside, and banged hard on the door, making a great noise. As soon as I heard it, I knew at once that it was the head jailer—the other jailer would never have dared to treat me in this way. Immediately I sent off a man downstairs to say that I would be

[3] 1594.

back in a moment. Then instead of carrying on with the adoration of the cross of wood, I prepared to accept the spiritual cross which Our Lord was preparing for me. I slipped off my vestments. Then I hurried downstairs to stop the jailer coming up and finding us all, for then, indeed, many would have had to suffer. As he saw me, he called out.

"What are you doing out of your cell? You ought to be locked up and closely confined."

I knew the kind of man he was. Pretending to be angry with him, I asked him why, if he was really the friend he professed to be, had he come here at a time like this, when he knew we would be saying our prayers, if ever we did.

"So you have been at Mass", he said. "I'll go up myself and see."

"You will do nothing of the kind", I answered. "It's obvious you don't know the first thing about us. There is not a single Mass said to-day anywhere in the whole Church. Go up, if you like. But if you do, you must realize that you won't get another farthing from me or from any of the Catholics here for our cells. You can put the whole lot of us with the paupers in the common jail if you wish, but there we won't have to pay anything and it's you who'll be the loser. On the other hand, if you are friendly and don't come upon us suddenly like this without warning, you won't find us ungrateful. You can't say you have found us ungrateful so far."

This pacified him, so I said,

"And why do you come along now?"

"Just to give you Mr. Topcliffe's greetings."

"His?" I said. "Why this sudden friendship between him and me? Isn't he shut up in such and such a prison? He must be powerless against me at present?"

"Yes," he answered, "but all the same he sends you his good wishes. When I visited him to-day he inquired after you. I told him you were very well, and he said, 'But he doesn't bear his imprisonment as patiently as I do. I want you to give him my good wishes and tell him what I've just said.' So I've come here to tell you."

"Very well", I answered. "Now tell him from me that, thanks to the grace of God, I am glad to be in prison for the faith. I only wish he were there for the same reason." [4]

So the jailer went off, rating his servant for not keeping me in close confinement. Thus Topcliffe's prophecy came true; he had interrupted me in the very act of making the adoration of the cross, not that he had recalled what he had said, for at the time he had meant something quite different. Yet Saul was among the prophets, but he did not stop me going upstairs and carrying on with the service he had interrupted.

The jailer in charge of my cell would do nothing about our cells without my leave. Our first jailer did not live long and his successors were very obliging to me. One of them, whom I received into the Church, held the office by right of succession; but after his reception he sold his hereditary right and entered the service of a Catholic gentleman, a friend of mine. Later he accompanied the gentleman's son to Italy and received a vocation to the religious life. Now he is a prisoner for the faith in that same prison where he was my jailer.

---

[4] Had J. G. been able to see the letter which Topcliffe, possibly at this very moment, was writing to the Queen, he would have sent him a very different message. In this letter, dated "At the Marshalsea this Good or evil Friday, 1595" and described by Jessop as perhaps the most detestable composition on record, Topcliffe boasted that "I have helped more traitors [to Tyburn] than all the noblemen and gentlemen of the court, your counsellors excepted", and went on, "In all prisons rejoicings; it is like that the fresh dead bones of Father Southwell at Tyburn and Father Walpole at York, executed both since Shrovetide, will dance for joy." Jessop, 71.

The man who succeeded him had a wife and family, and it was only fear of poverty that prevented him, too, becoming a Catholic. But he became such a great friend of mine, and, in fact, of all ours, that whenever a special hunt was being made for any particular Catholics, he took them into his house and hid them there. At the time of my escape from the Tower he was one of the three people who exposed themselves to very grave danger on my behalf. Although he was nearly drowned on the night of the first attempt, nevertheless he rowed the boat on the second night. I shall tell you about this in a moment, for it was only a short time after that they removed me from this prison and put me in the Tower of London. This is how it came about.

There was in this prison a priest[5] whom I had occasion to help many times. On his arrival in England I had arranged for him to live in a fine house with some of my best friends. I had received his mother and brother into the Church, and when he was put in prison I found him friends and made him many gifts, and had always been kind to him. However, I noticed that he was a little unsteady and seemed rather too anxious to be free again, so I was careful not to confide in him, as I did in some other prisoners, for instance, in Brother Emerson and John Lillie. Nevertheless, this good man for some reason I do not know got me removed. Perhaps he hoped that after I had gone all the people he saw coming to me would then go to him. Possibly he wanted to ingratiate himself with the authorities and so secure his liberty or something of the kind. I cannot say; but whatever it was, he informed on me. He said he had been standing next to me when I handed a packet of letters from Rome and Brussels to Father Garnet's servant, "Little John", whom I mentioned

---

[5] William Atkinson, who later apostatized.†

above. (Now after he had been captured with me and examined without giving away anything, as I told you, some Catholic gentlemen had paid down a sum of money and had him released. They, and many others besides, needed his services badly, for there was no better man in the country at making priests' hiding-places.) As I was saying, this priest reported that I had handed "Little John" these letters and that I was in the habit of receiving letters from priests abroad addressed both to me and my Superior. Acting on this information, the authorities sent along one day a Justice of the Peace to interview me. There were two of the Queen's messengers or pursuivants with him and without warning they came to my room with the head warder. Providentially they found no one with me except two boys—I was giving them instructions before sending them abroad. One, if I remember right, got away; the other was put in prison for a time. But they found nothing in my cell that I was afraid they might find, for I kept all my important possessions and my papers in small hiding-holes. Brother Emerson knew about them, and after I had been taken away he took everything out, including my reliquary which I still possess. There was also some money laid aside for the upkeep of my house in town, about a thousand and three hundred florins. He sent this to the Superior who took charge of the house for me until I was rescued from prison.

These officials, then, came along and began their examination, but it was soon over, because they could get none of the information they were after. Then they started to search my cell, hoping to find some letters or other incriminating evidence. While the Justice of the Peace was going through my books, one of the pursuivants searched my person. He undid my doublet and came on my hairshirt. At first he did not know what it was:

"What's this?" he asked.

"A vest", I said.

"Oh, it's a hairshirt", he said.

Then he got hold of it and tried to pull it off me by force.†

The impudence of this vulgar creature, I must confess, made me more angry than anything I have ever had to suffer. I very nearly seized him and thrust him away. But I am glad I did not. Instead I called to the Justice of the Peace, who ordered him to stop at once.

They found nothing they wanted to find in my cell except myself.

15. THE TOWER AND TORTURE

April 1597

They led me away and took me to the Tower of London. There they handed me over to the Governor, a knight called Berkeley, who had the title of Queen's Lieutenant. At once he took me to a large, tall tower, three stories high with lock-ups in each story.[1] (There are many such towers inside the fortifications.) For that night he assigned me a room on the first floor and handed me over to a warder[2] in whom he had special confidence. The warder then went off and returned with a little straw. He spread it on the ground and went away again, shutting the door of my cell and fastening another door above it with a great bar and iron bolts.

So I commended my soul to God who, "going down as He does, into the pit with His people", never abandoned me in my bonds; and then to the Blessed Virgin, Mother of Mercy, and to my patrons and my guardian angel; and after I had made my prayer my mind was at rest, and I lay down to sleep on the straw. That night I slept very well.

The next morning I walked round my cell. In its dim light I found the name of the blessed Father Henry Walpole cut with a chisel on the wall. Then, close to it, I discovered his little oratory, where there had been a narrow

[1] The Salt Tower at the south-east corner of the Inner Ward. J. G. was taken there from the Clink on April 12, 1597. C.R.S., vol. 4, 233.
[2] His name was Bonner, as appears from the Hat. Cal., 7:417.

window. It was now blocked with stonework, but there on either side he had chalked the names of all the orders of Angels. At the top, above the Cherubim and Seraphim, was the name of Mary, Mother of God, and then above it the name of Jesus; above that again the name of God written in Latin, Greek, and Hebrew characters.† It was a great comfort to me to find myself in a place sanctified by this great and holy martyr, and in the room where he had been tortured so many times—fourteen in all, as I have heard. And as they tortured him more often than they wanted known, they did not do it in the ordinary public chamber. And I can well believe that he was tortured that number of times, since he completely lost the use of his fingers. For when he was taken back to York to be executed in the place where he was arrested on his landing in England, he wrote out with his own hand an account of a discussion he had with some ministers there. Part of it was given to me later with some meditations on the Passion of Christ which he wrote in prison before his own passion. I was hardly able to read what he had written, not only because he wrote in haste but because his hand could barely form the letters.† It looked like the writing of a schoolboy, not that of a scholar and gentleman. Yet he was a courtier before Campion's execution and while he was still a layman wrote some beautiful English verses in his honor, telling how the martyr's blood had brought warmth into his life and many others' too, inspiring them to follow the more perfect way of Christ's counsels.†

So I was very glad when I found myself in Father Walpole's cell; but I was too unworthy to inherit the place where such a noble soul as he had suffered. The next day, either on orders or with the idea of doing me a service, the warder removed me to a cell on the floor above. It was large and,

by prison standards, fairly comfortable. I told him I preferred to stay in the cell below and explained why, but he
would not allow it. Then I begged him to let me go down
there occasionally to say my prayers, which he promised
and allowed. Also, he offered to fetch me a bed if any friends
of mine were willing to send me one, for beds are not provided in this prison, but the prisoner must find his own
bed and any other furniture he wants, on condition that
they go to the Lieutenant of the Tower, even if the prisoner is liberated. I told him my only friends were my old
companions in the prison I had just left. If he went there
they might give me a simple bed as an alms. So the warder
went off at once, and they gave him the kind of bed they
knew I liked—a simple mattress stuffed with wool and feathers in the Italian style. They gave him also a coat and some
linen and told him always to come and ask them for whatever I needed—he had only to bring a note signed by me
mentioning the thing I wanted. Then they put some money
into his hands and begged him to treat me well.

On the third day the warder came to my room straight
from his dinner. Looking sorry for himself, he said the Lords
Commissioners had arrived with the Queen's Attorney-
General and that I had to go down to them at once.

"I am ready," I said, "but just let me say an Our Father
and Hail Mary downstairs."

He let me go, and then we went off together to the
Lieutenant's lodgings inside the walls of the Tower. Five
men were there waiting for me, none of whom, except
Wade, had examined me before. He was there to direct the
charges against me.[3]

---

[3] The names of the five men who constituted the board are given in the
signatures below the official report of his examination. They were Richard

The Attorney-General took out a sheet of paper and solemnly began to write out a form of juridical examination. They put no questions about individual Catholics—they were all about political matters—and I answered on the general lines I had always done before. I said that matters of state were forbidden to Jesuits and consequently I never had anything to do with them; if they wanted confirmation they had it. I had been in prison now three years and had been examined time and time again, and they had not produced a scrap of writing or a single trustworthy witness to show that I had taken part in any activities against the Government.

Then they asked me about the letters I had recently received from our Fathers abroad; and I realized for the first time why I had been removed to the Tower. I answered:

"If I have ever received any letters from abroad at any time, they have had nothing to do with politics. They were concerned merely with the financial assistance of Catholics living on the Continent." [4]

"Didn't you receive a packet a short time ago", said Wade, "and hand it over to so-and-so to give to Henry Garnet?"

Berkeley, the Lieutenant of the Tower; Edward Coke, who had been launched on his great legal career by his recent appointment as Attorney-General in preference to Bacon in 1594; Thomas Fleming, appointed Solicitor-General in November 1595 and later Lord Chief Justice of the King's Bench; Francis Bacon, the future Chancellor, who was then struggling through his years of disappointment in uneasy association with Essex; and William Wade, who was then Secretary of the Privy Council and later Lieutenant of the Tower. Their report is dated April 14, 1597. *S.P.D.*, vol. 262, no. 123.

[4] The exact words of J. G.'s reply are written in his own hand in the report of his examination. "I refuse", he said, "not from any disloyal mind, as I look to be saved, but for that I take these things not to have concerned any matter of state, with which I would not have dealt, nor any other but matters of devotion as before." The report shows that J. G. made an attempt to escape from the Clink by means of counterfeit keys. This was probably an additional reason for his removal to the Tower. *C.S.P.D.* (1595–1597), 389.

"If I have received any such packet and forwarded it, I did what I was bound to do. But, I repeat, the only letters I have received or forwarded are those, as I have said, dealing with the dispatch of money to religious and students on the Continent."

"Very well," they said, "then tell us the name of the man you gave the letters to, and where he lives."

"I don't know, and even if I did, I could not and would not tell you", and I gave them the usual reasons for this answer.

"You say", said the Attorney-General, "you have no wish to obstruct the Government. Tell us, then, where Father Garnet is. He is an enemy of the State, and you are bound to report on all such men."

"He isn't an enemy of the State", I said. "On the contrary, I am certain that if he were given the opportunity to lay down his life for his Queen and country, he would be glad of it. But I don't know where he lives, and if I did, I would not tell you."

"Then we'll see to it that you tell us before we leave this place."

"Please God, you won't", I answered.

Then they produced a warrant for putting me to torture.[5] They had it ready by them and handed it to me to read. (In this prison a special warrant is required for torture.)

I saw that the warrant was properly made out and signed, and then I answered:

"With God's help I shall never do anything that is unjust or act against my conscience or the Catholic faith. You have

[5] This warrant is entered in the Privy Council Register without the names of the signatories (vol. 27, 38). It instructs the Lieutenant of the Tower: "You shall by virtue hereof cause him to be put to the manacles and such other torture as is used in that place." The warrant shows that this severity was due to the information that J. G. was receiving intelligence from abroad.

me in your power. You can do with me what God allows you to do—more you cannot do."

Then they began to implore me not to force them to take steps they were loath to take. They said they would have to put me to the torture every day, as long as my life lasted, until I gave them the information they wanted.

"I trust in God's goodness", I answered, "that He will prevent me from ever committing a sin such as this—the sin of accusing innocent people. We are all in God's hands and therefore I have no fear of anything you can do to me."

This was the sense of my answers, as far as I can recall them now.

We went to the torture-room in a kind of solemn procession, the attendants walking ahead with lighted candles.[6]

The chamber was underground and dark, particularly near the entrance. It was a vast place and every device and instrument of human torture was there. They pointed out some of them to me and said that I would try them all. Then they asked me again whether I would confess.

"I cannot", I said.

I fell on my knees for a moment's prayer.[7] Then they took me to a big upright pillar, one of the wooden posts which held the roof of this huge underground chamber.

---

[6] There is said to be an underground passage from the Lieutenant's lodgings where J. G. was examined, to the vaults under the White Tower, where he was tortured.

[7] "He used to fall down at the rackehowse dore upon both knees to commend himself to God's mercie and to crave His grace of patience in his paines. As also being upon the racke he cried continually with much myldeness upon God and the holy name of Jesus." Allan's *Death and Martyrdom of Father Edmund Campion* (ed. 1908), 13. The reading of this passage can certainly be taken as part of J. G.'s preparation for his own ordeal, so that Campion's behavior had by now established a ritual among all the martyrs.

Driven in to the top of it were iron staples for supporting heavy weights. Then they put my wrists into iron gauntlets and ordered me to climb two or three wicker steps. My arms were then lifted up and an iron bar was passed through the rings of one gauntlet, then through the staple and rings of the second gauntlet. This done, they fastened the bar with a pin to prevent it slipping, and then, removing the wicker steps one by one from under my feet, they left me hanging by my hands and arms fastened above my head. The tips of my toes, however, still touched the ground, and they had to dig away the earth from under them. They had hung me up from the highest staple in the pillar and could not raise me any higher, without driving in another staple.[8]

Hanging like this I began to pray. The gentlemen standing around asked me whether I was willing to confess now.

"I cannot and I will not", I answered.

But I could hardly utter the words, such a gripping pain came over me. It was worst in my chest and belly, my hands and arms. All the blood in my body seemed to rush up into my arms and hands, and I thought that blood was oozing out from the ends of my fingers and the pores of my skin. But it was only a sensation caused by my flesh swelling above the irons holding them. The pain was so intense that I thought I could not possibly endure it, and added to it, I had an interior temptation. Yet I did not feel any inclination or wish to give them the information they wanted.

[8] J. G., as his nickname "Long John" betokens, was very tall and well built, and would therefore have suffered more acutely from this form of torture than a lighter man. Suspension by the hands in the manner described by J. G. avoided the dislocation and damage effected by the rack. There had been a revulsion of public opinion in London against the cruelties practiced by Norton, the Queen's "rack-master", and Topcliffe, licensed by Elizabeth to torture in private, introduced this refinement which was known as the "manacles or gauntlets".

The Lord saw my weakness with the eyes of His mercy, and did not permit me to be tempted beyond my strength. With the temptation He sent me relief. Seeing my agony and the struggle going on in my mind, He gave me this most merciful thought: the utmost and worst they can do to you is to kill you, and you have often wanted to give your life for your Lord God. The Lord God sees all you are enduring— He can do all things. You are in God's keeping. With these thoughts, God in His infinite goodness and mercy gave me the grace of resignation, and, with a desire to die and a hope (I admit) that I would, I offered Him myself to do with me as He wished. From that moment the conflict in my soul ceased, and even the physical pain seemed much more bearable than before, though I am sure it must, in fact, have been greater with the growing strain and weariness of my body.

When the gentlemen present saw that I was not answering their questions, they went off to the Lieutenant's house, and stayed there. Every now and again they sent to find out how things were going with me.

Three or four robust men remained behind to watch and supervise the torture, and also my warder. He stayed, I think, out of kindness, for every few minutes he took a cloth and wiped the perspiration that ran in drops continuously down my face and whole body. That helped me a little, but he added to my sufferings when he started to talk. He went on and on, begging and imploring me to pity myself and tell the gentlemen what they wanted to know. And he urged so many human reasons for this that I thought that the devil had instigated him to feign this affection or that my torturers had left him behind on purpose to trick me. But I felt all these suggestions of the enemy like blows in the distance; they did not seem to touch my soul or affect me in any way. More than once I interrupted him:

"Stop this talk, for heaven's sake. Do you think I'm going to throw my soul away to save my life? You exasperate me."

But he went on. And several times the others joined in.

"You will be a cripple all your life if you live. And you are going to be tortured every day until you confess."

But I prayed in a low voice as well as I could, calling on the names of Jesus and Mary.[9]

Sometime after one o'clock, I think, I fell into a faint. How long I was unconscious I don't know, but I don't think it was long, for the men held my body up or put the wicker steps under my feet until I came to. Then they heard me pray and immediately they let me down again. And they did this every time I fainted—eight or nine times that day—before it struck five.

After four or before five o'clock Wade returned. Coming to me he asked,

"Are you ready now to obey the Queen and her Council?"

I answered:

"You want me to do what is sinful. I will not do it."

"All you have to say", said Wade, "is that you wish to speak to Cecil, Her Majesty's Secretary."†

"I have nothing to say to him", I said, "except what I have said to you already. If I asked to speak to him, people would be scandalized. They would think I had given way, that at last I was going to say something that I should not say."

In a rage he suddenly turned his back on me and strode out of the room, shouting angrily in a loud voice:

"Then hang there until you rot off the pillar."

---

[9] "The inquisitors say that he [J. G.] is very obstinate, as they cannot draw the least word out of his mouth, except that in torment he cries, 'Jesus'." Garnet to the General, May 7, 1597. Stonyhurst MSS *Anglia*, vol. 2, no. 27.

He left. And I think all the Commissioners left the Tower then, for at five o'clock the Tower bell is rung, a signal for all to leave unless they want to have the gates locked on them. A little later they took me down. My legs and feet were not damaged, but it was a great effort to stand upright.

They led me back to my cell. On the way we met some prisoners who had the run of the Tower, and I turned to speak to my warder, intending them to overhear.

"What surprises me", I said, "is that the Commissioners want me to say where Father Garnet's house is. Surely they know it is a sin to betray an innocent man? I will never do it, even if I have to die."

I said this to prevent them spreading a report, as they so often do, that I had confessed something. And I also wanted word to get round through these men that it was chiefly concerning Father Garnet that I had been questioned, so that he might get to hear and look to his own safety. I saw that the warder was not pleased at my talking in their hearing, but that made no difference to me.[10]

When I reached my cell the man seemed really sorry for me. He laid a fire and brought me some food, as it was now nearly supper time. But I could eat only a little; and I lay down on my bed and rested quietly until the morning.

In the morning after the gates of the Tower were opened, my warder came up to say that Wade had arrived and that I had to go down and see him. I put on a cloak with wide

[10] This ingeniously dispatched message got through to Father Garnet. Writing to the General of the Society on June 10, eight weeks later, Father Garnet says: "He [J. G.] hath been thrice hanged up by the hands until he was almost dead and that in one day twice. The cause was (as I now understand perfectly) for to tell where his Superior was, and by whom he had sent him letters which were delivered him from Father Persons." Stonyhurst MSS, Grene's *Collectanea P.*, vol. 2, 548.

sleeves—I could not get my swollen hands through the sleeves of my own gown—and I went down.

When I entered the Lieutenant's house, Wade said to me:

"I have been sent here in the name of the Queen and her Secretary, Cecil. They say they know for certain that Garnet meddles in politics and is a danger to the State. And this the Queen asserts on the word of a Sovereign and Cecil on his honor. Unless you choose to contradict them both, you must agree to hand him over."

"They cannot be speaking from experience", I answered, "or from any reliable information; they don't know the man. I have lived with him and know him well, and I can say for certain that he is not that kind of man." [11]

"Come," said Wade, "why not admit the truth and answer our questions?"

"I cannot", I said, "and I will not."

"It would be better for you if you did", and saying this he called out to a gentleman waiting in the next room. He was a well-built man whom Wade called "Master of Torture". I knew such an officer existed, but I found out later that this was not the man. He was Master of the Artillery. Wade gave him this title to terrorize me.

"By order of the Queen and Council", he addressed this gentleman, "I hand this man over to you. You are to torture him twice to-day and twice every day until he confesses."

The man took charge of me. Wade left. In the same way as before we went to the torture chamber.

[11] On November 19, 1594, while J. G. was in the Clink, Garnet wrote to Father Persons in most loyal terms about the Queen: "Her Majesty hath been in danger by a short sickness; but thanks be to God, well recovered; and was yesterday at the triumphs all in yellow, that it was comfortable to behold her so fresh and lusty." Stonyhurst MSS, *Anglia A*, vol. 1, no. 82.

The gauntlets were placed on the same part of my arms as last time. They would not fit anywhere else, because the flesh on either side had swollen into small mounds, leaving a furrow between; and the gauntlets could only be fastened in the furrow. I felt a very sharp pain when they were put on.

But God helped me and I gladly offered Him my hands and my heart. I was hung up in the same way as before, but now I felt a much severer pain in my hands but less in my chest and belly. Possibly this was because I had eaten nothing that morning.

I stayed like this and began to pray, sometimes aloud, sometimes to myself, and I put myself in the keeping of Our Lord Jesus and His blessed Mother. This time it was longer before I fainted, but when I did they found it so difficult to bring me round that they thought that I was dead, or certainly dying, and summoned the Lieutenant. I don't know how long he was there or how long I remained in a faint. But when I came to myself, I was no longer hanging but sitting on a bench with men supporting me on either side. There were many people about, and my teeth had been forced open with a nail or some iron instrument, and hot water had been poured down my throat.

When the Lieutenant saw that I could speak, he said, "Don't you see how much better for you it would be if you submitted to the Queen instead of dying like this?"

God helped me and I was able to put more spirit into my answer than I had felt up to now.

"No, no I don't!" I said. "I would prefer to die a thousand times rather than do as they suggest."

"So you won't confess, then?"

"No, I won't", I said. "And I won't as long as there is breath left in my body."

"Very well, then, we must hang you up again now, and a second time after dinner."

He spoke as though he were sorry to have to carry out his orders.

"*Eamus in nomine Domini*", I said. "I have only one life, but if I had several I would sacrifice them all for the same cause."

I struggled to my feet and tried to walk over to the pillar, but I had to be helped. I was very weak now and if I had any spirit left in me it was given by God and given to me, although most unworthy, because I shared the fellowship of the Society.

I was hung up again. The pain was intense now, but I felt great consolation of soul, which seemed to me to come from a desire of death. Whether it arose from a true love of suffering for Christ, or from a selfish longing to be with Christ, God knows best. But I thought then that I was going to die. And my heart filled with great gladness as I abandoned myself to His will and keeping and contemned the will of men. Oh! that God would grant me the same spirit always, though I am sure that in His eyes it was far from a perfect spirit, for my life was to be longer than I then thought, and God gave me time to make it more perfect in His sight, since, it seems, I was not then ready.

Perhaps the Governor of the Tower realized he would gain nothing by torturing me any longer; perhaps it was his dinner-hour or maybe he was moved with genuine pity for me; whatever the reason, he ordered me to be taken down. It seemed that I had been hanging only an hour in this second period to-day. Personally, I believe he was moved by compassion, for some time after my escape a gentleman of position told me that he had heard Sir Richard Berkeley, this same Lieutenant, say that he had freely resigned his office because he no longer wished to be an instrument in such torture of innocent men. At all events it is a fact that he did resign, and only three or four months after his appointment. His place was taken by another knight[12] and it was under him that I escaped.

My warder brought me back to my room. His eyes seemed swollen with tears. He assured me that his wife, whom I had never seen, had wept and prayed for me all the time.

He brought me some food. I could eat little, and the little I did eat he had to cut up into small pieces. For many days after I could not hold a knife in my hands—that day I could not even move my fingers or help myself in the smallest way. He had to do everything for me. But in spite of this on orders from the authorities he took away my knife, scissors, and razors. I thought they must be afraid that I would attempt suicide, but I later learnt that they always do this in the Tower when a prisoner is under warrant for torture.

I expected to be taken again and tortured as they had threatened to do.[13] But God knew the weakness of His soldier and gave him a short struggle lest he be defeated. To others stronger than me, to Father Walpole, Father Southwell, and others, He offered a hard fight that they might

[12] Sir John Peyton, who became Governor of the Tower in June 1597, held the office until July 1605 when he was succeeded by William Wade.

[13] J. G. was taken a third time to the torture chamber. Father Garnet mentions the incident in his letter of May 7: "They lately took him to the rack, and the torturers and examiners stood ready for work, but when he entered the place he straightway threw himself on his knees, and with a loud voice prayed God that as He had given strength to some of His saints to be torn asunder by horses for the sake of Christ, so He would give him strength and courage to be rent in pieces before he should speak a word that would be injurious to any one, or to the Divine glory. And so they did not torture him, seeing him so resolved." Stonyhurst MSS, *Anglia A*, vol. 2, no. 27.

conquer. These men "in a brief time fulfilled a long space"; but I was clearly unworthy of their prize and was left to fulfill the length of my days, to make good my failings, and wash with many tears a soul which I was not counted fit to wash—once and quickly—with my blood. It was God's good pleasure; and what is good in His sight, be it done.†

16. CLANDESTINE CORRESPONDENCE

Left to myself in my cell I spent most of my time in prayer. Now, as in the first days of my imprisonment, I made the Spiritual Exercises. Each day I spent four or sometimes five hours in meditation, and so for a whole month. I also had my breviary with me; and every day, too, I rehearsed the actions of Mass, as students do when they are preparing for ordination. I went through them with great devotion and longing to communicate, which I felt most keenly at those moments when in a real Mass the priest consummates the sacrifice and consumes the *oblata*. This practice brought me much consolation in my sufferings.

At the end of three weeks, as near as I can remember, I was able to move my fingers, and to hold a knife in my hand and help myself.[1] When I had finished the Spiritual Exercises I asked permission to have some books, but they allowed me only a Bible which I got from my old prison. Then I asked for a little money, hoping gradually to bribe

[1] Cardinal Allen describes the similar helplessness of Edmund Campion after his torture. "And his said keeper asking him the next day [after his racking] how he felt his handes and feet: he answered, 'Not ill, because not at all'. And being in that case benomed both of hand and fote, he likened himselfe to an elephant, which being downe could not rise; and when he could hold the bread he had to eate between both his handes, he did compare himselfe to an ape; so mirry the man of God was in his minde in all his bodely miseries." Allen, *Edmund Campion*, 14.

the warder to bring me secretly several things I wanted—
even, possibly, some books. Thanks to my friends everything I asked for reached me safely by his means.

Then I asked my warder to buy me some large oranges.
As he was particularly fond of this fruit, I presented him
with them, but I was thinking of another use I could put
them to in time.

Every day I did exercises with my hands after dinner, for
I never took supper, though it was always offered. The food
there was provided at the Queen's expense, and it was
plentiful—every day they gave me six small rolls of very
good bread. (The grades of diet in this prison vary according to the rank of the prisoner. The scale is a purely social
one, and taking no account of the religious state, it puts
first what ought to be esteemed last.) [2]

My finger exercises consisted of cutting up the orange
peel into small crosses; then I stitched the crosses together
in pairs and strung them on to a silk thread, making them
into rosaries. All the time I stored the juice from the oranges
in a small jar.

My next move was to ask the warder to take some of the
crosses and rosaries to my friends in my old prison. As he
did not think that any harm could come from this, he consented. Still, however, I had no pen and I did not dare to
ask for one. In any case, even if I had been allowed one I
was hardly able to write at all. Though I could now hold a
pen in my hand, I could scarcely feel I had anything between
my fingers. My sense of touch did not revive for five months,
and then not completely. Right up to the time of my escape,

[2] There are numerous entries in the Tower Bills of J. G.'s expenses, e.g.,
"Midsummer 1597: John Gerrat, Gent., 12 April–S. John Baptist ... diet,
keeper, fuel, washing. 12 pounds, 11 shillings, 7 pence." Tower Bills, *C.R.S.*,
vol. 4, 233.

which was after six months, I always had a certain numbness in my fingers.[3]

As I did not dare to ask my warder for a pen to write with, I asked whether I could have a quill for picking my teeth. The warder gave permission, and I sharpened the end into a point, cut it off, and fitted it into a piece of wood. With the rest of the quill I made a toothpick, taking care that it looked long enough for the warder not to suspect that I had cut a piece off. Later I showed it to him and then asked him for some paper to wrap the rosaries in, and, lastly, I obtained his leave to write a few lines in charcoal, begging my friends to pray for me. All this he allowed, suspecting nothing at all in my action; but, in fact, on the same sheet of paper I wrote to my friends in orange juice, telling them to reply in the same way if they received the note, but not to say much at first, and to give the warder a little money, promising him something each time he brought them a rosary or cross and a short written message from me assuring them that I was well.

My friends received the rosary wrapped in the paper. They knew that, given the chance, I would have written something in orange juice as I used to do when I was with them, and immediately they went to a room upstairs and putting the paper by the fire, read what I had written. They replied in the same way, sending me a gift of some sweetmeats and other delicacies, which provided them with a pretext for the paper which they wrapped them in.

---

[3] In June J. G. evidently asked for permission to take exercise in the open air, since he was unwell. His petition was forwarded by the Lieutenant, Sir Richard Berkeley, to Cecil on June 20. "Gerrat, a prisoner in the Tower, being ill and weak, hath importuned me to signify his petition to be allowed to take the air on a wall near his prison. I am bold to advertise you of this, being their mouth, as they term me. The man needs physic." *Hat. Cal.*, 7:260.

We continued to communicate like this for the next six months. When we found that the warder never failed to deliver the messages faithfully, we became much more confident.

For the first two or three months he had no idea that he was carrying letters to and fro. At the end of three months I asked him whether he would allow me to write some letters in pencil, and he gave me permission. I always handed him my letters unsealed, so that he could see what I said. In the penciled letter I confined myself to spiritual topics, but in the white spaces between the lines I gave detailed instructions to different friends of mine outside. Of course he knew nothing about this.

Actually, as I was soon to discover, my warder could not read. But he pretended very cleverly that he could, and used to stand behind me looking over my shoulder while I read out all that I had written in pencil. Yet I began to suspect that he was illiterate and decided to try him out.

One day while he was looking over the paper, I read out something quite different from what I had written down. I did it again four or five times, and when he did not correct me I turned to him with a smile and said frankly that there was no need for him to go on watching me. He admitted then that he could not read and explained that he liked listening to what I read out. Thereafter he let me write whatever I wanted and carried everything indiscriminately to my friends. Finally he allowed me some ink, and took sealed letters to and fro.

When he saw that I dealt only with a few people, who could be relied on for their discretion, and realized that neither they nor I were likely to betray him, he did whatever we asked. He received, of course, some payment each time. But he begged me not to ask him to go to the Clink so often, because he would eventually come under suspicion and both of us suffer. He suggested that a friend should meet him at a place near the Tower and take the letters from him. But I did not want anyone to put their trust in him, apart from the prisoners, who ran no risk in acknowledging that they knew me or in sending me presents and alms. And I knew that the warder would mention the letters to no one, for it would have done him as much harm as the persons to whom he carried the letters. This he knew well. And even if he had wished, there was not much harm that he could do me and my friends. I never wrote down their names in my letters, not even when I was at liberty, but I used other names which were recognized by the people I addressed. I called one "my son", another "my friend" or "my nephew", and their wives, "sister", "daughter"—so that if the letters were intercepted, which, in fact, they never were, no one would know to whom I referred. And besides I never used lemon or citron juice. There was one occasion when I did in my previous prison and that was for the letters which Wade intercepted; but then there was a special reason. They were letters of recommendation and had to be read in one place and then taken on to another; and lemon juice has this property, that it comes out just as well with water or heat. If the paper is taken out and dried, the writing disappears, but it can be read a second time when it is moistened or heated again. But orange juice is different. It cannot be read with water—water, in fact, washes away the writing and nothing can recover it. Heat brings it out, but it stays out. So a letter in orange juice cannot be delivered without the recipient knowing whether or not it has been read. If it has been read and contains something that compromises him, he can disown it. I was certain, therefore, that all my letters reached my friends and that theirs reached me safely, and in this way I got all the information I needed from them, and they received the spiritual help they sought from me.

To make doubly sure that nothing went amiss, I secured the release of John Lillie through the kindness of friends who bought him out. Then I arranged for everything addressed to me from outside to be given to him and to no one else, and for him to hand it to the warder. Later it was through his help that I was able to make my escape, but I had no thought of this at the time I first used him to carry my letters. Then my only object was to make it easier to send and receive more letters.

The next four months passed quietly. By the end of the first month I had received some books and begun to study a little. And it was at this time that an incident occurred that caused me a great deal of anxiety.

Francis Page (I have spoken about him before) was residing with my former host[4] who had now been released from prison. When I was removed to the Tower, Page found out what part I was confined in, and with his customary kindness, used to come every day to a place some distance off, but near enough to be able to watch my window, where he hoped to catch sight of me. Eventually one day—it was summer time and very hot—I was standing by my window and he saw me. He uncovered his head and then started walking up and down. At each turn he stopped in the same place, faced my direction, and took off his hat. In order not to attract attention he pretended to be arranging his hair or doing something else to his head, just to give himself an excuse for taking off his hat. He did this a number of times before I recognized him by the clothes he was wearing. I

[4] William Wiseman.

signed my greetings, then I blessed him and stepped back from the window. Though the signs I made could not be seen, there was always a danger that someone might be watching him and become suspicious.

But the good man was not satisfied. Every day he came for my blessing and spent a good deal of time walking up and down, facing my cell, and doffing his hat at each turn. I signed to him to stop, but he went on, and eventually the authorities noticed that he came and behaved in the same manner every day. It filled me with great grief when one day I saw them seize him and carry him off.

He was taken to the Lieutenant and questioned about me and my friends. He gave nothing away. He said simply that he liked walking by the broad flowing Thames and came there merely for pleasure. Nevertheless, they kept him a prisoner in the Tower for several days while inquiries were made. They found out that he was living in my host's house, and this confirmed their suspicion that he had been sent to communicate with me by signs. But he admitted nothing, and eventually they summoned me. The other men who usually examined me were called in.

Master Page was walking up and down with my warder in the hall as I passed through into the dining-hall where the examination was being held. The first thing they said was:

"There is a certain Francis Page here. He says he knows you well and very much wants to have a word with you."

"If he wants to, he can", I answered. "But who is this Francis Page? I don't know anyone of that name."

"You can't mean that", they said. "He knows you all right. At any rate he knows you well enough to recognize you a long way off. He comes here every day just to see you."

I went on denying that I knew him, but they had no further information to go on, and they were going to get nothing out of me either by bluff or threats.

So they ordered me back to my cell. On my way I passed through the hall. There was Page standing with a number of other people. I looked all round and called out at the top of my voice:

"Is there anyone here called Page? The man says he knows me well, and comes to watch me at my window. I don't know the man from Adam. Why should anyone want to get himself into trouble talking like this?"

The warder tried to silence me, but it was no good. It never, of course, entered my head for a moment that Page had confessed anything. But I wanted to stop them telling Page that I had said the sort of things about him that he was reported to have said about me. That was, in fact, their plan. Already they had told him I had admitted that I knew him. Now they wanted him to watch me going in to the examination room, so that they could tell him afterward that I had just confirmed all I was supposed to have said before. I spoilt that game. When he was called in, Page merely repeated what he had just heard me say in the hall as I passed through. They had been outwitted, and in their disappointment they stormed at the warder and cursed me.

A short time afterward Master Page purchased his release.[5] He crossed the sea, did his studies in Belgium, was ordained priest, and later returned to England. For the most part he worked in London, where he was loved by all the many souls he helped. At my request he had particular care of Mistress Line, and it was in her apartments that he was

[5] Page was in prison from "the Vigil of Pentecost [May 14] till 13 October" 1597. *C.R.S.*, vol. 10, 1.

captured (I told you the story) and escaped. Then he obtained his desire and was admitted into the Society. But before he could cross to Belgium to do his noviceship, he was captured. "Like gold in the furnace he was tested, and was accepted like the victim of a holocaust: he washed his robe in the blood of the Lamb." Now he no longer walks up and down by the waters of the Thames watching me in the Tower, but serene and happy in heaven he looks down on me, still tossed on the waters by the winds and storms. But he is, I trust, anxious still for my safety.[6]

Often he had told people how heartened he had been that day, when he heard what I said as I passed through the hall. It enabled him to see the ruse and protect himself against it.

During my confinement in the Tower I was allowed no visitors, and it was impossible therefore to deal directly with souls. I was able to do something, however, by correspondence, but only in the case of people I could trust not to reveal my secret arrangements for writing and receiving letters.

John Lillie happened one day after his release to be walking the streets of London, when two noble ladies, mother and daughter, came up and asked him whether he could possibly take them to see me and my prison cell. He knew how difficult this would be and tried to dissuade them. But they persisted and gave him no peace until he had promised to broach the matter to my warder, asking him, perhaps, to let them in as two of his own relations.

The warder was promised a large sum and consented; and the ladies presented his wife with a new gown. Then they dressed themselves up like simple London citizens (ordinary people dress very differently from fashionable women) and came along with John Lillie. They pretended they wanted

---

[6] Page was executed at Tyburn on April 20, 1602.

to see the warder's wife and visit the lions that are kept in the Tower and the other animals which curious people come to see. After doing the sights, the warder took them inside the walls, and waited his chance to bring them along to my room—he was running a great risk for a small gain. The moment they set eyes on me they rushed forward and fell down and tried to kiss my feet. They almost fought each other to be the first to kiss them.

How could I refuse, when they had risked so much for this? They begged me so earnestly to allow them, that in the end I did, for I knew they were honoring not me personally, but a prisoner of Christ's.

We had a short talk together, then they gave me some presents they had brought and went away very comforted. They believed they would never see my face again, for they had heard in the city that it was at last intended to have me tried and condemned.†

One day Father Garnet, my Superior, sent me a letter giving me the same good news. It was a letter full of consolation. He told me to prepare myself for execution, and, I must admit, "I rejoiced at the things that were said to me." But my great unworthiness prevented me from entering the house of the Lord. A grace like this is the gift of God. It cannot be had for mere willing or striving, and it was hidden from Father Garnet that this mercy was in store for him, not for me. And now I can only pray that God may permit me still to follow him from afar to the Cross which he reverenced and loved so much. God gave him his heart's desire, for on the feast of the Finding of the Holy Cross his soul found its true love. Now I must merely mention that on the same feast of the Finding of the Holy Cross, the day on which that dear priest was crowned in heaven, God in His goodness granted me two great favors through his intercession. I will tell you briefly what they were at the end of this narrative. Now I must hurry on. Already I have given these slight and trivial incidents in my life-story much fuller treatment than they deserve.

Father Garnet, then, sent me a warning letter; and the way my captors acted and spoke at this time held out the same promise. For they came again, all the men who on the previous occasion had examined me with authority to torture me.[7] But this time their purpose was different. They were going to put me through an examination before bringing me up for formal trial.

The Queen's Attorney-General put to me a series of questions, following, as he said, the same phrasing, order, and form that he would observe in the actual prosecution.

He started with my priesthood and my coming to England as a priest and a Jesuit. Then he asked whether I had dealt with any people with the intention of seducing them from the faith and religious profession approved by law, to the Pope's allegiance. I confessed straightway that I was guilty on all these counts—that was sufficient for a legal sentence. But when they asked me to name the persons with whom I had plotted against the Government, I denied I had done any such thing. Nevertheless they persisted: how could I be so anxious for the conversion of England, they urged, and yet keep out of politics, which were the best means to my purpose?

As near as I can recall now, this is what I answered:

---

[7] From George Abbot's *Sex Quaestiones* it is clear that Francis Bacon was not a member of the board on this occasion. His fortunes were in eclipse after the preference shown to his rivals Coke and Fleming to the discomfiture of his patron Essex. He had just published his first collection of essays in February and at this time was attempting to arrange a match with Lady Elizabeth Hatton, the granddaughter, or Burghley. But in this project he was again defeated by Coke.

"I will speak my mind plainly in this matter of conversion and politics, so that you will be left in no doubt and have no need to question me further. I call on God and His Angels to bear me out—I am not lying. I am hiding nothing from you that I have at heart. If I could have fulfilled all that I wish and desire, I would want the whole of England to return to Rome and the Catholic faith: the Queen, her Council, and yourselves also, and all the magistrates of this realm; yet so, my Lords, that neither the Queen, nor you, nor any officer of state forfeit the honor or right he now enjoys; so that not a single hair of your head perish; but simply that you may be happy both in this present life and in the life to come. But do not think that I want this conversion for any selfish reason of my own— that I may be freed and may enjoy the good things of life. I call on Almighty God to witness: I would gladly go out tomorrow morning to be hanged just as I stand before you now. These are my thoughts, my aspirations. I am not at enmity with the Queen nor with you, nor have I ever been."

For a few moments the Attorney-General was at a loss for an answer. Then he asked me to name the Catholics I knew. Did I know so-and-so?

"I don't", I said, and, as usual, I explained that even if I did know I could not mention their names. Then he went off on to the question of equivocation and began to disparage Father Southwell's character.

Now at his trial Father Southwell had refused to admit that he knew the woman who was brought in to give evidence for the prosecution.[8] Though she swore he had visited

---

[8] This was Ann Bellamy, who when in prison was ruined by Topcliffe and married by him to Nicholas Jones, the underkeeper of the Gate House. *Troubles*, 2nd series, 61–64.

her father's house and had been received there as a priest, Father Southwell denied it—and he had been captured in that very house and in the very hiding-place which that woman had betrayed to the pursuivants. She was a monstrous creature and thought nothing of bartering away her own father's life and Father Southwell's too. But Christ, who came not to set peace, but a sword between the wicked and the good, separated this wicked daughter from her good parents.

Father Southwell was astonished at the woman's impudence, but he denied everything she alleged. And he explained why he did so, putting his reasons well and showing clearly and convincingly that it was wrong for him to increase the burden of those who were already suffering for their faith and had been kind to him. Then, following up, he argued very learnedly that it was lawful and in some cases even necessary to resort to equivocation. Though many, he said, abhorred the doctrine, he showed there were solid reasons for it, and it rested on ample authority in Sacred Scripture and the Doctors of the Church.[9]

The Attorney-General reprobated such teaching and tried to show it countenanced lying and undermined social intercourse between men. Against this I maintained that equivocation was different from lying. In equivocation the intention was not to deceive, which was the essence of a lie, but simply to withhold the truth in cases where the questioned party is not bound to reveal it. To deny a man what he has no claim to was not deception. I showed that this teaching in no way destroyed the bonds of society, or made human intercourse impossible. "Equivocation", I said, "could not be invoked in contracts, since every man is bound

---

[9] For Southwell's defense of equivocation see Appendix E.

to give his neighbor even his smallest due, and in contracts truth is due to the contracting party. Nor could it be invoked in ordinary conversation to the prejudice of plain truth and Christian sincerity, and still less in matters falling under the lawful cognizance of the State. For instance, a man cannot deny a crime if he is guilty and lawfully interrogated." [10]

"What do you mean by lawful interrogation?" asked the Attorney-General.

"The question must be asked by a person who has authority or jurisdiction, and it must concern an action in some way harmful to the State, otherwise the law cannot take cognizance of it. Wrong acts, that are merely internal, are reserved to God's judgment alone. Again, there must be some evidence adduced against the accused person. In England it is the custom for the accused, when asked whether he is guilty or not, to answer 'Not guilty', until witnesses are produced against him or a verdict of guilty returned by the jury who examine the case. This is the general practice and no one calls it lying. In general, equivocation is unlawful save when a person is asked a question, either directly or indirectly, which the questioner has no right to put, and where a straight answer would injure the questioned party."

Then I explained that this was the practice of Our Lord and of the saints and all sensible men. "The board examining me now", I said, "would do the same if, for example, they were questioned about some secret sin or were attacked by thieves and asked where their money was hidden."

"When did Our Lord use equivocation?" they asked.

---

[10] The official report of the examination helps to explain J. G.'s statement: "He saith, that a witness being examined *juridice*, and of temporal things, not concerning religion or Catholics, cannot answer with equivocation." Strype, *Annals IV* (ed. 1824), 428.

"When He told His Apostles", I answered, "that no one knew the Day of Judgment, not even the Son of Man; and again, when He said He was not going up to Jerusalem for the feast, and then went. He knew He was going when He said He was not."

Wade broke in.

"Christ was ignorant of the Day of Judgment as Son of Man."

"The word 'ignorant'", I said, "cannot be used of the Incarnate Word of God; His human nature was hypostatically united to the divine. He was constituted Judge by God the Father, and would therefore know all that touched His office. Moreover, He was infinite wisdom and knew all that concerned Himself."

Now, Protestants don't admit all Saint Paul teaches. They claim, of course, to follow him, but this was a case in point: Paul teaches that the fullness of the Godhead resided in Christ, corporeally, and that in Him were all the treasures of the wisdom and knowledge of God. However, this passage did not occur to me at the moment.†

They had practically no answer to make. But the Attorney-General wrote down every word and told me he would use it against me before very long when I came up for trial.† But he did not keep his promise, for I was unworthy to enter the house of God. Nothing defiled can enter it, and I was still to be cleansed and made to pass much time in exile; and then, if it please God, be saved, yet as by fire.

This examination took place in Trinity Term, as it is called.[11] There are three terms in the year when the courts

---

[11] The exact date was May 13 (cf. Coke's letter to Burghley. Strype, *Annals IV* [ed. 1824], 427). Trinity Term 1597 opened, in fact, on May 23, ten days after J. G.'s examination.

are open and many people come to London with their suits. Because of the greater crowds in town then, they choose these times to try the priests they have decided to sentence to death. It seemed now that this is what they planned, but man proposes and God disposes; and He disposed differently in my case.

This term passed and it looked as if there were no hope that they would prosecute me in public after all. In my enforced rest, I turned more to my studies, and began to think that they were keeping me here because they wanted to cut me off from outside, and that this was why they had moved me to a stricter and more secluded prison.†

17. ESCAPE

October 4, 1597

I tried my best to reconcile myself to God's will, and accept all the restrictions imposed on me.

It was the last day of July and the feast of our blessed Father.[1] I was making my meditation and was longing to have the opportunity of saying Mass again, when the thought suddenly came to me—I might be able to do it in the cell of a Catholic gentleman in the tower opposite me. There was only a garden between his cell and mine.[2]

He had been in prison there for ten years and lay under sentence of death, but the sentence had not yet been carried out. Every day he used to go up on to the lead roof above his cell where he was allowed to walk up and down for exercise. From there he used to greet me and wait on his knees for my blessing.

When I turned the idea over in my mind later, I thought it might be done, if only the warder could be persuaded to let me go over. The gentleman's wife was allowed to visit him on fixed days and bring him clean linen and other things he needed. She carried them in a basket, and as she

---

[1] Saint Ignatius, the founder of the Society of Jesus. He was beatified on July 27, 1609, the year in which J. G. was writing. He was not canonized until March 12, 1622.

[2] This was John Arden, who was imprisoned in the Cradle Tower, which was at the opposite corner of the Queen's Privy Garden.†

had now been doing this for years the warders had got out of the way of examining its contents. With her help I hoped we might be able little by little to bring in everything we needed for Mass. My friends, of course, would supply them.

I decided to try. So I signed to the gentleman to watch the gestures I was going to make; I dared not call to him because it was a good distance across and I might easily be overheard. He watched me as I took a pen and paper and pretended to write; next, I placed the letter over the coal fire and held it up in my hands as though I were reading it; then I wrapped up one of my crosses in it, and went through the motions of dispatching it to him. He seemed to follow what I was trying to indicate.

The next step was to get the warder to take one of my crosses or rosaries to my good fellow-prisoner—the same man had charge of us both. At first he refused, saying that he could not risk it as he had no proof that the other man could be trusted to keep the secret.

"If the man said something to his wife and it became known, it would be all up with me", he said.

But I put heart into him and told him that this was most improbable. Then I placed some money in his hand as I always did, and he agreed. My letter was taken and delivered, but the gentleman wrote nothing back as I had asked him to do. The next day, when he came out for his walk on the roof, he thanked me by signs, holding up in his hands the cross I had sent him.

When at the end of three days he had not replied I began to suspect the reason for it. So I went through the whole series of signs again with greater precision, showing him how I squeezed the juice out of an orange and dipped my pen into the juice, and then, to bring out the writing, held the paper to the fire. This time he understood and held my next letter to the fire and read it. In his reply he said that the first time he thought I wanted him to burn the paper, because I had scribbled a few words in pencil on it, and he had done this.

He answered my query, saying he thought the scheme was practicable, provided the warder allowed me to visit him in the evening and stay over the whole of the following day; his wife would bring all the Mass requisites that were given her.

The next step was to sound the warder—would he allow me over to see my fellow-prisoner just once? I said I wanted to dine with him and promised to let him share the feast. He refused absolutely—he was frightened lest I might be seen walking across the garden or lest the Lieutenant should choose that very day to pay me a visit. But I pointed out that this had never happened and was most unlikely to happen and, to end the argument, I produced the golden reason—I promised to pay him cash for his kind offices. He agreed.

I fixed the day for the feast of the Nativity of Our Blessed Lady.[3] In the meantime I arranged for the prisoner's wife to go to a certain place in the city. There she would meet John Lillie, who, following the instructions in my letter, would hand her the things needed for Mass. I had also told Lillie to bring a number of small hosts and a pyx as I wanted to reserve the Blessed Sacrament.

Lillie collected everything, and the woman brought them in.

When the evening arrived, I went across with my warder and stayed with the gentleman all that night and the following day. According to the promise we had made with the warder, not a word was said to the gentleman's wife.

[3] September 8, 1597.

That morning I said Mass. I felt very great consolation, and I gave Communion to the noble confessor of Christ, who had been so many years without this comfort. I also consecrated twenty-two hosts and placed them in a pyx with a corporal and brought them back with me to my own cell, and renewed the divine banquet for many days afterward with fresh relish and delight.

When I went across that evening I had no thought of escape—I had only looked to the Lord Jesus, prefigured as our Redeemer in the ash-baked loaf of Elias, to give me the strength and courage I still needed to journey the rest of my hard way to the mountain of the Lord. But while we were passing the time of day together, it struck me how close this tower was to the moat encircling the outer fortifications, and I thought it might be possible for a man to lower himself with a rope from the roof of the tower on to the wall beyond the moat. I asked the gentleman what he thought about it.

"Yes, it could be done easily", he said, "if we only had some really good friends who were ready to run the risk of helping us."

"We have the friends all right," I said, "if only the thing is practicable and really worth trying."

"As far as I am concerned," he said, "I am all for attempting it. I would be much happier if I could live in hiding with my friends, and with the consolation of the sacraments and with pleasant companions, instead of passing my days like a solitary between these four walls."

"Good", I said. "Now, we'll pray about it, and meanwhile I'll put the matter to my Superior and do whatever he thinks best."

For the rest of the time we were together we discussed the details of the plan we would follow, if we decided on the attempt.

When I got back to my cell that night I wrote to my Superior through John Lillie and laid all the details of the scheme before him. Father Garnet replied that I certainly ought to attempt it, but I was not to risk my neck in the descent.

I then wrote to my former host[4] and told him that we were going to attempt an escape, and warned him to mention it to as few people as possible. If the plan got out, it would be all over. Then I asked John Lillie and Richard Fulwood (he was attending Father Garnet at the time) whether they were prepared to take the risk, and, if they were, to come on a certain night to the far side of the moat, opposite the squat tower I had described, near the point where Master Page had been seized. They were to bring a rope with them and tie it to a stake; we would be on the roof of the Tower and throw them an iron ball attached to a stout thread, the kind used in stitching up bales. They must listen in the darkness for the sound of the ball touching the ground, find the cord, and tie it to the free end of the rope. This done, we would draw up the rope by pulling the other end of the cord, which we held in our hands. I told them to pin a piece of white paper or a handkerchief on the front of their jackets, for we wanted to be sure of their identity before throwing the cord. Also, they were to bring a rowing boat so that we could make a quick get-away.

When everything was arranged and the night fixed, my former host, who was afraid of the risk I was taking, was anxious that I should first see whether the warder could be bribed into letting me walk out of the prison, as I could easily do in borrowed clothes. Therefore, in the name of a friend of mine, John Lillie offered the warder a thousand

[4] William Wiseman.

florins down and a yearly allowance of a hundred florins for life. The warder would not hear of it. If he allowed it, he said, it would mean that he would be an outlaw for the rest of his life, and he would be hanged if he were caught. So the matter was dropped and we went ahead with our first plan.

I begged the earnest prayers of all who were let into the secret. One gentleman, the heir to a large estate, bound himself by vow to fast one day in the week for life, if I got away safe.

The night came. I begged and bribed my warder to let me visit my fellow-prisoner. I walked across. The warder locked the pair of us in the cell, barred the door as he always did, and went off. But he had also bolted the inside door which gave on to the stairs leading up to the roof, and we had to cut away with a knife the stone holding the socket of the bolt. There was no other way out.

At last we climbed silently up the stairs without a light, for a guard was posted every night in a garden at the foot of the wall, and when we spoke, it was in a faint whisper.

At midnight we saw the boat with our friends approaching. John Lillie and Richard Fulwood were at the oars and a third man sat at the tiller. He was my old warder in the Clink, and he had obtained the boat for us. As they pulled in and got ready to land, a man came out from one of the poor dwelling-places on the bank to do something. When he saw the boat draw up, he started talking to the men, thinking they were fishermen.

He went back to bed. But the rescue party were afraid to land until the man had been given time to get to sleep again. So they paddled up and down. Time passed. It became too late to attempt anything that night.

They rowed back toward the bridge, but by now the tide had turned and was flowing strongly. It forced their little boat against the piles driven into the bed of the river to break the force of the water. It stuck, and it was impossible to move it forward or back. Meanwhile the water was rising and was striking the boat with such force that with every wave it looked as if it would capsize and the occupants be thrown into the river. They could only pray to God and shout for help.[5]

We were on the top of the tower and heard their shouts. Men came out on to the bank, and we were able to watch them in the light thrown by their candles. They rushed to their boats and pulled off to the rescue. Several boats came quite near, but they were afraid to pull alongside—the current was too strong. Forming a semi-circle round them, they stayed like spectators watching the poor men in their peril without daring to assist.

Amid all the shouting I recognized Richard Fulwood's voice.

"I know it", I said. "It's our friends in danger."

My companion would not believe that I could pick out anyone's voice at such a distance,[6] but I recognized it only too well, and I was miserable at the thought that such devoted men were in danger of their lives for my sake.

We prayed fervently for them. Though we had watched many people go out to help them, they were not saved yet.

---

[5] This was the famous old London bridge opened in 1209. It was 926 feet long and had nineteen arches buttressed by great piers, which obstructed the flow of the river. The existence of water works added to the hazards of the passage. There was a saying that wise men go over the bridge, fools under it. The present bridge, which replaced it in 1831, was built sixty yards west of the old bridge.

[6] The distance was about half a mile.

Then we saw a light lowered from the top of the bridge, and a kind of basket at the end of a rope. If only they could get into it, they could be pulled up. However, God had regard to the peril of His servants, and at last a powerful sea-going craft came along with six sailors aboard and, hazardously drawing up to the craft in danger, pulled on deck Lillie and Fulwood. Then immediately the small boat capsized before the third man could be rescued—as though it had only been kept afloat for the sake of the Catholics it carried. However, by the mercy of God, the man who was washed over into the river was able to grasp the rope let down from the bridge; and he was hauled to safety.

So all were rescued and got back to their homes.

The next day John Lillie sent me a letter as usual through the warder. I might reasonably have expected him to say something like this: "Now we know—and our peril last night has taught us—God does not want us to go ahead with the escape." But quite the contrary. The letter began:

"It was not God's design that we should succeed last night, but He mercifully snatched us from our peril—He has only postponed the day. With God's help we will be back to-night."

Determination like this and the man's devout sentiments reassured my companion. He felt certain we would succeed. But I had great difficulty in getting leave of the warder to stay a second night out of my cell, and we were very much afraid he might notice the loosened stone when he came to bolt the door in the evening. However, he did not see it.

Meantime I had written three letters which I intended to leave behind in the cell. The first was to my warder, justifying myself for contriving my escape without letting him know. I said I was merely exercising my rights—I had committed no crime and was wrongfully held in prison. I told him I would always remember him in my prayers, if there was no other way I could help him. The purpose of this letter was to put him less at fault, in case he was imprisoned for our escape.

The second was to the Lieutenant. In this letter I made further excuses for the warder, protesting before God that he was not privy to my escape and would never have allowed it if he had known. And to prove this, I mentioned the attractive offer we had made, which he had refused. As for my going across to another cell, I had extorted his permission only with the most persistent entreaties, and it would be wrong to put him to death for this.

The third letter was to the Lords of the Council. In the first place I stated my motives for regaining the freedom that was mine by right. I did it not from love of freedom for its own sake, but from love of souls—souls who were being daily lost in England. I wanted to get out and reclaim them from sin and heresy. Concerning the affairs of state they knew my clear record and could count on my not soiling it in the future. Finally, I protested and proved that neither the Lieutenant nor the warder could be charged with connivance or consent. They had known nothing about it; my escape was entirely due to my own exertions and my friends'.

I left these letters to be picked up by the warder. One last letter I wrote and took with me. It was delivered to the warder (as you shall hear) next morning—but not by John Lillie.

At the right time we went up on to the tower. The boat came along. No one interfered and it pulled in safely to the bank. The schismatic stayed in the boat; the two Catholics got out with the rope. It was a new one, as they had thrown the old into the river when they ran into trouble the previous night. Following my instructions they fastened it to a stake, and then listened for the sound of the iron ball we threw down to them. It was found without difficulty and the cord fastened to the end of the rope. But it proved very difficult indeed to pull up—it was a good deal thicker and doubled. This was Father Garnet's instruction, to guard against the rope snapping under the weight of my body. But actually he had increased the hazards.

Now a fresh difficulty arose which we had not foreseen. The distance between the tower at one end and the stake at the other was very great, and the rope, instead of sloping down, stretched almost horizontally between the two points. We had therefore to descend by working our way along the rope—it was impossible to slide down with our own weight, and this we discovered by making up a bundle of books and other things which we wrapped in my cloak and placed on the double rope to see whether it would go down of its own accord. It didn't. Fortunately, it stuck before it got out of our reach, for if it had gone beyond recovery we would never have gotten down ourselves. We hauled the bundle back and left it behind.[7]

My companion now changed his mind—he had always said it would be the simplest thing in the world to slide down. Now he saw the hazards of it.

"But I shall certainly be hanged if I remain here", he said. "If we throw the rope back now it will fall into the moat and the splash will betray us and our friends as well. I'll go down and God help me. I'd rather take a chance of escape than stay locked up here with no chance at all."

---

[7] The height of the wall beyond the moat had not been allowed for and prevented the rope inclining. As J. G. had not ventured to appear on the roof in daytime he had been unable to make an accurate reckoning.

So he said a prayer and took hold of the rope. He got down fairly easily for he had plenty of strength and the rope was still taut. But his descent slackened the rope and made it much more difficult for me. I only noticed this when I started to descend.

I commended myself to God and Our Lord Jesus, to the Blessed Virgin, my guardian angel, and especially to Father Southwell, who was imprisoned near here until he was taken out to martyrdom, and to Father Walpole and to all our martyrs. Then I gripped the rope with my right hand, and took it in my left. To prevent myself falling I twisted my legs round the rope, leaving it free to slide between my shins.

I had gone three or four yards face downwards when suddenly my body swung round with its own weight and I nearly fell. I was still very weak, and with the slack rope and my body hanging underneath I could make practically no progress. At last I managed to work myself as far as the middle of the rope, and there I stuck. My strength was failing and my breath, which was short before I started, seemed altogether spent.

At last, with the help of the saints and, I think, by the power of my friends' prayers below drawing me, I moved along a little way and then I stuck again. Now I thought I would never be able to get down. But I was determined not to fall into the moat as long as I was still able to hold the rope. I tried to recover a little strength and then, using my legs and arms as well as I could, I managed, thank God, to get as far as the wall on the far side of the moat. But my feet just touched the top of the wall, and the rest of my body hung horizontally behind, with my head no higher than my legs—the rope had become so slack. I don't know how I would have gotten over the wall, if it had not been for John Lillie. Somehow or other (he could never say how he did it), he got up on to the wall, seized hold of my feet, pulled me over, and put me safely down on the ground. I could not stand upright, I was so weak. So they gave me cordial waters and restoratives which they had taken care to bring with them, and I was able to reach the boat. Before getting in they untied the rope from the stake, cut off part of it, and let the rest hang down against the wall of the tower. Our first plan had been to pull it away altogether, and we had accordingly passed it round a big gun on the roof without knotting it. But providentially we could not tug it loose; had we done so it would almost certainly have dropped into the moat with a big splash and we would have been in trouble.

We stepped into the boat and thanked God, "who had snatched us from the hands of our persecutors and from all the expectation of the Protestant people". We also thanked the men who had done so much and undergone such risks for us.

We rowed a good distance before we brought the boat to land. Then I sent my fellow-prisoner with John Lillie to my house, where Mistress Line, that saintly widow, was in charge, while I took Richard Fulwood and went with him to Father Garnet's house.[8] It was on the outskirts of the city, and horses were there ready for us. "Little John", Father Garnet's servant, was holding them, and before dawn broke "Little John" and I were in the saddle.

Father Garnet was in the country at the time.[9] We rode straight to his place and had dinner with him. The rejoicing was great. We all thanked God that I had escaped from the hands of my enemies in the name of the Lord.

---

[8] In Spitalfields. See below, p. 196.
[9] At Uxbridge.†

Meanwhile I had sent Richard Fulwood to a place we had decided on beforehand, where he was to hold a horse and be ready to fly with my warder if the man was prepared to make off at once. As I said, I had written a letter to be delivered to the warder when he came for his usual morning meeting with John Lillie. But it was not Lillie who came that morning. I had ordered him not to stir out of doors until the storm that was to be expected had blown over. In his place I chose another messenger whom the warder knew. He was surprised, of course, to find another man, but he said nothing. Just as he was turning back, as he thought, to deliver the letter in his usual way, the messenger seized hold of him.

"The letter is for you; no, not for anyone else", he said.

"For me? Who sent it?"

"A friend," replied the other man, "but I don't know who he is."

The warder was dumbfounded.

"But I can't read. If it is urgent, please read it for me."

The man read the letter he had brought. In it I informed the warder that I had escaped from prison, and, in order to put his mind at rest, briefly explained why I had done so. Then I pointed out that, though I had no obligation in the matter—I had merely made use of my rights—yet I would see to his safety. He had always been faithful in his trusts, and I would stand by him now. If he wanted to save his skin I had a man ready with a horse to take him to a safe place a good distance out of London. I would give him two hundred florins a year and he could lead a decent life. But I added this condition. If he accepted the offer he must settle his affairs in the Tower quickly and go off at once to the place to which the messenger would lead him. He was on his way back to the Tower to settle his business and see his wife safely away, when a fellow-warder ran into him.

"Off with you, as fast as you can make it", he said. "Your prisoners have escaped from the small tower. The Lieutenant is searching the place for you. If he catches you, God help you."

Shaking all over the man rushed back to the messenger. He begged him for the love of God to take him to the place where the horses were waiting. The messenger took him and found Richard Fulwood waiting with two horses.

He rode off and Richard took him to the house of one of my friends about a hundred miles from London. Already I had sent a letter asking this gentleman whether he would be so kind as to put the warder up and look after him, should he come. But I warned him not to confide in him or let him know that he knew me. Richard Fulwood, I said, would reimburse him for all his expenses. If the warder wanted to talk about me or about his own affairs, he should refuse to listen.

All went off as I had planned. My friend was not troubled, and the warder was safely away in his house. After a year he moved into another county. There he became a Catholic and lived comfortably with his family on the annuity which I sent him regularly according to my promise. And there too he died after four or five years. By this flight for dear life God had snatched him from the temptation of sin, and, I trust, given him a place in heaven. While in prison I had probed him frequently on his faith—his mind was made up, but I could not work on his will. My escape from prison was, I hope, in God's kind disposing, the occasion of his escaping from hell.

When the Lieutenant discovered that his prisoners and their warder had made off, he went to the Council, taking with him the letters I had left behind. The Lords of Council were amazed at the way I had escaped. One of them, a leading Councillor, said to a gentleman in attendance (as I was told afterward) that he was glad I had gotten away. The Lieutenant asked for authorization to search the whole of London and any place suspected, but the others told him it would be no use.[10]

"You can't hope to find him", they said. "If he has friends who are prepared to do all this for him, you can count on it, they will have no difficulty in finding him horses and a hiding-place and keeping him well out of your reach."

A search was made in one or two places. As far as I could discover, nobody of note was taken.

[10] "1597, Oct 5—This night there are escaped two prisoners out of the Tower, viz. John Arden and John Garret. Their escape was made very little before day, for on going to Arden's chamber in the morning I found the ink in his pen very fresh. The manner of their escape was thus. The gaoler, one Bonner, conveyed Garrett into Arden's chamber when he brought up the keys, and out of Arden's chamber by a long rope tied over the ditch to a post they slid down upon the Tower wharf. This Bonner is also gone this morning at the opening of the gates. . . . I have sent hue and cry to Gravesend and to the Mayor of London for a search to be made in London and in all the liberties." Sir John Peyton, Lieutenant of the Tower of London to the Privy Council. *Hat. Cal.*, 7: 417–18.

18. LONDON AND HARROWDEN

1597–1598

For a few days I remained quietly with Father Garnet. I wanted to get my strength back and allow time for the talk about my escape to die down. Then my hosts and very loyal friends begged me to come and stay with them in their London house, near my second prison, for they were still living there. I accepted the invitation and was safe with them. However, I allowed few visitors in, and I went out only at night, a practice which I nearly always observed in London. At this time I called on only a few of my very best friends.

However, I visited my house which was in charge of Mistress Line, the future martyr. Mr. Robert Drury, another future martyr, was still living there. And at this time I gave shelter here to a gentleman who had been the Earl of Essex's chaplain in the expedition against Spain which captured Cadiz.[1]

He was a learned man and spoke several languages. In order to become a Catholic he had declined many offers of high preferment in his church. Already he had had a taste of prison, and when he was offered the chance of escaping, I told him he could stay at my house.

---

[1] William Alabaster, whom Anthony à Wood calls "the rarest poet . . . that any age or nation produced."†

I looked after him there for two or three months. During this time I gave him the Spiritual Exercises, and he made up his mind to enter the Society. He was a man who had been nurtured, so to speak, in Calvin's bosom. He had spent his life in the army, and he was used to having his own way over other people. When he announced his intention, I asked him to tell me frankly why he chose the Society when he knew, or should know, that it meant just the contrary of all he was used to.

"There are three principal things", he answered, "that have induced me to make this decision. First, the fact that heretics and all enemies of God hold the Society in far greater detestation than any other body. I presume this must be because it has the Spirit of God, which the devil cannot abide; and because in God's providence, it is destined to destroy heresy and combat sin of every kind. The second is this. The Society will not allow its members to accept ecclesiastical preferment. Ambition therefore is less likely to affect them, and as their best men are not drawn off they are better able to maintain a tradition of holiness and learning. And thirdly, it has a special regard for obedience. And this is a virtue which I place first in order, both for itself and for the good it can do to people's souls. And, besides, all will be in order with a body of men, if they are all united in purpose under the direction of God."

These were his reasons for joining the Society, so I sent him to Father Holt in Belgium and asked him to see him on to Rome. I gave him three hundred florins for his expenses.†

Before I gave up the house, I gave the Spiritual Exercises to several other people. A good and devout priest, Mr. Woodward, was one of them. He, too, wanted to join the Society, and he went over to Belgium to do so; but there was a great scarcity of English priests for the army at the time, and he was temporarily appointed to that work. He died in the field, very much loved and respected by everyone who knew him.

I retained my house only for a short time after my escape. During my imprisonment people had come there in far greater numbers than I would have tolerated myself had I been free. Too many people, in fact, knew about it. But my main reason for giving it up was that it was known to the man[2] who had been responsible for my removal to the Tower. He had professed to be sorry for what he had done, and I had forgiven him willingly and felt the same affection for him as before; but soon after my escape he was released, and I learned that he was not very highly thought of by the people he lived with. Therefore I thought it unwise to have such a man in a secret which involved the safety of so many people. Mistress Line, who was a woman of much prudence and good sense, thought the same. So we found her another house where she could continue her good work.

A short time before this, an opposition movement against the Archpriest had begun. This prelate had been appointed by Rome to secure some measure of subordination and Government among the English clergy. But a group of restless priests did all they could to defeat the Pope's decree. They worked up the people against the Archpriest and against the Society, and, as always happens, they gathered a party of opposition round themselves.

Several priests whom I used to take in and entertain at the house were affected, and all the same, they came expecting to find a welcome in the house which, as they had

[2] William Atkinson. See above, p. 126.

been told, Mistress Line kept. So the house which was meant for myself and my close friends became a place of call for many people, some of whom were no friends of mine at all and might even have been traitors. And it was this that forced me to make other arrangements.

As it seemed advisable to scotch the idea that Mistress Line kept an open house for any and everybody, she took a lodging for a time by herself in a rented room in a private house. But I still wanted to have a place of my own in London, where I could put up all my good friends in safety, and lodge priests. So I came to an arrangement with a prudent and pious gentleman, whose wife was like him,[3] whereby we jointly rented a large house and shared the expense. One half of it was for them, the other for me. In my part I set up quite a large and well-equipped chapel.

Here I lodged whenever I was in London, and I sent my friends here too, giving them a little money for their board. This new arrangement cost me scarcely half as much as the old one, which had involved my maintaining a staff whether the house was used or not, though, in point of fact, it was seldom empty.

I made this change just in time to save myself and my friends. Had I stayed on in the old house, I should almost certainly have been recaptured. This is what happened.

The priest who had me removed from the Clink to the Tower (I told you the story) now began pestering me with letters. He wanted me to give him an interview, but I put him off at first; and later, when he persisted, I did not even answer his letters. I made the excuse that I had far too much to do. This went on for six months. And then he sent me a very pressing request and moaned that I had no time for

---

[3] Mr. and Mrs. Heywood.†

him. I did not reply. Instead, I bided my time. I knew where he lived, and I sent a friend to tell him that if he wanted to see me, he must come along at once with the messenger. I warned the messenger to see that he did not hang about in the streets, or write any note, or talk to anyone on the way; and I arranged for the messenger to bring him, not to a house, but to a field near one of the Inns of Court.[4] It was a popular place for walks, and he could stroll up and down with the man until I arrived.

It was night and there was a bright moon. I took two friends with me in case an attempt was made on me. As I wanted him to believe that I lived in a different part of London, I walked round the outside of the field, so as not to enter from the direction in which my house lay. By chance, however, I passed by the house of a Catholic adjoining the field, and the good man caught sight of me entering the field near there and possibly thought that I had just come out of the house—for the Archpriest[5] was living in it at the time. Anyhow, I found him walking up and down waiting for me. I listened patiently to all he had to say; there was nothing new: he had said everything before in his letters, and he had had my answers. This increased my suspicion, and with reason too.

Within a few days both that corner house near which he saw me enter the field and my old house which I had just left (though he did not know it) were both surrounded and thoroughly searched, the same night and at the same time. The Archpriest was almost caught. He just had time to escape into a hiding-place.† The other house, which the priest knew I had once occupied, was searched for two whole

---

[4] Lincoln's Inn Fields.†
[5] George Blackwell.†

days. The Lieutenant of the Tower and Knight Marshal[6] took charge of the search in person—a thing they do only when one of their own prisoners has escaped. This made it quite clear that they were after me and that the priest had given them information about the house. Incidentally, there was a priest living in the house at the time with a Catholic to whom I had let it. However, they did not find him.

When they failed to find me they posted pursuivants the next day to my host's house, for he had by then gone back to live in the country. But, thank God, I wasn't there that day.

As you can see, it was a good thing that I had been cautious with this priest and had given up my old house in time.

I was convinced now that I would also have to leave his house in the country and go elsewhere. It seemed that I would always be causing those good and dear friends of mine[7] some sort of trouble; but when I put the suggestion to them, they would not hear of it, though in all other matters they were always ready to listen to me. Yet, as there was no other way of giving them peace and quiet, I brushed aside their pious wishes and put my proposal to the Superior who agreed to it. Then I asked Father Garnet to give them another Jesuit, a Father Banks, who is now a professed Father, a good and devout man who was then working with the blessed Father Oldcorne. Father Garnet consented, and I introduced this Father to the family, and we were there for a short time together. Meanwhile, I was out and about much more than usual.†

[6] The Knight Marshal was J. G.'s cousin Sir Thomas Gerard, the son of Sir Gilbert Gerard of Brandon, who had been Coke's predecessor as Attorney-General.

[7] The Wiseman family.

And so I happened, by God's good providence, to visit a noble household. I had often been invited there before and had been expected for a long time, but other business had always kept me elsewhere.

The lady of the house was a widow, a devout and pious soul.[8] But when I came to the house[9] I found her completely overwrought by her husband's untimely death. So much had it affected her that she hardly moved out of her room for a whole year; and for three years after that (when I was visiting her) she had been unable to bring herself to enter the wing of the house in which her husband had died. Besides this grief, she was worried by anxiety for the future of her son, who was still under his mother's care.[10] He was one of the first barons of the realm, but his parents had suffered very heavily for their faith. Much of their property and income had gone in fines exacted by a heretical Government, and, to meet their heavy debts, their estate had been heavily mortgaged and it was difficult to find enough for current expenses. But a wise woman builds up her house and proves herself in it.

I found one of our Fathers living with the family. He was a learned man and a good preacher, and had been with them a year now.[11] Some of the household, however, were prejudiced against him, though the mistress always showed him great respect and went to the sacraments frequently. When I arrived, all this good lady's wishes appeared fulfilled.

[8] Elizabeth Vaux.†

[9] Irthlingborough, a manor of the Vaux family, two miles north-west of Higham Ferrers, Northants.

[10] Edward Lord Vaux, born on September 13, 1588. His father, George Vaux, had died on August 20, 1595, leaving three sons and three daughters to the care of J. G.'s new hostess.

[11] Father Richard Collins, a Yorkshireman and first cousin of Guy Fawkes. He came to England in April 1596. *Troubles*, 3rd series, 288.

She welcomed me with great kindness, and her grief seemed to change to joy. Some of the household came and assured me that if I could come often, or better still, if I could live with them, the lady would put aside her long mourning—she would be a different person and all would be well with her. I think the lady herself must have told them this. For later, when she got the opportunity, she sang the praises of my hosts—she had heard so much about them, about their chapel and vestments, their patience and goodness proved in the fire of persecution. She said it was no matter of surprise that they were so remarkable, seeing the director they had. If only she had the same advantage, she would be like them and, so she hoped, all would go well with her.

Seeing what a false idea she had formed about me—how she was led to believe that I was a much better person than I really was—I told her the truth: that she had much greater helps than they. But she answered: her director was a good and pious man and she reverenced and liked him very much. Yet he had never mixed with men; he had always been absorbed in his studies, so that whenever any business or practical matter was under discussion he could give no helpful advice. This was why some of the people in the house did not like him. I objected:

"What's wrong with them", I said, "is that they are ungracious and they don't know how to submit to authority; they would treat me in exactly the same way if I lived with them."

"If they did," she said, "they wouldn't stay long in the house, even if they were much more indispensable than they are." They had, in fact, charge of the whole household under her.

So she begged me to put her to the test and see for myself whether she really meant to be amenable in carrying out any changes which, before God, I judged necessary. An offer like this from a person of her standing seemed difficult to reject, coming as it did at a time when I had to find a new residence. It seemed clearer than daylight to me that God's hand was here. From the moment I first set foot in England right up to the present time, His providence had shifted me from one house to another; and each house in turn was better placed for extending the range of my acquaintances, and particularly among persons of quality, and for comforting and guiding them in His service. I told her, therefore, that I was deeply grateful and would bring her offer to the notice of the Superior. I added that one thing particularly made it attractive to me—that here I would be living with another Jesuit, a man whom I liked very much; elsewhere I had always been with secular priests.

On my return to London I put the proposal to Father Garnet. He was very glad of the offer, for he realized that in time the place could be developed into a splendid center. The offer, he said, was most timely. He was being constantly petitioned by a family in a county farther north, where there were many Catholics and no priest of the Society, to let them have the very Father who was stationed here, and they would be delighted if he could come to them. But I objected that there was work for two priests and more in the house and that I was very anxious to have a Jesuit companion. Father Garnet, however, had already made up his mind. Because of the opposition this priest had roused he was replacing him here by another Father, and could not let me have him. So I begged him, instead, to give me Father John Percy.† I had never met him personally, but I had gotten to know him through a frequent correspondence I had with him in prison. He had been captured in Flanders and taken off to Holland, where he had been recognized and tortured and later thrown into that terrible Bridewell prison. But after some time he managed to escape with another priest by lowering himself by a rope from a window. Mistress Line had welcomed him in my house, but he had moved off after a short time into Yorkshire. He was living there with a pious Catholic, and had endeared himself so much to the people that, even with Father Garnet's consent, it took me a full year to get him away.

Now that the gentle widow wanted it and Father Garnet approved, I settled everything and left my old hosts as safe and well-provided as they had ever been. In fact, they were much better off now, for I left Father Banks with them, and he was a finer man than me in every way. At first my old friends seemed not to think so highly of him, but when they came to know him better they found everything I had said about him was true. Soon they came to regard him as their father. Afterward I frequently visited that house where I had found such true devotion and fine loyalty.

I settled, then, in my new residence. By degrees I healed my hostess' excessive sorrow. I told her our grief for the dead should be tempered; we were not to mourn like men who had no hope. Her husband, I pointed out, had become a Catholic before he died, and a single prayer would do him more good than many tears. Tears should be reserved for our own and others' sins. Indeed our souls needed a tide of tears, and all our thoughts and strivings should be turned to the well-being of our souls. Then I taught her how to meditate, for she was capable of it—in fact she had intelligence and talents of a high order. So I gradually brought her round to turn her old sorrow into a sorrow of another and nobler kind, and then to set cares of the next world before those of this—to reflect that though her life hitherto

had been a good and holy life, it could be made holier still
by following as closely as possible the pattern of Our Lord's
life and of His saints.

First of all, then, she decided to stay a widow. As she
could not give God her virginity, she would offer Him a
chaste life. She would practise poverty, in the sense that she
would put all she possessed or came to possess at the service of God and His servants; and she herself would be a
kind of handmaid to them to wait on their wants. Lastly
and before all else, she would be obedient. She would carry
out what she was told to do as perfectly as if she had made
a vow—in fact, she complained that our priests were forbidden to receive such vows. Briefly, she decided, and I
could see she was resolved, to fulfill as nearly as she could
the role of Martha, and of other holy women who followed Christ and ministered to Him and His Apostles. She
was ready to set up house wherever and in whatever way I
judged best for our needs—whether, she protested time and
again, it was in London or in the remotest part of England.

A house in or near London, of course, had the great
advantage that it would be much better placed for apostolic
work, but, on the other hand, London was too dangerous
for me at the moment. In any case, she would have no
privacy there, and it would be unsafe for her. She was a
marked Catholic, and the Lords of the Council wanted to
keep in touch with her son, the baron, and watch where
and how he was being brought up. Besides this, she had
the management of the estates during her son's minority
and her officials and bailiffs would be constantly coming to
see her; and this alone made it impossible for her to live
near London under an assumed name, as she would have to
do, if she was going to continue her good work for any
length of time. The two ladies who looked after Father

Garnet followed this practice. They were sisters-in-law of this widow, the daughters of the same baron. One was unmarried and the other a widow.[12]

Therefore I could not see how she could do better than live where she was among her own people. She was connected by ties of blood or friendship with all the leading families of the country.

The only question to be decided was the exact place. The house she was living in at present was old and tumble-down. Her father-in-law had moved there, and his wife was a much better hand at spending money than saving it. The house had by now become unsuitable to a family of their standing; but about three miles off they had another larger mansion, which had been the ancient and principal family seat.[13] But this too had been neglected, and in many parts it was quite dilapidated, almost in fact a ruin. Certainly it was no place where she could give hospitality, as she intended, to all the Catholic gentlemen who would come to see me for their spiritual comfort and consolation, for these were the only guests she wanted. Moreover, it was ill-suited for defense against the sudden incursions and raids of the pursuivants, and, consequently, she would never be as free as she wished to be. What she desired, in fact, was a house where life could go on in as nearly the same way as in our colleges, and this she achieved in the end.

We searched everywhere for the perfect house, looking over many in this county, but they all had some feature that made them not quite suitable for our purpose. Eventually, however, we found a princely mansion built by the

---

[12] Anne Vaux and her sister, Eleanor, widow of Edward Brooksby. See above, p. 50, note 4.

[13] Great Harrowden, two miles north of Wellingborough, Northants.

Chancellor of England who had recently died childless. Now it was to let for a term of years.[14]

It was large and well-built, and stood remote from other dwellings, surrounded by fine orchards and gardens—people could come and go without anyone noticing them. She took the lease for fifteen thousand florins, and started getting it ready for us, since she was anxious to have all the alterations finished before we moved in; but man proposes and God disposes—always, it is true, for the best interests of His children.

[14] This was Kirby Hall, the great mansion built by John Thorpe between 1570 and 1575, about twenty miles to the north. To-day it is a ruin in a very secluded part of the Northamptonshire countryside. Some improvements had been made by the Chancellor, Sir Christopher Hatton, who died childless on November 21, 1591, and J. G. was under the impression that he had built the place. There are two leases of Kirby Hall dated March 24 and April 1, 1599.†

19. JOHN THE PRIEST

July 1599

This lady had many servants in her house when I came to live with her. A number were non-Catholics; others were Catholics of a sort, but all enjoyed too much liberty. Gradually I got rid of the abuses. By talking privately with them and by my sermons in public I brought them slowly, with the help of God's grace, to better ways. Some I instructed and received into the Church, but there were a few I had to get dismissed, since there seemed no hope of their reform. Among them was the man who had formed the center of opposition to the previous chaplain, but there was another also who responded very slowly to correction.

This man happened to be up in London with us. It may have been only thoughtlessness or careless talk—possibly it was just impatience at the stricter discipline that now ruled— anyhow, he informed a treacherous friend of his that I had recently come to live at his lady's house and had made a number of changes there; and he added that I was now in London, and mentioned the house where I was staying. (This was the half-house I had rented.) He said that he had gone there with his lady, and that, while I had been in town with her on business connected with her son, the master and mistress of my house had frequently been round to visit her.

My hostess had left London taking this servant with her. But he had done the damage. The Council got to hear that

I was residing at this lady's mansion, and that I was now in town in such and such a house. Straightway they instructed two Justices of the Peace to search the place.

I had no inkling of any danger, and had stayed in London on business, and was giving a retreat in the house to three gentlemen. One was Mr. Roger Lee, who is now bursar at the English school at Saint Omers. He was a gentleman of good family and a very fine character, and his charming manners made him a favorite with everyone, particularly with the gentry. He was always with them, hunting, hawking, and the rest. Everything he did, he did well, and he was a Catholic too; in fact he was such a good man that he was thinking of withdrawing from the world to follow Christ more closely. When I was in the Clink, he came to visit me frequently, and it was easy to see that he was called to higher things than catching birds—that he was called in fact to be a catcher of men, not beasts. I had, therefore, fixed a date to give this good friend of mine a retreat, for I wanted him to discover by means of the Exercises the straight road that leads to life, with Him for guide who is Himself the Way and the Life.

After finishing my business in town, I had given out that I had returned to the country. Actually I had taken the chance of this seclusion to begin my own retreat. Mr. Lee and some others I was instructing were meditating privately in their own rooms. Then without warning the storm burst. It was the fourth or fifth day of my retreat about three o'clock in the afternoon. Suddenly John Lillie rushed up the stairs and burst into my room without knocking. He held a drawn sword in his hand.

I was a little taken aback by this sudden intrusion and asked him what was happening.

"They're making a search", he said.

"Where?" I asked.

"Here! This house! They're here already!"

They had been very clever and knocked gently as though they were friends, and the servant had opened to them at once. He suspected nothing—then he saw them rush past and scatter through the house.

While John was telling me what had happened the Justices came upstairs with the mistress of the house. They came to the room where we were. But straight opposite was the chapel, with a door facing the door of my room on the other side of the passage. The magistrates saw the chapel door open, went in, and discovered a beautifully furnished altar with Mass vestments laid out beside it. Even these heretics were amazed at them. Meanwhile, in the room opposite, I was completely at my wits' end what to do. There was no hiding-place in the room, and the only way I could get out was along the passage where the searchers were. However, I took off the soutane I was wearing, but I could see no place where I could hide my books and pile of manuscript meditations.

We stood listening with our ears to the door. I heard one of them say, "Good God, what have we got here? And to think that we almost didn't raid the house to-day." This made me think it must have been a chance search, that probably they had no warrant for it and came with only a few men; and we began to wonder whether it would not be worth trying to rush down with drawn swords and force our way out, snatching the keys from the search party as we passed. Mr. Lee would help us, and the master of the house and two or three manservants. On the other hand, we knew that if we were taken in the struggle, the law would fall much harder on the master of the house for contempt and resistance to search.

While we were discussing what was best to do, the searchers came to my room and knocked. We made no answer,
and as there was no bolt or lock on the door, we pressed
down the latch with our fingers. Then they knocked again,
and we heard the mistress saying: "Perhaps the servant who
sleeps here has taken the key away with him. I'll go and
look for him."

"In that case, we're coming with you", they said, "You
may be hiding something away."

Without staying to see whether there was a lock on the
door they went off with the lady, for God "blinded the
eyes of the Assyrians that they should not find the place
and injure His servants, and He led them off they knew
not whither."

They went downstairs. With great presence of mind, the
mistress took them into a room where two ladies were
sitting—the sister of my hostess[1] and Mistress Line. The
moment the magistrates started questioning them, she rushed
upstairs to us.

"Quick", she said. "Quick, get into the hiding-place."
She just had time to say this and run down again when the
magistrates made for the staircase. But she stood on the
bottom step. Immediately the searchers' suspicions were
aroused and they wanted to push past, but they could not
do this without laying violent hands on the lady and, being
gentlemen, they held back.

One of the searchers, however, stuck his head past her
while she stood there occupying the whole width of the
staircase. Peering upstairs to see what was going on, he only
just missed seeing me scramble into my hiding-hole—for
immediately I got the lady's warning I opened the door of

[1] Mary Lady Lovel, sister of Mrs. Vaux. See above, p. 30, note 1.

the room and as quietly as I could took a stool and climbed up into the hiding-place which was built in a secret gable of the roof. When I was up I beckoned John Lillie to follow. But he was more concerned about my safety than his own. He refused.

"Father," he whispered, "I can't come. There's no one to own the books and papers in the room, for they're after you. If there's no owner, they won't stop till they've found you. Just say a prayer for me."

Here was a truly "faithful and prudent servant", a man full of charity, ready to lay down his life for a friend.

Reluctantly I agreed and closed down the little door through which I had got in. But I could not open the door of the proper hiding-place inside, and I would certainly have been found if they had not taken John and, presuming he was a priest, given up the search. For this was what God was pleased to arrange, thanks to John's wise and intrepid action.

He had just time to take away the stool, get back into my room, and shut the door, when the two leading searchers came up the stairs and knocked violently. It was clear that they intended to break down the door if they could not find the key; so this gallant soldier of Christ opened and stood fearlessly facing them.

"And who are you?" they asked.

"A man. Can't you see?"

"Say who you are. Are you a priest?"

"I won't tell you whether I am a priest", he answered. "It's for you to prove it. But I am a Catholic."

On the table they saw all my meditation notes, my breviary, and several Catholic books, and, what I valued most, my manuscript sermons and notes for sermons which I had collected together over the last ten years. I treasured them more than anything—more than all the precious things these men perhaps had hidden away in chests.

"Whose are these?" they asked when they saw them all.

"Mine", answered John.

"Then you must be a priest. And whose is this soutane?"

"It's just a dressing-gown anyone might use."

They were convinced now that they had found a priest.

All the papers and books in the room they carefully packed away in a case and carried off. Then they locked the chapel and put their seal on the door. Taking John by the arm they led him downstairs and handed him over to their men.

As he entered the room where the ladies were, this good man who never forgot his place and always stood in ladies' company with his head uncovered greeted them both, then took off his hat and sat down. With an air of authority he turned to the two chief searchers.

"These are gentlewomen," he said, "and you must take care to treat them well. I don't know them myself, but it is obvious they are persons deserving your respect."

When the ladies knew that I was safe and that the other priest had got away—Father Pollen was with me, an old man who had entered the Society late in life at Rome: he had slipped into a hiding-place—and when they saw, too, the grave airs John was assuming, they could hardly hide their satisfaction. Whatever they were fined or had to suffer on suspicion of harboring a priest seemed nothing at all to them now. They were amazed and delighted and almost laughed at John playing the priest, and doing it so well that he completely tricked those tricksters, who called off their search for priests.[2]

[2] John Lillie was captured in July 1599.†

The magistrates who had conducted the search now took John "the priest" off with them, also the master of the house—they hoped they would be able to confiscate all his property—and the two manservants. The ladies' story was simply that they had called in after dinner to see the mistress of the house and knew nothing about any priest. They were left undisturbed, but had to give bail to appear when summoned. Mr. Roger Lee got off in the same way, though he had greater difficulty in persuading the magistrates he was only a visitor.

In the end they went off satisfied. Their prisoner was locked up for the night. The next day he was to be examined.

The moment they left, the mistress of the house rushed upstairs with the other ladies to tell me the news. We all thanked God for saving us from almost certain capture, and under God we blessed the prudent action of our faithful servant. That same night Father Pollen and I moved to another house—we were afraid the searchers might discover that John was no priest and return.

The following day I hurried off to my friends in the country. It was a long journey. When I told them what had happened, I could see fear cloud their faces, then great relief. All of us from our hearts commended John to God in our prayers.

And it was well that we did. The following day the magistrates realized they had been tricked. They discovered that John had been an apothecary in London some seven years, that for eight or nine more he had been imprisoned in the Clink, that he was the go-between used by my warder when I was in the Tower (they had captured the warder's wife after her husband's flight and she had confessed everything she knew). So they realized that he was no priest at all, but a priest's servant, and mine at that. They knew now—when it was too late—that I had been hiding in the same house. They had my notes as proof of it, for there was no doubt they were mine. Again they went to search the house, but this time they found the nest deserted. The birds had flown.

John was taken to the Tower of London and put in chains. Then they questioned him about my escape and all the places he had visited with me since then. John knew now that the secret of his dealings with the warder was out, and as he had always desired, if it were given him, to lay down his life for Christ he admitted frankly that he had planned my escape. He added that he did not in the least regret having done it, and, in fact, would do it again, if occasion arose. But he exculpated the warder, protesting that he was not privy to the escape. On being questioned about the places he had visited with me, he answered as he had so often been taught to answer, that he would bring no one into trouble, for to name any house or family would be a sin against justice and charity. As it was clear that he would give nothing away, they did not press him. They said they would take action and that they had means of making him reveal all they wanted to know.

"Never", answered John. "Never, with God's help, will I do such a thing. True, I am in your power, but you can do with me only what God permits."

They took him to the torture chamber. There they hung him up in the way I have described already. For three hours on end they tortured him cruelly. But they could not wring from him a word of information against me or against anybody else. After that they gave up hope of getting him to implicate anyone either by threats or force; and, instead of torturing him, they tried to break his will into compliance by holding him for three or four months a solitary prisoner. Again they failed. But now they admitted their failure and sent him to another prison—the place where they usually held prisoners awaiting execution.[3] No doubt they intended to get rid of him that way, but God arranged differently. He was indeed a long time there, but he was given more liberty and he was allowed to mix with other Catholic prisoners. Then one day a priest approached him and asked his help to escape. John set to work on a plan, and found a way by which both he and the priest escaped.

As it is the kind of incident in which the providence of God stands out clearly, I must mention it now. It happened while John was in the Tower. Wade, the chief priest-hunter, was examining him about me and other Jesuits. Did he know Garnet? "No", was John's answer.

"No?" said Wade, with a cynical smile. "And you don't know the house he has in a place called Spital?"

"Now that we've got you safe here," he went on, "I don't mind telling you. We are quite sure that in a few days' time we will have this man Garnet here to keep you company. He is coming to London. He will stay in that house, and we will catch him there."

John knew quite well that Father Garnet used to stay in the house, and was very alarmed that the place had been betrayed. But within a few days he managed somehow or other to send through a parcel to a friend of his in London. It was wrapped in white paper and was received safely. All his friends knew that if John was given a chance, he would send a letter that way. They read his message, then, saying that Father Garnet's house had been betrayed and warning them to let him know at once. This they did. Father Garnet was saved, for sure enough, as Wade declared, he would have been at home within a few days. However, he kept

---

[3] Newgate prison.

well out of the way, and was able to have all his possessions removed from the place so that when the house was searched, nothing was found. You can imagine the haul they would have made—Father Garnet himself and all his books, his vestments, everything he had for the altar, and heaven knows what else. Under Providence this escape was John's good work. He saved Garnet, as before he had saved me.†

When John was free again, he came to see me. I would have liked very much to have kept him, but I did not dare to. He was too well known now and would have been a constant source of danger to my friends as well as to me. For whenever I visited the houses of the gentry, Catholic or Protestant, I went openly, and John might easily have run into men who recognized him, and, through my association with him, might have identified me. Only a few spies knew what I looked like,[4] for I had always been in close custody, and only a chosen handful of proved Catholics had spoken with me in prison. True, I had been examined several times in public, but then my examiners seldom went down into the country. Had they done so, I would have gotten word and taken care to keep out of their way.

For a time, therefore, I placed John with Father Garnet, where he could live a quiet life in hiding. Later, when I got the chance, I sent him over to Father Persons in order that he might do what he had so long wanted to do—namely, join the Society. He was admitted at Rome, and he lived there as a Brother for six or seven years. Everyone held him in high esteem. Now I, too, for the glory of God, can bear my own personal testimony to his character, and I can do it safely for I believe he has recently died in England—he went back there suffering from consumption.† What I want

---

[4] There are three descriptions of J. G. as a wanted man. See Appendix J.

to say is this: that during those five or six years he was with me in England, and engaged in every kind of business on my behalf in places far and near, with people in every walk of life—for often when I was upstairs with the master of the house and his friends, he was below with the servants, often gamblers and the like—all that time he guarded his heart and soul with the utmost care. Never was he near danger of mortal sin. Time and again in his confession he had to make mention of some venial sin he had committed long ago in order that I might have matter for absolution.[5] He was an innocent soul, if ever there was one. And he was so wise and prudent too.

Now I have finished the story of John Lillie, and I must get back to my own.

Barely had I escaped from this danger when I almost fell into another and much worse one, and I would certainly have done so, had not God intervened.

I have told you the story of how one of my hostess' servants gave us away, letting it out to a friend of his that I lived with his lady and was in London at that time in such and such a house, how the house was searched and my companion and all my notes carried off; finally, I explained how I escaped.

Now that the Council knew my country home they commissioned the Justices of the Peace in the county to search the lady's house for me. Already there was talk in the whole county that she had taken this splendid mansion because it was a remote place where she could entertain priests freely and in large numbers. The gossip had some foundation.

---

[5] At this time the discipline of the seal of confession was in certain details less strict than it has since become. It was then considered lawful for a confessor to bear witness in general terms to the exceptional virtue of a penitent.

It was at this time that we drove over to the new house. We were going to make the final arrangements for moving in; and as I wanted especially to decide at the same time where to locate the hiding-holes, we took with us "Little John" (Father Garnet had lent him to us for the occasion). We made all the arrangements, and left "Little John" behind with Hugh Sheldon, who has since taken Lillie's place in Rome as Father Persons' assistant.

These two men were to build the hiding-places. They had been proved trustworthy time and again; in fact they were to be the only two persons, apart from ourselves, to know where our hiding-places were. The rest of us returned the same day to the old house. God's providence was watching over us. One of the servants advised us to try a different road back; he said it was easier for the lady's carriage; and it was a happy chance that we did as he suggested. Had we not done so, the searchers would have been at the house early next morning, and almost certainly they would have come on us unprepared and found their quarry. The ordinary route home, which we did not take, passed through a town,[6] where the searchers were lying in wait, and almost certainly would have identified me. But as they did not see us return, they concluded we were spending the night at the new house. The first thing in the morning they were there to search it.

The house was so large that they could not surround it completely, and though they brought a large body of men with them, they could not even keep a watch on all the exits. "Little John" slipped away safely. But they caught Hugh Sheldon. They could get nothing out of him, and so they

---

[6] This was doubtless Kettering, which lies about halfway on the direct route from Kirby Hall to Irthlingborough.

put him in prison and later transferred him to Wisbeach. From there he was sent to some other prison with a large party of priests. He was eventually exiled with them all.

The Justices realized that they had been deceived and that the lady must have returned the previous day. Immediately they rode back their horses full out, and burst in on us at the dinner-hour.[7] A careless porter let them in, and they were up in the dining-hall before we knew they had arrived. Happily the lady of the house was indisposed that morning and we were about to start dinner in my room. (Mr. Roger Lee was with us; he had come from London to finish the Exercises we had interrupted there. Little did he suspect that God had arranged other "exercises" for him.)

I heard that men had come and that they were in the great hall and had pressed their way into the baron's room where he was dining privately.[8] (The boy, too, was sick that day.) Then I realized what the visit was about. Hastily I snatched up everything I wanted to conceal, and made a dash for the hiding-place with Father Percy and Master Roger Lee; if Roger was found, they would suspect my presence at once, for he had been with me in my London house and caught there.

Our only way to the hiding-place passed the door of the room where all the searchers were gathered. I heard them shouting out that they wanted to get on with their search without delay. One pursuivant actually pushed his head round the door to see who was passing, and some of the Catholics in the room told me afterward that he must have seen me as I went past. But God intervened, for how else can

---

[7] The party probably rode back across country via Grafton Underwood and Burton Latimer.

[8] He was aged ten at the time.

you explain it? There they were, straining and shouting to get through and search the house, yet they halted behind in an unlocked room just long enough to allow us time to reach the hiding-place and shut ourselves safely in. Then they broke out as though they had been let loose. They burst into the lady's apartment while others raged round the remaining rooms. Undoubtedly it was the finger of God, who did not want to cut at the roots of the lady's good works. Rather, by this manifestation of His providence He wished to confirm her in her resolve and keep her for a future full of service and fine achievement.

They searched the whole day and found nothing; then they left with their hopes frustrated and sent in a report to the Council. Meanwhile we traced the man who was responsible for it all and dismissed him in a kindly way. I gave it out that I was going to quit the house altogether, and for a time we took very special precautions.

Any move to the new mansion was out of the question now. The Justices of the Peace in the county—they were fierce heretics—and others who were Puritans declared they would never leave the lady quiet in that house.† They knew she was moving there in order to have a place where she could put up priests. Though they frustrated the move, she did not give up her purpose, and started at once to adapt her present house.[9] She built us separate quarters close to the old chapel where the former barons used to hear Mass when the weather was too wet for them to go to the village church. Here she erected a three-storied building for Father Percy and me. It was most conveniently designed and secluded. From our quarters we could pass out unnoticed into the private garden and through the broad walks

[9] Great Harrowden.

into the fields, and there mount our horses to go wherever we wanted.[10]

Now that our life was safe and undisturbed, I used frequently to leave Father Percy at home and make journeys abroad in the hope of establishing similar centers with other families. Father Roger Lee, as he is now, was a great help to me in this work, before he left England. First of all, he took me to see one of his relatives whose father was a member of the Council.[11] This gentleman lived in a princely mansion. He was a schismatic (that is, a Catholic by conviction), but there was no hope of converting him. He was content with wanting to be a Catholic, and refused to go beyond that for fear of offending his father.

The lady of the house was a Protestant, but she was already interested in the Catholic faith and there was a chance she might come over in time.[12] The house was full of Protestant servants, and every day Protestant noblemen came there either on business or to see the gentleman and his wife. As I had to go there publicly, it was essential that I should conceal the reason for my coming.

On our arrival we were received with kindness, and they welcomed me for the sake of their dear cousin. On the first day I had no opportunity of talking to the lady alone. There was always somebody with her and we were obliged to play cards—just passing the time like people who don't know or care about the value of time.

[10] A building, which is probably the wing referred to by J. G., is the only part of the old mansion still standing.

[11] Sir Francis, son of Sir John, Fortescue of Salden, Bucks., who was Master of the Great Wardrobe to Queen Elizabeth and from 1589 Chancellor of the Exchequer.†

[12] Sir Francis Fortescue's wife was Grace, daughter of Sir John Manners, second son of Thomas, first Earl of Rutland.

But the next day when the lady, suspecting nothing, went aside to the window of the dining-room to set her small clock, I joined her there. First I talked to her for a short time about her clock and then brought the subject round to the state of her soul, trying to convince her that she should give more attention to that than to anything else. She looked at me in astonishment—I was the last person in the world she expected to speak in this fashion. As I did not know when I would get another opportunity, I abandoned my guise. I told her she was the whole reason of my visit, and that I was ready to settle on the spot any doubts she might have about the faith, and then instruct her. Later I would set her in the way of virtue, and show her how she could make continuous progress toward perfection—a thing she would never discover in a false religion where no account was taken of perfection. She was impressed and promised to find a suitable time for further discussion. As she was a remarkably modest woman and had many moral virtues I thought it well to set a high ideal before her.

A time was arranged and she was satisfied on all points of faith and became a Catholic. After she had been received I converted other people in the house and recommended to her a Catholic maid-in-waiting, and, finally, suggested she should have a priest permanently in her house, for it would be easy to arrange it. There was no need to make his presence generally known, as mine was in the house in which I was staying, where all were Catholics. Here a priest could live comfortably at the top of the house, and, as she now had some Catholic servants, Protestants could be kept away from him. Actually I had never come across a house in the whole of England where a priest could live so conveniently in secret. There was a fine room for him opening on to a spacious corridor about eighty feet long, which looked out on to a garden laid out, as I heard, at a cost of ten thousand florins. In the same corridor was another big room which might serve as a chapel, and a third which the priest could use as his dining-room. It was the right size and had a fireplace and everything he might want.

It would be a great pity, I pointed out, if there were no priest in a house like this, where the lady was a devout Catholic and the master so friendly that he was glad to have priests. Sometimes he came to my sermons, and, later on, even prepared the altar for Mass and said the breviary every day. Still, he stayed outside the Ark, and had he fallen suddenly into the waters he would have been swept away by the deluge. In his presumption he thought he was certain to have time to repent before his death.

The lady fell in completely with my proposal to place a priest there. So I introduced Father Anthony Hoskins, a very able man who had recently arrived in England from Spain, where with remarkable results he had spent ten years studying as a Jesuit. While he was stationed here he did much good and in many directions. He remained with the family until recently when he was called away to a more important post. But he was far from passing all his time in the house, for he was the sort of person whom people would want to see and consult once they had met him.† Now they have another Jesuit in his place, a very devout man, but Father Percy is still the lady's director, and it was only this week that he wrote to me saying:

"So-and-so [meaning this lady] is making great progress. She has dedicated her household and herself to the Blessed Virgin of Loreto, to be her handmaid and the handmaid of her Son, offering herself and all she has, for ever. And as a symbol of this offering she has had a heart of gold made, very finely wrought, and is anxious to send it to Loreto as soon as she can. I should be grateful if you could tell me the best and safest way she can send her offering."

So he wrote about this lady, and in this way, by God's grace, was this house, with its private church, founded and developed.

20. WITH SIR EVERARD AT CARDS

Master Roger Lee introduced me also to several neighbors, including a knight of the Queen's court.[1] This man had inherited a large estate and had married a lady who was heiress to all her father's property.[2] There was no Catholic or person inclined to Catholicism in the whole family. In fact, the lady's father who was master of the house at the time was a convinced Protestant, and his only interest was to amass money and estates for his daughter. His son-in-law devoted all his time to youthful sports. Whenever he was in London he attended court and was one of the Queen's Gentlemen Pensioners;† and at home he had no interest apart from his hounds and hawks.

Now Master Roger Lee was his neighbor[3] and a keen sportsman himself; he often joined him in the hunt or brought his falcons to hawk in company. So we took advantage of this, and I was introduced to the gentleman's house as Master Roger's close friend. We went frequently, and I took every opportunity that offered to introduce the subject of Catholic doctrine and practice. But, to avoid suspicion, I saw that Master Lee did most of the talking and let him show more enthusiasm than me. This he did so well that the gentleman, far from guessing who I was, actually

[1] Sir Everard Digby.†
[2] Mary Mulshaw of Gayhurst, North Bucks.
[3] At Pitstone, seven miles east of Aylesbury, Bucks.

asked Master Lee's opinion as to whether I would make a good match for his sister.† He wanted to see her married to a Catholic because, as he said, they were good and honorable people.

We fell into frequent conversations on the subject of salvation. First we made an impression on his wife when she was alone at home during one of her husband's absences in London. Now that her parents were dead and she was mistress of the house, we could talk to her more freely. Eventually one day she expressed her wish to become a Catholic, and told me she was anxious to talk to a priest just once. I smiled to myself and said it could be arranged and promised to discuss the matter with Master Roger Lee. Meanwhile, I told her that I would first teach her a method of examining her conscience, which I had been taught myself by experienced priests.

So I told Master Roger Lee that the lady had now made up her mind and was ready to become a Catholic and that all she was waiting for was to see a priest. I asked him therefore to break the news that I was one.

This he did but the lady would not believe it. She was amazed. "How can he possibly be a priest?" she protested. "Why, the man lives like a courtier. Haven't you watched him playing cards with my husband—and the way he plays, he must have been at the game for a long time. And he's been out hunting with my husband, and I've heard him myself talking about hunting and about hawking, and he never trips in his terms. No one could do that without being caught out unless he was thoroughly familiar with the sport."

So she objected. She said other things such as this, to show that I could not possibly be a priest. But Master Lee explained:

"He did indeed talk and behave like this", he said. "That's true. But if he hadn't, how do you imagine he could have entered the house and spoken to you and brought you slowly to the faith? If he had come here dressed like a priest—and I can assure you he would have much preferred to, if it had been possible—do you think you would ever have let him into the house, to say nothing of your father, for he was alive then?"†

All this she was forced to admit, but still she would not believe it.

"Please don't get angry with me", she said, "if I ask you a question. What other Catholic, apart from yourself, knows that he is a priest? Does so-and-so", and she mentioned the name, "does he know it?"

"Yes," he said, "and he has often confessed to him."

Then, after several other names, she mentioned my hostess,[4] who lived about ten miles away in the same district.

"And tell me," she went on, "does she know he's a priest and is she glad to have him about?"

"Of course," said Master Roger Lee, "she knows it and she's handed herself over to his direction with her whole house. She would not wish to have anyone else."

At last she admitted she was satisfied. So Master Lee said: "And you will see he's quite a different person when he drops the part he has been playing."

This she admitted herself the next day when she saw me in clerical dress—she had never before seen me in priest's clothes. She made her confession very carefully, and formed a flattering opinion of me that I did not deserve, and wholly

---

[4] Probably Roger Lee's mother at Pitstone. Harrowden, Mrs. Vaux's house, was rather more than ten miles from Gayhurst.

accepted my guidance and planned great things. Indeed she achieved them and still does to this day.†

This done, all three of us got together and discussed the best way of catching her husband in Saint Peter's net.

Now it so happened that he had fallen sick in London, and his wife decided to go up and visit him. But we were there before her.

His illness gave me the opening I wanted. From the uncertainty of human life and the certainty (unless we guarded against it) of suffering both in this world and the next I showed how "here we have no abiding city", but must look to a heavenly one. I found him very responsive, for misfortune makes men think seriously, and this gentleman had always been a man of sound sense and good heart and had laid a firm foundation for the faith.

I instructed him, and he prepared himself carefully for confession. Unlike his wife, he was not the least bit astonished to be told that I was a priest. He had met men in my case before. Moreover, he was glad to have a confessor who understood men like him and who could help him when called upon and could appear in company without danger of his priesthood being discovered.[5]

When I had done everything for him he began to be anxious about his wife and wanted us to help him to bring her into the Church. We smiled to ourselves, but said nothing. We would wait till she came and then watch to see how each would try to bring the other over.

They were a happy pair. They both dedicated themselves to the service of God, and the husband later was to sacrifice

---

[5] At this time William Atkinson, foiled in his attempt to catch J. G. in London, was watching his movements in the country and sending reports to Cecil.†

all his property, his freedom, and his life too for God's Church. I shall tell you the story later, for this was Sir Everard Digby. If so much had not been written and published already about him and his companions, I would have had to say much about him at the end of this narrative. However, no account of him so far has done justice to his sincerity of purpose or set forth all the circumstances in a way that gives him his due.†

After this meeting they both visited me in my country place. But while they were there Sir Everard was taken very seriously ill. His life was in danger, and all the Oxford doctors said they could do nothing for him. As it seemed that he only had a short time to live he began to prepare himself earnestly for a good death, and his wife began to dispose herself for leading a more perfect life. She gave several days to learning the way to meditate, seeking out God's will in regard to her future, for she wanted to direct her life entirely to His greater glory. In brief, she had it in mind, in the event of her husband's death, to devote her life to good works, and observe perpetual chastity and exact obedience. Regarding her property—and it was considerable, for she had no children[6]—she would devote it all to good causes under my direction. She was prepared also to go and live wherever and in whatever way I suggested, as God's honor and the good of her own soul required. It was her wish, she said, to go about in poor clothes and observe true poverty, wherever she might be. This she was to do as long as the persecution lasted. Should England become Catholic again she would give her house (it was large and well-built) and all the property her father had left her to the foundation

[6] Her first son, the famous Sir Kenelm Digby, was born after this, on July 11, 1603.

of a college—and it would have been more than sufficient for a splendid foundation.

That was her plan, but for the time being God happily decided otherwise. All the physicians from Oxford, as I said, gave up Digby's case as hopeless, but I, who loved him very much, did not give up hope. Without telling him I sent for a Cambridge doctor, a Catholic and a learned and experienced man who, to my certain knowledge, had cured other cases abandoned by physicians.† On his arrival at the house where this good man and his wife were staying, I told him all I knew about the patient's illness. Then I made sure that he asked Digby himself to tell him all he could about his condition. When he had done this I asked him whether he thought there was any hope.

"Yes," he said, "if Sir Everard is ready to put himself entirely in my hands, we might save him still with God's assistance."

"As your Reverence knows the doctor and has called him, I will put myself under him."

Against everyone's expectations the doctor cured him, and so completely that it was hard to find a more robust or healthy man in a thousand.

To me he was always a most loyal friend, and we might have been brothers in blood. In fact we called each other "brother" when we wrote or spoke to one another.† You can gauge the extent of his attachment to me from this incident.

Once when I had gone to a certain house to help a dying man, he got to hear that I was in danger. Straightway he expressed great concern and told his wife that, if I was taken, he would watch all the roads along which they might carry me a prisoner to London, and would collect a sufficient body of friends and servants and rescue me from my captors by force. If he missed me on the road, he would liberate me somehow or other even if he had to spend his whole fortune in the attempt. That was how he felt toward me, nor did he change to the end. Rather his affection increased, as he showed at his trial when he spoke in my defense before the court.†

However, as I said, he had just now recovered his health, and he and his wife set up a small domestic church like the one in the house where I was staying. They built a chapel and sacristy and provided it with rich and very beautiful vestments. As a chaplain they received a Jesuit priest who stayed with them to the day of Sir Everard's death.[7]

What this family did others did too. Many Catholic gentlemen, when they visited this house and saw the arrangements there, took it as a model. They founded congregations centered round their own homes, furnished their chapels, and designing accommodation suited to a priest's needs, maintained one there with reverence and respect.†

Among others who did this was a lady who lived near Oxford.[8] Her husband was a Catholic but his interests were worldly. Nevertheless, as far as she could do so with such a husband, she gave herself up to my direction. I often called to see them, and both welcomed me warmly. There I sent one of our Fathers to work—Father Edward Walpole, whom I mentioned early in this story, where I told you how during my first year in England, he left a large patrimony in order to follow Christ our Lord.

---

[7] Father Percy; cf. below p. 244. At the time of the Gunpowder Plot Sir Everard's houses were ransacked; at Gothurst was found a pair of wafer irons for making altar breads, and at Stoke Dry his haircloth valued at 6s. 8d. P.R.O. *Exchequer* (*Various*), 178–3574.

[8] Waterperry, seven miles east of Oxford and for some centuries the seat of the Curzon family, was a Jesuit mission station for a long period. Clare, daughter of Sir Francis Curzon of Waterperry, entered the Benedictine convent at Brussels on August 15, 1603. *C.R.S.*, vol. 14, 178.

There was another lady[9] who wanted to do the same thing. She was a relative of my hostess. She, too, lived in Oxfordshire and was married to a knight with a large estate, who hoped one day to become a baron, and is still hoping. When she visited our house, this lady said she wanted to learn how to meditate, so I showed her. Her husband, however, was a Protestant, and though she was very anxious to do it, she could not keep a priest in her house. Instead, she arranged to support a priest who could visit her regularly during her husband's absences. Also, she determined to devote an hour every day to meditation and, when she had no guests, another one or two hours to spiritual reading, and every six months make a general confession—a practice taken up by all the men and women I have just mentioned and by many others as well, more than I can mention individually. Twice a year she came to make her general confession to me, and I found she never omitted her hour's meditation or her daily examination of conscience, except on one occasion when her husband insisted on her staying with the guests. Yet she had a large household to keep her busy, and she was seldom without people staying with her.

Once in this lady's house I was sitting with her in the dining-room after dinner—her maids-in-waiting were there, but the servants had gone downstairs for their own dinner. We were discussing spiritual subjects and sitting at the table. Suddenly some servants came up with a guest who had just arrived. He was a Doctor of Divinity from Oxford and a well-known persecutor of Catholics. His name was Abbot.† Just recently he had published a book against Father Southwell, who had been executed, and Father Gerard, the man

[9] Lady Agnes Wenman of Thame Park, twelve miles east of Oxford.†

who had escaped from the Tower. These two priests had defended the doctrine of equivocation which he set out to refute. After its publication this good man was promoted to the Deanery of Winchester, which carried with it an annual income of eight thousand florins.

The gentleman, as I said, was shown upstairs and walked into the dining-room.[10] After the fashion of these dignitaries, he was wearing a silk soutane that came down to his knees. He found us, or so he thought, playing cards. Actually we had put the cards away to attend to better things as soon as the servants had gone downstairs, and we had resumed our game when this gentleman was announced. So he found us sitting at the card-table piled with money.

I should explain that whenever I was with Catholics and we had to stage a game in circumstances like these, we had an understanding that everybody got his money back at the end and that the loser said an *Ave Maria* for every counter returned. In this way I often played with brother Digby and others, when there was occasion to act a part and make bystanders think that we were playing for money in good earnest.

The good Minister, therefore, did not have a moment's suspicion. After an exchange of courtesies he began talking volubly. It is all these men can do; they have no solid knowledge, but with their persuasive words of human wisdom they lead poor souls astray and "subvert whole households,

---

[10] Had J. G. read Abbot's book, *Sex Quaestiones*, to which he refers, he would have appreciated the irony of this situation. Before beginning his refutation of J. G.'s doctrine of equivocation, Abbot exclaims: "Gerard, as we all believe, is still alive. Only a few months ago he cunningly escaped from captivity. He can answer for himself, if I misrepresent his words even in the slightest measure." *Sex Quaestiones*, 5.

teaching what they ought not". So after a good deal of frivolous talk, this man came out with the latest news from London: the story of a Puritan who had thrown himself from a church tower and had left behind a note in which he claimed that he was certain of his eternal salvation. The doctor did not mention that, but I had heard it from another source.[11]

"Poor fellow", I said. "What could have induced him to destroy his body and soul in one fell act?"

"Sir", answered the doctor, in a learned and magisterial manner. "Sir, it is not for us to pass judgment on any man."

"Quite so", I said. "It is possible, of course, that the man repented of his sin as he was still falling, *inter pontem et fontem*, as they say. But it is very unlikely. The man's last act which we have any means of judging was a mortal sin and merited damnation."

"But," said the doctor, "we don't know whether this was such a sin."

"Pardon me," I said, "it is not a case here of our own judgment. It is a question of God's judgment; He forbids us under pain of hell to kill anyone, and particularly ourselves, for charity begins at home."

The good doctor was caught. He said nothing more on the point, but he turned the subject, saying with a smile:

"Gentlemen should not dispute on theological questions."

"I agree", I said. "We don't, of course, pretend to know theology, but we should at least know the law of God, even if our profession is to play cards."

[11] Dorrington, a rich Puritan, threw himself from the steeple of Saint Sepulchre's on April 11, 1600. A paper was found on his person inscribed: "Lord, save my soul and I will praise Thy name." G. B. Harrison, *Last Elizabethan Journal*, 77, quoting Sidney Papers, 2, 187.

When the lady I was playing with heard this retort she could hardly keep a straight face. What would he have thought if he had known whom he was talking to? But the doctor did not stay much longer. He went away after about an hour. I don't know whether he left sooner than he had intended, but I do know that we much preferred his room to his company.†

21. FRIENDS AT COURT

1599–1605

I must now return to events in London and tell you what happened after they had taken John Lillie and imprisoned the gentleman who rented that house with me for my own and my friends' needs.

As I could not keep it any longer, I looked out for another. And I found one and rented it. But a partnership was out of the question, for I did not want to live in the house of any-one who was known to be a Catholic. So I arranged for this new place to be let to Master Roger Lee's nephew, whom I had received into the Church with his wife.[1] People did not know he was a Catholic, and consequently the house was above suspicion. I used it for three years, and during all that time it was not once searched. Even during the general searches made before the Queen's death, when the prisons were crowded with Catholics, no one came near it.

For housekeeper I employed a schismatic, a good and hon-est man, and while I was in residence, he attended to all my wants, and when I was away I sent him instructions by post.

To all appearances he was the servant of the gentleman who had rented the house, and this is what his neighbors took him to be. As a schismatic he went to their church, so no suspicion was cast either on himself or on the house.

---

[1] Probably Sir Edmund Lenthall of Lachford, Oxon, whose mother was Eleanor Lee.

However, when I came to town, I always entered the house after dark, and in the summer months I hardly ever went out. My friends used to visit me, either singly or in pairs, some one day, some another, for I did not want a throng of visitors to attract attention to the house. No one ever came with a servant, even if they were highly placed persons used to moving about with numerous attendants. It was better both for them and for me that they didn't, for I was able to carry on like this much longer.[2]

It was from this house, not long after I had taken possession, that Master Lee and three others left for the noviceship.† They are all priests now and doing good work in the Society. The only one of them not active at the moment is Father Strange, who is in prison in the Tower, where he had suffered much cruel torture and long solitary confinement. From a natural standpoint he is bound to find this solitude hard and oppressive, but a man is never alone who has God as companion, to console him and abundantly make up for the lack of those comforts we go seeking in created things. When I was imprisoned in the Clink Father Strange used to visit me. He was a Catholic before I met him, but I saw that he was a talented and attractive youth, an only son and the heir of a big property. As he could move at his ease in good company, I got him to come and see me often, and in the end, he made the Spiritual Exercises. In course of them, he saw that it was his duty to follow Christ our Lord and enter the Society. But until he could make all the

---

[2] About this time Cecil received a false report that J. G. had gone to Ireland. "John Gerrard the Jesuit was supposed to direct himself for Ireland by Westchester. He hath been lately in London, and hath disguised himself with an artificial beard and periwig of a brown colour, somewhat dark. His beard is very long cut after the spade fashion and very even and formally. He was met in Clerkenwell after this manner." *Hat. Cal.*, 14:194.

necessary dispositions (he had to sell his property) I arranged for him to live in Father Garnet's house so that he should not lose the ideals he had conceived, but rather strengthen them. He was with Father Garnet for nearly two years, but he succeeded finally in disentangling himself from his worldly commitments. And then, as it were, cutting the last coils that tied his craft to the English shore, he crossed to the Continent a free man.†

Before he left he introduced me to a friend of his, who is now Father Hart.† He, too, was an only son; his father, a wealthy man, is, I think, still alive. Though I did not give him the Exercises, I was able to see him from time to time (it was after my escape), and in place of the Exercises, I taught him the method of daily meditation. I also gave him some devout books to read, including Father Jerome Platus; and this worked in him a desire for religious life and the Society. He is now a useful man on the English mission and is well-fitted to move in good society, to which he was accustomed before he left the world.

The third was the present Father Thomas Smith, who has been at Saint Omers for the last three years. He was a Master of Arts at Oxford, and when I first met him he was acting as tutor to the young baron, my hostess' son;† and I had plenty of opportunity of talking with him. He was, however, a schismatic, and I found I could do nothing with him—not even shake his complacent state of mind. He was the type of person who can say truthfully with the prophet: "My belly cleaveth to the ground", and they are much more difficult people to move than heretics, as we have all experienced. However, he often listened to my conversation and attended my public instructions. But he lay like one asleep in a heavy dream, as if in a lethargy, and you could almost sense the resistance of the strong man armed and set to guard the house in peace. But eventually a stronger than he overcame and despoiled him, and, binding him, made a prize of all his defenses. This stronger one who conquered him was the infant Child who was born and given to us.

On the very night of Christmas,[3] while all of us and almost the whole household were together celebrating the birthday of the Lord, he alone lay in bed. He could not sleep and began to feel a sense of shame stealing over him when he realized that the three boys[4] whom he taught were up and praising the Lord and teaching him, by conduct and not by words, a lesson which he should have been teaching them. Roused from sleep by the Infant's cries, he began to reflect on all the time he had wasted and how children and unlettered folk were pressing before him into the kingdom. A trembling overwhelmed him. He fretted at the delay and got out of bed and came at once to the chapel and knocked. He asked to see me urgently. As I was engaged, I told the messenger that he must let his business wait till the morning, when I would gladly speak to him. But this did not satisfy him. He said he must speak to me now, so I told him to have a little patience; and when I had finished Matins, I came out to him, dressed just as I was in my alb. As soon as he saw me he threw himself down at my feet.

"O Father," he said with tears, "for the love of God I beg you to hear my confession."

Wondering at the change that had come over him, I told him to be of good heart and assured him that I would hear him at a convenient time, but he must first prepare himself well.

---

[3] Christmas 1599. Thomas Smith entered the English College, Rome, on October 24 the following year.†

[4] There seems to have been here the beginnings of a small school such as are found frequently later centered around recusant houses.†

"Father," he answered, "I have put it off much too long already. For the love of God don't ask me to put it off any more."

"You're right", I said. "There is need to act at once. But it is one thing to postpone your confession, another to give a reasonable time to preparation. If you don't prepare and examine your conscience carefully, when there is nothing to prevent you, it would be no good my hearing and absolving you."

"But what if I die before then?" he pressed.

"In that case," I said, "I'll answer for you before God. Now, go and conceive in your heart a true sorrow for having offended so good a God."

He gave in, but he was still in tears when he left me. After a few days spent in a careful examination of conscience, he became a Catholic and joined us in celebrating the last days of the feast, the first of which he had missed.

These three men crossed to Belgium with Master Lee. From there they went on to Rome to do their noviceship at Sant'Andrea, all except Father Hart. He joined later, but some special business brought him back to England before the others. He is there still doing useful work.

During my visits to London, I did not allow everyone I thought it well to meet to come to my house. Sometimes I went to their homes, especially after dusk in winter time.

Once a lady asked me to her house to hear the confession of a nobleman who was attached to the court. He was a close friend of the lady's husband, who was also a Catholic and well known to me; and though he was quite a young man, he was one of the principal officers in the Irish war.[5]

---

[5] Perhaps Sir Henry Norris, a soldier in Flanders, Brittany and Ireland, who was in London in the winter of 1598–1599.†

The courtier whom he brought to see me was a baron, and he has now, at the time of writing, succeeded to the earldom on his father's death.[6]

This young baron, then, wanted to make his confession. As I had not met him before, I started, as I usually did, by asking him whether he had prepared.

"Yes", he answered.

"And how often do you come to the sacraments?"

"Twice or three times a year."

"It would be better", I said, "if you came more often. And then you would not have to prepare so carefully. As things are, my advice is that you spend a few days making a good and exact examination of conscience—I will show you how. Then, when you come to confession you will get more benefit from it, and we will both be satisfied. For the future I would urge you to come to the sacraments more frequently." And I gave him the reasons why he should.

He listened to me very patiently. Then, when I had finished he said:

"I will do what you suggest most willingly, but next time. Now it is quite impossible for me to put off my confession any longer."

"Why?" I asked.

"Because tomorrow I shall be in danger of my life, so I want to make my preparation now."

"What do you mean?" I asked.

"I've been insulted by a gentleman at court," he said, "and in a way I cannot overlook. Honor obliges me to challenge him to a duel. We meet tomorrow at a place outside the city."

---

[6] Richard de Burgh, Baron Dunkellin, who succeeded his father shortly after this meeting as fourth Earl of Clanricarde. As J. G. says later that Essex was in disgrace at this time, the incident he proceeds to narrate occurred sometime in 1600.

"Heavens", I said. "Don't you know what it means to receive the sacrament in that state? That's not how to prepare for danger; you won't cleanse your conscience that way. I can well believe you were in good faith when you proposed to confess. But all you'll do will be to rouse God's anger more and put yourself still farther from Him. The sacraments can have no effect, if you come to confession with your mind made up to take revenge. And moreover the thing you propose doing is not merely a sin; it involves you in excommunication. I beg you put the idea out of your head. There must be some other way of defending your good name. If it's your honor you are out to defend, that's not how to go about it. What you are really defending is your good name with men who count for nothing—men who put their worldly standing before God's honor and pleasure."

"I cannot withdraw now", he answered. "Too many people have heard about it. Even the Queen knows; she has given an express command that we should not go through with it."

"Well, there," I said, "what better reason could you want for calling it off than obedience to the Queen's orders? And also you are known as the Earl of Essex's close friend, and he's now in the Queen's disfavor.† If you defeat your opponent, the Queen, to spite your friend the Earl of Essex, is certain to punish you for flouting her wishes. And if you kill him she will take your life for the same reason. On the other hand, if you lose, then in the shame of defeat you've lost the honor you were out to defend. What's more, if you're killed with your intent of revenge, you plunge into everlasting shame and fall into eternal punishment. And while you're parrying the man's thrusts at your body, the devil at every pass is working with his sword to pierce the guard to your soul."

In spite of everything, regard for what men would say
got the better of him, for, given his commitments, this is
what influenced him. He answered:

"I beseech you, Father, pray for me, and if you possibly
can, hear my confession."

"That's out of the question", I said. "You are under no
necessity to defend your honor, as perhaps a man might be
who is under engagement in war. You are the challenger,
and you could have avoided the duel, for there were other
ways of defending your good name. If there is any necessity, it's of your making. It was you who persisted in this
evil enterprise. But I'll tell you what I shall do. Here's a
fragment of the true Cross from my reliquary. I shall place
it on an *Agnus Dei*† and you can wear it on your person.
Then you may hope that perhaps for its sake God will protect you from danger and give you time to repent. Mind
you, I'm not giving it to you to speed you in your wicked
resolve. I'm giving it to you to wear with reverence and
regard, so that if you are in danger—not that I want you to
be—then God may be moved to give you your life for the
good will you show in honoring His Cross."

He took the gift gratefully and reverently and had it sewn
inside his shirt close to his heart, for they had arranged to
fight in their shirts without cuirass. It so happened that God
allowed his opponent to make a lunge at his heart; he pierced
his shirt but did not touch the skin. Then in turn he
wounded his man and had him on the ground. But he spared
his life and walked away the victor. In high spirits he came
and told me how he had been saved by the power of the
Holy Cross. Then he thanked me warmly and promised to
be more careful in future.

Later the Queen took a strong liking to him and kept
him in close attendance at court. But he soon tired of the

life, and when his father died, he married the Earl of Essex's widow.[7] She was a heretic, but he made her a Catholic, and they are living now as Catholics in Ireland, as I am told.†

To come back to the knight who introduced me to this baron. Following my advice, he spent several days examining his conscience carefully and then made a general confession of his whole life, with a view to leading a better life in the future. When, afterward, he told me he was anxious to return to the Irish wars, I was doubtful whether this was lawful in conscience, so he promised that if the priests over there, to whom I referred him, decided it was unlawful (they were on the spot and in a better position to judge), then he would resign his commission and return to England. Soon after arriving in Ireland he was killed in battle by a musket ball while he was assaulting a wall and waving on his men to follow. But he had consulted the priests (he told me this in a letter), and they had said that it was lawful to fight against the Catholic faction, because no one had seemed at all clear why they had taken up arms.

After his death a remarkable incident occurred, which should be told here. His wife was a devout lady. The last thing she was expecting was news of her husband's death, but about that time she heard a knocking every night on her bedroom door. It was a loud knock and it woke her. The maids in the room also heard it, but when they opened the door they could see nobody there. So she called a priest to watch with her in the room with the maids until the

---

[7] Frances, daughter and heiress of Sir Francis Walsingham, Secretary to Elizabeth, and widow, first of Sir Philip Sidney and then of Robert Devereux, second Earl of Essex, the Queen's favorite, who came to his tragic end in 1601. Thus the only child of Walsingham, the great persecutor of Catholics under Elizabeth, became a Catholic under J. G.'s influence.

knocking started. As soon as he heard it (it always began at
the same time) the priest went to see what was happening,
but again there was nobody there. The noise and knocking
went on from the day he died until the day she received
news of his death. It looked very much as if it were an
angel warning her to pray for her husband's soul.

During my visits to London I got many opportunities of
meeting men of rank, and I was able to strengthen them in
their faith, and direct them, and, in some cases, bring them
back to the Church. Many of them brought members of
their family and their friends to see me.

One man asked me to ride out and see a friend of his,
whom he would bring to meet me at a place two miles
from London. This friend was a person of wealth and influence and unquestionably the most important man in his
county. His rank was just below that of a baron—he was
not an earl or a peer—and his whole life was given to
pleasure-seeking.

So I met him. Informed who I was, he greeted me courteously, but at the same time he did not want to show that
he knew me. So I played the part of the Catholic layman
who was anxious that everyone should become a Catholic,
and told him that I had heard he was a friend of Catholics,
but his own worst enemy, for he stayed outside the Church.
At once he raised the question whether he had to become
a Catholic to save his soul, and I showed him that it was
necessary. But it was much harder to wean his will from
the pleasures of the world, and it was to this that I directed
my attack. With God's grace I cast down his defenses and
made a breach through which good and salutary counsel
found a way into his heart. Up to that time he had spoken
to me and addressed me as a gentleman and as a friend of
one of his friends. Now, he said, "You're the man to hear

my confession." So we arranged a convenient time and place where we could dispatch the business at our leisure.

A few days later he came to my friend's house near London and stayed on there until with proper preparation he was able to make his confession. Thereafter he was one of my principal benefactors. Every year, until I left England, he provided me with a thousand florins, and also horses and other things I occasionally needed.[8]

This same gentleman introduced me to his brother-in-law, the son and brother of an earl, and himself the heir to the earldom.[9] I rode to meet him at the same place. Before we parted God touched his heart also and he was given the grace of conversion. He was satisfied on all points of faith and morals, and a few days later I made him a Catholic. I am confident that he will, please God, become one of the chief supports of the Church.

I used my own house to administer the sacraments to these and other gentlemen, but I was careful to keep the place from public attention, lest it became known as a Catholic house. I wanted to use it as my London shelter (the risk, of course, for all priests, and for me especially, was far greater in London than anywhere else). Men of position and influence knew they could visit me without risk of a sudden raid, and so they came with greater confidence. I found by experience that this caution was appreciated by them, since it made as much for their safety as it did for mine.

---

[8] Richard Bancroft, Bishop of London, makes a reference to J. G.'s horses in a letter to Cecil on April 11, 1603: "For Mr. Gerard is a tall black man, very gallant in apparel, and being attended with two men and a foot boy is exceedingly well horsed." *Hat. Cal.*, 15:25.

[9] In spite of the accumulation of detail, it is difficult to identify this person with certainty. It may well have been Francis Manners, son of John Manners, fourth Earl of Rutland and brother and heir of Roger Manners, the fifth Earl.†

I had this house for three years and then leased it to a Catholic friend, and took another just off the Strand, the main street in London. Most of my friends lived in that street, and I could visit them more easily, and they me. After I had moved out, I discovered how completely free from suspicion was the house I had just vacated, and had used for three years. One day my servant happened to send for the gardener he had known while in my old house—my new garden needed tidying up.[10] He came and remarked casually: "You know, the people who have taken over your old place are Papists"—as much as to say that the previous occupants had been good Protestants.

It was a convenient and very suitable place, with private entrances front and back, and I had some very good hiding-places constructed in it. I might have stayed there without the slightest risk or suspicion for a very long time, had it not been for some friends who made very indiscreet use of the house while I was out of London.[11] However, it remained safe right up to the time of the terrible commotion known as the Gunpowder Plot, as I shall explain briefly a little later.

In the meantime some friends introduced me to another gentleman, who at the time was heir to a barony, and is

[10] J. G. enjoyed gardening. In a letter of July 15, 1606, written soon after his escape, he submitted to Father Persons a number of suggestions about his future employment, and added: "I could have care of the garden, for I am excellent at that (if you will permit me to praise myself) for that was much of my recreation in England, and I hope my brother [probably Sir Oliver Manners] will witness with me that he hath seen a good many plants of my setting, and tasted the fruit of some of them." Stonyhurst MSS, *Anglia A*, vol. 6, no. 59.

[11] Probably "the house in the fields behind Saint Clement's Inn" where the oath of secrecy was taken by the conspirators before the Gunpowder Plot.

now himself a peer. With God's grace I was able to persuade him to take on the yoke of Christ's law and the Catholic faith, and I received him into the Church.

Another gentleman[12] whom I had known and met frequently before I became a Jesuit, fell sick. His life had been one of pleasure-seeking, for he was exceedingly rich and dissipated. His only thought had been to enjoy himself, and he might have come to a bad end any moment had not God been patient with him and at the right time brought him to repentance. Though he was seriously ill, the thought of death had not crossed his mind.

When I got news that he was lying ill, I arranged to be taken to his room about eleven o'clock at night after all his friends had left. He recognized me and was glad I had come. Then I explained what had brought me and warned him to think seriously on his state of soul while there was still time. I told him that no matter how much he had squandered his estate, he would do well to make God not his Judge, but his Friend and loving Father. His failing strength disposed him to hear me and "in the acceptable time God heard us and in the day of salvation helped us", for he said that he was ready there and then to make his confession. However, I told him I would be back the following night and urged him meanwhile to ask a friend of his whom I knew to read him Father Louis of Granada's *Explanation of the Commandments*. After each commandment I suggested he should spend a little time in reflection and try to recall the ways and the number of times he had offended against each, and make an act of sorrow before passing on to the next. He promised

[12] Sir Thomas Langton, baron of Newton-in-Makerfield, Lancashire. He was created a Knight of the Bath at the coronation of James I and died in Westminster on February 20, 1604, aged forty-four. *C.R.S.*, Lord Burghley's map of Lancashire, 19.

to do this, and I undertook to return the next night. I did, and heard his confession, giving him all the help I could. For his time of preparation had been short and, although he still had some strength left, I did not want to risk deferring his confession any longer. I warned him to be sure he discharged all his debts—they were substantial, for he had been very extravagant—and I exhorted him also to "redeem his sins by alms-giving". He arranged for both in the will he drew up the next day. He left, besides, a large sum for pious purposes, which, I am told, was duly paid.

Then I asked him to prepare to receive Holy Communion and Extreme Unction the following night, and to have a book of devotion read to him in the meantime. He did this and more: he exhorted all who came to see him the next day to waste no time setting their lives straight with God and not wait to the last moment as he had done.

"Don't count on the special mercy God has given me; it would be presumption and an offense against God. On this score I have deserved hell a thousand times over." He said many other things like this, earnestly and without any inhibition, and made everyone marvel at the sudden change in him. When his friends urged him to hide the crucifix that was hanging round his neck (I had lent him my own cross full of relics so that he could kiss it and make acts of reverence and love), "Hide it!" he said. "I would not hide it if the most fanatical heretic were in my room. I have been away from the profession of my faith too long. If God gave me life now, I would proclaim myself a Catholic openly." Everyone was astonished at the way he spoke, and he greatly edified and moved them all. He spoke in this way to all the peers and great men who visited him.

So his conversion became public knowledge, and many courtiers spoke about it afterward. When I came to him on the third night, as I had promised, he confessed again with great sentiments of sorrow. Then he begged to receive the sacrament of Extreme Unction. As I was administering it, he arranged himself so that I could conveniently reach the parts of the body I was to anoint—you might have thought he had been a Catholic for many years. He was in such high spirit that I asked him: "Do you trust completely in the merits of Christ and in the mercy of God?"

"Yes", he answered. "How could I do otherwise? If it were not for His great mercy to me I would be damned in hell. When I look at myself I see no ground for hope, but only for trembling. But I am full of hope in the mercy and goodness of God. He has waited for me so long and now He has called me when I was the last to deserve it."

Then, taking my hand, he went on:

"And, Father, I can't tell you how much I owe to you. God sent you to bring me this happiness."

I found also that he had no temptations against the faith. He believed and professed every article of the Creed most firmly, and it was clear that God had infused into his soul the habits of many virtues.

I then set up an altar in his bedroom (I had brought all I needed with me), and I said Mass at which he assisted with very great devotion and comfort. Later I gave him Viaticum, and he could not have received it with more reverence. When all was done, I gave him a few words of advice to help him if he should fall into his agony before I returned. He was full of consolation when I left.

How remarkable is God's providence! A few hours after I had gone he gave his soul to God. To the last he was petitioning for mercy and thanking God for all the mercy he had received. Before he died he asked the people by his bed to see that certain purple and red robes of his were turned to use at the altar—he had received them from the King when he was made a Knight of the Bath. The investiture of this Order takes place only at the anointing and coronation of the King, and these knights have precedence over all other knights except those of the most noble Order of the Garter, almost all of whom are earls or other peers. (He was a Knight of the Bath, as I said, and he wanted all the robes with which he had been invested at the Coronation to be devoted to the use of the altar.) My own vestments had pleased him. Though light and easy to carry about, they were beautifully made from red silk embroidered with silver lace. After his death I was duly given the robes and had them made up into two sets of vestments of different colors, one of which is now at Saint Omers College. In this way I was able to carry out the pious wish of a gentleman whose conversion, as I saw it, was a great mark of God's goodness and providence.

Also about this time I received into the Church a lady, the wife of a knight who is now a very good and helpful friend of our Fathers. Her husband was at that time a Protestant, but I had assisted his brother by means of the Spiritual Exercises to set the world at naught and follow Christ's counsels. It was he who introduced me to his sister. And after I had seen her once or twice, she became a Catholic; though she was well aware that as soon as her husband got to know, she would suffer heavily for it. And indeed she did.

First he was gentle with her; then he used threats—he tried every way of shaking her resolution. For a long time it looked as if there were nothing for her to do but separate from her husband and lose everything she had in the world, in order to possess her soul in peace. Because of her action her husband was deprived of his office in the State; and this trial she bore with great fortitude. She was staunch and

unruffled, and by the example of her patience and goodness she worked on her husband—first he became a friend
to Catholics and then a Catholic himself. Father Walpole,
whom I introduced to him before I left England, received
him into the Church.

There were many other conversions, but I cannot give
them all separate mention. Already my narrative is quite
out of proportion to the insignificant things it records. What
I did is nothing compared with what others did. But there
is one thing I cannot pass over; it gave me very special
pleasure because of the person concerned, for I don't think
I loved anyone more dearly.

Sir Everard Digby, about whom I spoke above, had a
friend to whom he was deeply attached.[13] He had often
sung his praises to me, and he was anxious that I should
meet him and if possible win him over. But the gentleman
held an office at court which required daily attendance on
the King, and as he could not be absent for long at once, it
was a considerable time before a meeting could be arranged.

At last Sir Everard met his friend when we were both
together in London, and asked him to come to his room at
a certain time to play cards—cards are, as it were, the books
which nearly all these gentlemen in London study day and
night. He agreed to come, but when he arrived, instead of
a card party, he found the pair of us sitting and talking very
seriously. Sir Everard asked him to sit down for a little while
until the rest of the party arrived. Then, in an interval of
silence, Sir Everard said,

"The two of us have been engaged in a very serious conversation. In fact, we have been talking about religion."

[13] Sir Oliver Manners, fourth son of the fourth Earl of Rutland. He was
Clerk of the Council.

Then, addressing the gentleman, he added: "You know I am well disposed toward Catholics and the Catholic faith. I have, however, been arguing against the faith with this gentleman, who is a friend of mine, just to see what kind of defense he can make. He is an earnest Catholic, I don't mind telling you." Then, turning to me he begged me not to be angry for betraying me to a stranger. "I must admit," he went on, "he made such a good defense of his position that I didn't know how to answer. I am so glad you have come in now to help me out."

The visitor was young and confident. With his ability and such a good case to argue, he thought he would be able to carry all before him, and, as he told me afterward, he rather looked down on me.

He began by bringing objections against everything I had been saying. I waited patiently, and when he had finished speaking, I answered in a few words. Then he pressed again and we went on arguing with one another for the best part of an hour. At the end of it I explained my standpoint more fully and confirmed it with texts from Scripture and passages from the Fathers, and with arguments that came to hand. I felt, as so often I did on occasions like this, that God was giving me words as I spoke with great fervor on His behalf—not, I mean, for my own sake, nor for any deserts of mine, but just as He gives milk to a mother when she has an infant who needs milk from her breasts. The gentleman was willing to learn. He could not bring himself to argue against what he saw to be true, so he listened in silence and, meanwhile, in tones more persuasive and forceful than mine, God was speaking to his heart. God, too, gave him "ears to hear", and "the word fell not upon stony ground, nor among thorns, but upon good soil"—such good soil that it yielded with God's grace a hundredfold in season.

Before he left he resolved to become a Catholic. He took away with him a little book to help him to prepare his confession, which he made before the end of a week.

From that time on he wanted to do more than just keep the commandments; indeed God was preparing him for higher things. Whatever advice I was called upon to give, he accepted readily; he never let it slip his memory, but always acted on it most promptly. He examined his conscience carefully every day, learnt how to meditate, and made a meditation every morning. To do so, he had to rise very early before the King. In summer this meant daybreak, for the King went hunting every day, and he by reason of his office had to be in attendance at the King's breakfast.[14] He read devotional books eagerly, and always carried one in his pocket. You might see him in the court or in the Presence Chamber, as it is called, when it was crowded with courtiers and famous ladies, turning aside to a window and reading a chapter of Thomas à Kempis' *Imitation of Christ*. He knew the book from cover to cover. And after reading a little he would turn to the company, but his mind was elsewhere. He stood absorbed in his thoughts. People imagined that he was admiring some beautiful lady, or wondering how to climb to a higher position. Actually he had no need to worry about this. He was the son and brother of an earl, and his office at court was a very honorable one, and gave him the King's ear every day. He was also a man of intelligence and knew the right time to make requests. In fact the King gave him an office (he sold it later) which, had he kept it, would have brought him in more than ten thousand florins a year. He was certain to receive high promotion before very long, for he had exceptionable ability in making himself most

[14] He was the King's Carver. Birch, *Court of James I*, vol. 1, 49.

agreeable and loved by everyone. Indeed, after he had turned his back on the court and left all worldly honors behind, I heard people of high position and much experience at court say that in all their forty years they had known nobody who had been so universally loved and esteemed by one and all. But what is much more important, he was a chosen favorite in the court of the King of kings, and had his heart set on a larger and more lasting prize. He asked me to go through the Spiritual Exercises, and in the course of them decided to leave the court and devote himself to the things that would make his life more pleasing in God's sight and more profitable in his neighbor's service. As quickly as he could, he made the necessary disposition of his estate to free himself for his escape from England. Then, to everyone's astonishment, he asked and obtained the King's leave to go to Italy, where he is living now. He is so very well known to the Fathers of the Society that there is no need for me to say more. I will just add this. All my information is that wherever he has been he has left behind him a high reputation and high expectations.[15]

Apart from Sir Everard Digby, this gentleman had another close friend, a man of influence and large properties, richly talented, but a man of the world. He brought him to see me and through my means made him a Catholic.

Among his friends there were two gentlewomen. They loved and were captivated by him, but it was a laudable attachment with a view to marriage, for I am sure they would have preferred him to the greatest earl in England. One of them belonged to the court and was a maid-of-honor of the Queen; the other lived in the country and came from a noble Catholic family.

---

[15] He was ordained priest at Rome on April 5, 1611.†

He introduced me to the first lady and by my ministry made her a Catholic. Then he suggested that she should set her heart on something nobler than his person—on God, to whom all our love is due. He went on to tell her that he would never love any woman save with the love of charity, and he was resolved never to marry.

The second lady, who was already a Catholic, he persuaded to become a nun. She is in religion now and is making good progress.

I am sure this gentleman was chosen and set apart by God in order to bring many souls to follow the counsels of Christ and to be a help to ours in many ways.

22. LAST DAYS OF WORK

The conversions which occurred in the country were numerous, and some converts were the heads of families. However, as I have been very long already, I will confine myself to a single instance, which had a happy beginning and a happy ending.

The lady was a kinswoman of my hostess. Though she had married a gentleman who had been a Catholic for many years, no one, not even her husband, or any friend, or even my hostess, who loved her like a sister, could induce her to become a Catholic. The lady did not in the least mind listening to Catholics, even priests, for she enjoyed a keen argument with them, but she would follow no one's advice but her own. She had indeed gifts that I have seldom seen in a woman, and my hostess often shed tears over her. It made her sad that she could find no cure, and she was anxious that I should see her just once. For her intelligence, her character, her way of life, and all about her, she had only praise; the one fault she found in her was her persistence in heresy.

Although she lived in a distant county, my hostess asked her to stay with us. She accepted the invitation, and on her arrival she found me, as we had previously arranged, sitting about and talking in company, and dressed as if I were a guest just down from London. We did little the first day or two. We knew there was plenty of time, and I wanted her to feel at her ease with me. On other visits she had met priests in the house, but for the most part they had kept to themselves in their rooms.

As soon as I thought she realized I was a Catholic—there was no question of her taking me for a priest—I slowly introduced the subject of religion. At first I said very little, but what little I said was to the point, and she seemed lost for an answer. Then I left her. I did not want to press home my advantage; it was enough to make her want to hear more.

At length, after a few more days, I judged her ready. I arranged for my hostess to open a serious conversation on religion, and then, when she saw me come in and take over the conversation, to leave us together with perhaps one or two of her daughters—three had come with her.

This we did. We joined issue, and the advantage, so it seemed to her, shifted to and fro. We went on for an hour or two, at the end of which she listened to me without interruption for two or three hours more, and though she answered little, she would not admit herself defeated. But she thanked me cordially, and went away all flushed and red in the face. Clearly she was moved, or rather, changed in heart, for she ran at once to my hostess.

"Cousin," she cried, "what have you done?"

"What have I done?" asked my lady.

"Who's this man you brought to me? Is he what you said he was?" And she asked questions about me and spoke much too favorably about my eloquence and learning, saying she could not hold her own or answer back.

The next day God confirmed what He had begun in her. She surrendered at discretion, and I gave her a book to help her prepare for confession. Meanwhile, with the mother's consent and help, I instructed the three daughters, and when they had learned their catechism, I heard their confessions.

However, in the course of her own preparation the lady felt troubled and downcast. It was not the thought of giving up heresy, but the prospect of confession that upset her. So I encouraged her as best I could, telling her she had no reason to fear. But now, when she had examined her conscience sufficiently, she began postponing her confession from day to day on the plea that she was not ready. I would not agree. I told her that it was the devil at work on his own ground, and she herself admitted later that this was true. For, when in obedience to me she confessed, she felt a great burden lifted and was filled with consolation, and said she was very glad she had not put it off longer.

I have often found that some people have great difficulty in making their confession when they are received into the Church. Some work themselves up to the point of feeling sick and almost faint—they have to sit down and rest, and then carry on when they have recovered a little. This has happened in cases where the penitent was in good health and anxious to confess. Then, sometimes, on recommencing they have fallen faint again, perhaps two or three times in the course of their first confession. But at the end of their confession they have felt all right, and after absolution gone away full of comfort and joy. In fact some have remarked to me that if people only knew the consolation to be had from confession, nothing would make them miss it.

This lady was one of these people. She rose from her confession completely comforted, and ran to thank her cousin who was the means of bringing her this happiness. God, indeed, was merciful to her. She became very devout, and on her return home, she took to making beautiful vestments, and, whenever she had the chance, she gave shelter to priests. This, however, did not satisfy her. She wanted to return and live with us so that she could come to the sacraments more often and hear the talks I gave every Sunday and feast day. She stayed with us, in fact, about two years, and during all that time she grew in devotion and read many ascetical books, and it was clear that a special grace and providence of God was guiding her life.

At the end of this time—she was then in wonderful health—she was struck down with a disease and in a few days became so weak that the physicians could do nothing for her. So we warned her to prepare for the next life, and she again made a good and careful confession of her past life. Then, when she saw that she was nearing her agony, she asked to write to her brother—he was a heretic and perhaps the worst enemy Catholics had in his county. She wanted to send him a letter, written in her daughter's hand and signed by herself, to this effect: that he was aware how for a long time she had been a very keen supporter of the new religion. He could be quite sure therefore that she would never have changed without very solid reasons—she had in fact excellent and impregnable grounds for the faith she had adopted. And she protested that from the day she became a Catholic she had lived at peace with herself, never before having enjoyed true peace of soul. Finally, she begged him to look to his own soul. "I, your sister," she said, "now at the point of death, with these last words of mine beg and beseech you to embrace the Catholic and the ancient faith; and I protest that in none other can men be saved." These were her sentiments when she had almost reached her agony, and they were sure evidence of the sincerity of her conversion, since she had true charity toward her neighbor.

I put a few questions to her and, finding that she had no temptation either to presume on God's mercy or to despair, I helped her as much as I could to make acts of trust in God. Then, when she was at the point of death, I offered her a picture of Christ in His sufferings, and she took it and kissed it affectionately. Then I placed a blessed medal in her hands, and reminded her, in order to gain the indulgences, to invoke the name, Jesus, at least in her heart, for she could no longer speak, and I told her to make a sign that she did so. She signed, and took the medal firmly and kissed it, and did this several times. Then I told her to renew her sorrow for ever having sinned against God, who was so good in Himself and had shown her so many mercies, and to raise her hand as a sign that she did. Again she signed fervently. Then I told her to show that she was sorry that she had lived in heresy, and had resisted God and His Church, and she signed once more; and lastly, that she wanted all heretics to return to the faith, and was ready to offer her life for their conversion. Again she signed her readiness. And with a hand that was already chill she grasped mine and held it tightly, and signed to show how comforting she found the suggestions I made to her. Up to her last gasp I consoled and encouraged her, telling her to give praise to God in her heart and to desire that all His creatures might praise and serve Him, and to offer her life for this end. She answered me, raising and lowering her hand, just as I had told her to do earlier when I wanted her to signify her assent. There were many persons standing by and among them a priest. All were full of admiration and said they had never seen such a death as hers. And so, just as I have described, up to her last breath, she still responded to my suggestions, raising her hand slightly when it was impossible to raise it more. In this state she gave up her soul to God, without any disturbance of mind or convulsion of body; but like a person falling asleep, she went to her rest in peace.

Her youngest daughter had died before her in our house. Her death, too, was holy. The second daughter married a wealthy gentleman, and brought him to me from a long way off to make him a Catholic. The eldest is still living in the same house. She is waiting her espousals, not to man, but to God, for she has a vocation to the religious life. Meanwhile she is living devoutly there, and gives her time to serving priests, as the lady of the house did and still does.

It is well past the time I should end. I exceeded long ago the limits I first set myself. Little remains to be told and I will be brief.

I was able to give the Spiritual Exercises to many people in this house, both to people who were living there and to visitors, and in every case the result I wanted was produced.

There were two people who made only the Exercises of the first "week"; they wanted to lead good and holy lives. One of them is now the father of a family. He does many good works and is a loyal friend of ours. As the other came uninvited and unexpected to do the Exercises with me, I asked him what had decided him to do this—he was a very young man, the grandson of an earl and the heir to a large estate.[1] He answered:

"I read in a book written against the Society[2] that you use this means to persuade people to enter the religious life and then rob them of their property. Among other names mine was mentioned as one of those who had made the Exercises under you. It was said that though you failed to make me a religious, you wheedled a large sum of money

[1] Henry Hastings, grandson of Francis Hastings, second Earl of Huntingdon.†
[2] A book called *Quodlibetical Questions* (1602) by the renegade priest William Watson, of whom Father Persons wrote: "He is so wrong shapen and of so bad and blinking aspect as he looketh nine ways at once."†

out of me." And he went on: "I know my wife is very devoted to you because you made her a Catholic, but I know also that you have never taken a penny from me or from her. As they have calumniated you so badly I am come to redress their lies."

He made the Exercises and profited a good deal from them. Later he wrote asking me to find him a priest who could move in society. I found the man and was about to send him when, suddenly, everything was upset for a time, and any possibility of doing good checked by the Gunpowder Plot, as it is called.

At this very time I had arranged for some friends to cross over to the Continent—and if there were no other proof, that by itself should prove that I knew nothing about the plot. One was a lady who was going to enter the Benedictine convent at Brussels†—I had sent over two others a short time before, and they now hold positions of responsibility in the convent. The other was a Protestant Minister whom I had instructed and received into the Church; the last I received before the upheaval.[3] As these and others were on the point of embarking, orders came to stop any ship leaving port. Every one of them was seized and imprisoned, and released only two years ago. The ex-Minister is doing his studies now in the Roman College; the lady is a professed nun in the convent she was on her way to join at the time she was captured.

Apart from this man, there was only one other Minister whom I converted, and he is now working as a priest on the mission. But while I was in this last place I sent over

[3] In his anxiety to "hurry on" J. G. has omitted a good story. This ex-Minister was John Golding. The day for his marriage had been fixed and later postponed. In the interval he was converted by J. G. He entered the English College, Rome, and was ordained in April 1615. Foley, 6:249.

many young men to the seminaries—and these men, please God, will be good harvesters in due season.[4]

But surely if we receive good things from God, we should be ready to bear with bad things too? Perhaps "bad" is not the right word for things that come from Him, since they are sent for our edification; indeed they are good for His servants, if they receive them in the right way and adore the disposition of Him who gives and who takes away. God had done many things to my great consolation while I was in this house. He had given me great comfort from the conversions that took place and the remarkable progress of so many souls in virtue. Nor were temporal comforts lacking. Everything there was well arranged, and I was given all I needed. I had several very fine horses for my missionary journeys, and all that was necessary to carry on my work. In the house itself everything was well arranged and convenient. My companions were Father Strange, who is now in the Tower (Father Percy had been given to Master Digby by the Superior), and another priest[5] who was with us a long time.

We were also well-off for good books and kept them in the library with no attempt to conceal them, for they were thought to belong to the young baron, a bequest from his uncle who was a very scholarly man,[6] well-known for his piety. This nobleman had resigned his right and title to his younger brother, the present baron's father, in order to

[4] It is possible to trace the names of over thirty students for the priesthood, sent over to the Continent by J. G., in the records of the English College, Rome, and the seminary at Valladolid.†

[5] Father Singleton; cf. below, p. 250.

[6] Henry Vaux, one of the Catholic gentlemen who gave an enthusiastic welcome to Campion and Persons on their arrival in England in 1580. He died not very long after his release from prison at the house of his sister, Mrs. Brooksby, at Great Ashby, Leicestershire, in November 1587.†

devote himself entirely to God and to his studies. Had he lived a little longer, he would have entered the Society. On his death-bed his only regret was that he could not there and then be admitted, for he was most anxious to become a Jesuit.

Also we had there many very fine vestments for the altar: two sets of each color which the Church uses—one for ordinary use, the other for greater feasts; some of these with figures of exquisite workmanship were embroidered with gold and pearls. Six massive silver candlesticks stood on the altar, and two smaller ones at the side for the elevation. The cruets, the lavabo bowl, the bell and thurible were all of silverwork; the lamps hung from silver chains, and a silver crucifix stood on the altar. For the great feasts we had a golden crucifix a foot high. It had a pelican carved at the top, and on the right arm an eagle with outstretched wings, carrying on its back its little ones, who were learning to fly; and on the left arm a phoenix expiring in flames so that it might leave behind an offspring; and at the foot was a hen gathering her chickens under her wings. The whole was worked in gold by a skilled artist.

I also had a precious ornament with the Holy Name engraved on it. My hostess had given it to me on the first Christmas after I came to live in her house. The Name was formed of pins of solid gold, and the surrounding "glory" had two pins in one ray and three in the next alternately. It was about twice the size of a sheet of this paper and contained altogether two hundred and forty gold pins, to each of which was attached a large pearl. The pearls were not perfectly shaped (had they been, the value of the ornament would have been fabulous, but, as it was, the whole thing was worth about a thousand florins). At the bottom there was a colophon, worked in gold and gems by the artist, in the form of a monogram, expressing the Holy Name, and in the middle of this a heart with a cross of diamonds radiating from it. This was a New Year's present from the devout widow in honor of the most Holy Name of Jesus, the day's feast.

All these treasures are still kept in trust for the Society;† and in the meantime they are used in the domestic chapel by our Fathers who serve the residence. I, who showed such little appreciation of these and many other things that God gave me, was forced to leave them to others who were more worthy of them and could use them to more advantage.

23. THE POWDER PLOT

November 5, 1605–May 3, 1606

As my principal friends were involved in the catastrophe of the Powder Plot, the Council was thorough and relentless in its hunt for me. They sent Justices of the Peace to the house. They were to search it scrupulously and if they failed to find me, stay on until they were recalled. Day and night guards were to encircle the house, and at night special watches set at a distance of three miles round, with orders to arrest any passing stranger. All this was carried out to the letter.

As soon as news reached us that a plot had been discovered and that some of our friends had been killed and others captured, we knew that we would have to suffer.† However, we had prepared, and although the search lasted many days nothing was discovered till my hostess revealed to the chief pursuivant a hiding-place which had only a few books in it. Her hope was that they would think that, if a priest was in the house, he would be hiding there, and that they would then call off the search. But they went on till the end of the ninth day.[1]

---

[1] This incident is described by William Tate, the Justice in charge of the search, in a letter to Salisbury, dated "Harrowden, November 15": "I required Richard Richardson, a servant of Mrs. Vaux, then present, to deal truly with me; who after some debate opened the door, whereat I entered and searched

I was in my hiding-place. I could sit down all right but there was hardly room to stand. However, I did not go hungry, for every night food was brought to me secretly. And at the end of four or five days,† when the rigor of the search had relaxed slightly, my friends came at night and took me out and warmed me by a fire. It was winter time, just before the season of Christmas. After nine days the search party withdrew. They thought I could not possibly have been there all that time without being discovered.

Meanwhile they had captured a priest who was on his way to our house for safety and knew nothing about the cordon of watchers. A few days before, when we first got word of the plot, he had left at my suggestion in order to see Father Garnet and ask him what we should do in the crisis. This good priest was Father Thomas Laithwaite, who is now a Jesuit and working in England.†

On his way he was captured but managed to escape. Seized on the road and brought to an inn, he was to have been examined and committed to prison at once. But entering the inn, he took off his cloak and sword and walked out again to the stables as if he were going to attend to his horse and take him to drink. There was a stream near the inn, and he asked the stable boy to lead his horse there at once. He went with him, and when he reached the stream he turned to the boy.

---

the same, and found it the most secret place that I ever saw, and so contrived that it was without all possibility to be discovered. There I found many Popish books and other things incident to their superstitious religion; but no man in it. I am assured that none could evade out thence after I entered the house, having guarded it day and night round about, and within myself and servants keeping keys of all the doors." *Hat. Cal.*, 17:490–91.

"Go and get the hay ready", he said, "and put down some straw for my horse to lie on. I'll be back myself when he has finished drinking."

The boy returned to the stable without further thought. Meanwhile the Father mounted his horse, spurred him into the stream, and swam him across to the other side. As his cloak and sword were lying in the inn his stratagem was unsuspected until they realized he had been away a long time and the boy told them what had happened. Immediately they set off in pursuit. But they were too late. The good Father knew the countryside well and reached a Catholic house before nightfall. There he hid for a few days. But when he found he could not get in touch with Father Garnet he tried to return to me, thinking the danger had passed. He avoided Charybdis to fall into the clutches of Scylla, for, as I have said, he was seized and dragged to London.[2] But his priesthood could not be proved, and his brother was allowed to pay a sum down for his release.

Two other priests were with me in the house when the troubles began—one, as I said, was Father Strange. They both wanted to go and stay with Father Garnet, but both were captured on their way. One[3] was thrown into Bridewell and was later exiled with some other priests. The other, namely, Father Strange, was put in the Tower and suffered much, as I wrote briefly above.

---

[2] "I commanded a strong watch to be kept day and night throughout all the country adjacent, and no man suffered to pass.... By this occasion many being stayed, one John Laithwoode was brought to me.... At his first examination he was insufferably insolent, but on the morrow he became of a better-tempered spirit." William Tate to Salisbury, November 15, 1605. *Hat. Cal.*, 17:490.

[3] Father William Singleton, one of the Assistants to the Archpriest. He was captured with Father Strange at Kenilworth on November 7, on his way to Hinlip. *C.S.P.D.* (1603–1610), 300.

The history of the conspiracy is well known. It has been written up by friends and enemies, but not perhaps as it will be written later.

When I left England I was ordered to write an account of the whole affair, and I did so as well as I could.[4] I am not going to repeat here what I wrote at length about the condition of England at the time, how at the accession of the King there was no relaxation of the persecution, but only a fresh persecution more bitter and grievous than the last.† The Catholic body now expected—some of them knew for certain—that new laws against them were to be passed in the next Parliament much more severe and cruel than the existing ones. There was to be no easing of the Queen's harsh rule. The yoke which Catholics had borne so long on their weary necks was to be made heavier still.

A group of young and eager Catholics, seeing that now they were going to be scourged not with whips but with scorpions, thought that there was no human hope left to them unless they chose to help themselves. Peace had now been made between his Catholic Majesty and the King of England—a peace in which Catholics had no share although they had more right to peace than the wicked. At the prospect of all this these people, I say, forgot that long-suffering and peace with which we should possess our souls. They could no longer bear to see holy things trodden underfoot and the faithful robbed of their possessions and loaded with innumerable wrongs. It was a daily and lamentable undoing of souls. They determined therefore to raise the people of God from the state into which they had fallen, to make war in deadly secret against the enemies of their souls and

---

[4] The reference is to J. G.'s *Narrative of the Gunpowder Plot*, printed in Morris' *Condition of Catholics under James I* (1871).

bodies and the enemies of the Catholic cause. I say "in secret" because there was no question of open opposition or of a Catholic rising. The strength of the Catholic body, it must be acknowledged, had been broken and shattered, and their arms taken from them. Thus it happened that the people I am speaking of devised this plot in order to deliver themselves and others with them from this fearful serfdom of soul and body. They thought that the only way of doing it was to remove at a single stroke all their enemies and the principal enemies of the Catholic cause.

I discussed all these points in the book I mentioned. There I also gave a detailed account of the method they decided to use, and explained how, when all was ready for the plan to be put through, one of them[5] disclosed the plot in confession to a Father of our Society. This Father refused to hear him further unless he was allowed to put the matter to the Superior under the seal of confession. The Superior, when he heard about the bloody plot, ordered this Father to do his utmost to stop his penitent going through with it. And he immediately wrote to the Pope, begging his Holiness to forbid Catholics resorting to external violence.[6] I have told how, after the plot had been discovered and made public, the Superior and Father Oldcorne were captured at the latter's house. They were discovered after a long search— they were twelve days in a hiding-hole.[7] With them were taken two servants or, as I have since heard and believe, two Brothers of our Society. Both were condemned to death and suffered martyrdom. One, Ralph, died with Father

---

[5] This was Robert Catesby, the instigator of the plot.

[6] For Father Garnet's knowledge of the Gunpowder Plot, see Appendix F.

[7] "When we came forth", wrote Father Garnet, "we appeared like two ghosts. . . . The fellow that found us ran away for fear, thinking we would have shot a pistol at him." They were captured on January 27, 1606.†

Oldcorne, whose companion and servant he had been. As the Father mounted the ladder to the scaffold, Ralph clasped his feet and kissed them and thanked him for his kindness and for all he had done for him. Then he blessed God for granting him such a happy end to his life in such good company.† The other was "Little John". For nearly twenty years he had been Father Garnet's companion, and I have had occasion to mention him frequently in the course of this story. He was well-known as the chief designer and builder of hiding-places in England, and was, therefore, a man who could hand over more priests and injure and betray more Catholics than any other single person. They tortured him long and mercilessly, and in the end, unable to get any information out of him, they killed him, but they had been unable to break his constancy.†

Also in that book I have told how Father Garnet and Father Oldcorne were brought to London. There they were examined time and again, particularly Father Garnet, and both were tortured, Father Oldcorne more often.[8] Father Oldcorne was taken back to Worcester. Though nothing could be proved against him, he was condemned, hanged, and quartered. It was a saintly martyr's death.†

At a special Assize in London Father Garnet was condemned but not proved guilty. He made such a clear defense of his conduct that people were amazed and praised the man until Cecil and others browbeat him and made it impossible for this most modest of men to clear himself of the calumnies against him.† Led out to the place of execution he bore himself bravely and meekly. His whole manner, and the way he accepted or rather welcomed his death and

---

[8] Father Garnet was tortured only once, but Father Oldcorne for five hours together on four or five consecutive days.†

suffering, touched the hearts of his most savage enemies, and they went away thinking well of him.[9]

All these details, which I have barely mentioned, I described fully in my other narrative. Here I will merely add something about the way we obtained the straw on which the miraculous likeness of Father Garnet appeared, for I attended afterward the death-bed of the man who found the straw or rather the man to whom God gave it.

A short time before he died, this man told me that he had felt an unusual fervor of soul on the morning of the holy priest's death. He wanted to attend the execution in order perhaps to secure some small relic. So he pushed his way close to the place where the executioner was hacking up the martyr's body, but he was afraid to touch anything as there were officers surrounding it. Just at that moment the butcher cut the venerable head from the body and threw it into a basket full of straw. As he did this, an ear of straw came up into his hand, or, at least so near his hand, that he was able to pick it up without drawing notice on himself. This ear was stained with blood, and he kept it with great reverence. For some days after, as he told me, he experienced a greater taste for spiritual things and for the counsels of Christ than ever before—in fact he had no peace of soul until he had renounced his property and made arrangements to cross the water and start his studies for the priesthood. He wanted very much to enter the Society, and this desire lasted till his death, which occurred at Saint Omers.

---

[9] The King granted Father Garnet the mercy of allowing him to hang until he was dead. A letter of Sir Charles Cornwallis speaks of the "sorrow expressed by the people for the Jesuit's putting to death, and ... when the executioner showed his head and bade 'God Save the King', there was not one would bestow an 'Amen'! but instead thereof fell upon the hangman, who escaped hardly with his life."†

When he lay dying he gave such edification that no one there remembers a holier death than his.

I will give here one more piece of information concerning Father Oldcorne's martyrdom. In my other account I mention that I received a letter from England telling me that when this holy martyr's intestines were thrown into the fire, according to sentence, they burned for sixteen days, the exact number of years he had worked in that county, kindling the fire of divine love and nursing it with his word and example. Now quite recently I was talking about this to a good priest, who at Saint Omers goes by the name of Father North.† This priest was in prison at Worcester at the time, and several people told him that the fire, besides lasting all that time, burst out into great flames, though heavy rain was falling, that crowds went to see it, and admitted the truth of the report when they returned home, and that, in the end, on the sixteenth or seventeenth day, the fire had to be extinguished or at least covered over with heaps of earth. This Father added that in the courtyard of the house where the two Fathers were taken he saw a crown traced out in grass, grass that was quite different in shade and texture from the surrounding grass; it was taller and shaped in the clearly defined form of an imperial crown. After the arrest of the Fathers the house had been abandoned, and he said that the animals which had gotten into the courtyard through the broken gates grazed there several months but never during all that time touched or trod on the crown. He regarded it as a symbol of the Fathers' innocence and an indication of their eternal reward.[10]

---

[10] For contemporary accounts of these occurrences and the sensation they caused see Appendix G.

I think I had better add these few lines about myself before I close. I said in the other book that a proclamation was issued against three Jesuit Fathers. I was one of them, and, though the least of them all my name was put at the head as if I were the chief of them—I who was the subject of the second-named and in every respect far inferior to the third.[11] All this—let me protest solemnly—was utterly groundless. I knew absolutely nothing about the plot from anyone whomsoever, not even, as the other two did, under the seal of confession. I had not even the vaguest notion that any such scheme was afoot, not until we heard the rumor that a plot had been discovered, and then the rumor reached us no sooner than everyone else living in that part of the country.

From the long search of nine days I realized that I was suspect and that they were after me in particular. So I wrote an open letter, in the form of a letter to a friend, in which I gave many proofs and protestations beyond cavil that I was altogether innocent of the charges against me. I had many copies of the letter made and had them scattered about the London streets in the early hours of the morning. Many people picked it up and read it. One copy was shown to the King by a member of the Council, a friend of mine or my cause. The King, as I heard, said it convinced him.† But afterward, when Father Garnet's whereabouts became known and there was hope of catching him and of loading the whole charge on to the Society, they thought it necessary to proclaim that some of our Fathers were the principal plotters.† My name was joined to those of the two

---

[11] The Proclamation is dated January 15, 1606, several weeks after all the conspirators had been captured. In a letter of January 22, Salisbury comments, "All these three described in the proclamation are the very pillars and oracles of their order."†

Fathers whom one of Master Catesby's servants had maligned. Before his death this man repented, confessing publicly that he had acted against his conscience when he said these things. He was afraid of death and hoped to be pardoned, and Secretary Cecil had lured and bribed him.

Possibly at that time some people really suspected that I was privy to the plot. It was known that many of the gentlemen in prison were my friends and had visited me regularly in my London house. One of them had confessed this at his examination but stated that I knew nothing whatsoever of their plot. After they had examined them all, still they could find nothing against me. Master Digby, who was my intimate friend and was for that reason most closely examined about me, protested openly before the court that he had never dared mention his intention to me for fear that I should dissuade him from the attempt.†

I came to hear this. I heard, too, several facts concerning Father Garnet, which showed that he had knowledge of the plot under the seal of confession, and had heard of it from a member of the Society[12] who also knew of it under the seal.

It seemed to me, therefore, that I was sufficiently cleared of the charge, and in order to bring the fact to notice, I wrote the three letters to three leading lords of the Council, a short time before the death of the condemned gentlemen. With very cogent arguments I proved that I knew nothing about the conspiracy and I showed them how they could satisfy themselves on the point while the gentlemen were still alive.†

Whether they did or not I don't know, but I do know that throughout the proceedings of Father Garnet's trial—it

[12] Father Greenway, *alias* Tesimond.

was after they received these letters—they never once mentioned me, although they did all they could to defame the entire Society and involve the whole English mission.† They named three Fathers as guilty—the two who had heard of it in confession, and Father Oldcorne, not as privy to the plot but as an accessory after the fact.

Nevertheless, I was most careful to lie in hiding.[13] I was at a house in London where I was then staying, which no one knew about.† By the protection of God I was safe, and if I had thought it well to do so I could have stayed longer. I did not leave England to avoid capture. It was no time to work, and as we had to lie quiet I took the opportunity to come over here and rest a little.[14] After so long a period of distracting work in all sorts of company I wanted a breathing-space to recover my strength for the work which lay in the future.

At that time I was on my own. Nearly all my friends were either in prison or so distressed that they could hardly look after themselves. Every place was watched. There was no safety anywhere.[15] Owing to an indiscretion on the part

[13] At least four renegade Catholics who claimed to know J. G. had offered their services to Salisbury as spies, and had been granted warrants for J. G.'s arrest. One, Lady Markham, gives this interesting testimony to the opinion in which J. G. was held in the Northamptonshire countryside. "I meet with many people", she says in a letter to Salisbury, "that will as easily be persuaded there was no gunpowder laid as that [this] holy man [J. G.] was an actor in the plot; and surely the generality did ever so much admire him that they were happy or blessed in hearing him, and their roof sanctified by his appearance in their house."†

[14] Under the strain of these events, Father Stanney, whom J. G. mentions earlier in this book (p. 52), went mad and was picked up in a raving condition at Ockingham and again later at Reading. *Hat. Cal.*, 17: 607.

[15] Father Greenway was arrested in the streets of London while he was reading a description of himself appended to the Proclamation for his arrest. There were many people about, and he allowed himself to be taken off quietly; but as he was passing down an unfrequented street, he threw off his

of others, as I said before, I had lost my house in London and had not yet made up my mind to leave England. But with all this I managed to rent another house in London, perhaps better suited to my present needs than the old one. I was able to furnish it with everything I wanted and make some good hiding-places in it, and there I was safe during the whole of Lent before I left. In addition to this I rented a second and much larger and finer house which I intended to share with Father Anthony Hoskins. After my departure it was used by the Superior for a considerable time.

About the end of Lent I brought the first of these houses into danger when I attempted to rescue one of our Fathers. It happened like this. The good priest, Father Thomas Everett,[16] had gone to stay at a gentleman's house in London, where he met some traitors or at least men who could not keep their mouths shut. The fact became known to the Council, and as this Father was about my height and had black hair, Cecil thought it was I who had been there. We shall catch him at once now, he said to a friend of his, naming me. But he missed both of us. As soon as I heard that the Father had gone to the house where his presence had not been kept secret, I asked the gentleman who had hidden me in his home before I got my own house to fetch the Father and keep him with him for the present. He did this, and the Father stayed there while the house he had just left was searched from top to bottom. A few days later they searched the house he had moved to, for they had found some of Father Garnet's books there, which the master of the house used to keep for him.† No one was found,

---

captor, escaped into Suffolk, and crossed to the Continent with a cargo of dead pigs.

[16] Cf. above, p. 30.

for Father Everett got away into a hiding-place, but they took off to prison the master and mistress.

I was alarmed when I got this news. There was now no Catholic in the house who knew where the Father was hiding, and I feared he would die of hunger or else come out and be captured. Therefore I sent some men there and described to them the place where the Father was hiding. They called out to him; they knocked on his hiding-place—still he refused to open. Though they said that they had been sent by me to rescue him, he did not answer. Their voices were unfamiliar, and he was afraid it was a ruse of the searchers. They do in fact pretend sometimes to go away, and then return a little later and, feigning a friend's voice, go round the rooms, announce that the searchers have left, and call out to all the people in hiding to come out.

This is what the good Father suspected was happening, and he made no answer. The men I had sent stayed a long time and were forced to return late. In the street they fell into the hands of watchers. That night they were kept in custody, but they were released after some difficulty the next day. One of them was known to have lived once with a Catholic and was therefore suspected of being a Catholic himself. This brought my house under suspicion, as it was now known that he lived there. Ostensibly it had been rented by a schismatic, who was not suspect, but that made no difference now. Four days later the chief magistrate of London, I mean the Mayor, came to search the place with a group of constables. In the meantime I had heard that Father Everett had refused to answer—I knew he was still there and was afraid he would die of hunger. So I sent the men back the following night and with them sent the man who had made the hiding-place and knew how to open it. With very great relief the Father emerged, and they took him to my house, where he stayed.

Meanwhile I had gone to stay with a friend whose house was very safe—he was afraid the arrest of the men I had sent to rescue the Father might set the searchers on my house. And three nights later this happened. It was Maundy Thursday.[17] Father Everett was saying Mass and had just finished the Offertory when there was an uproarious mob at the garden gate. The Mayor was violent, and he was so quick that he was through the garden and into the house and on his way upstairs just as the Father with his vestments on and altar things bundled under his arm got away into his hiding-place. It was so close that the Mayor and men with him smelt the smoke of the snuffed candles. Certain they had come on a priest, they searched more carefully. But they did not find even one of the three hiding-places. All those who were not hiding and who confessed themselves Catholics were taken off, and the schismatic with them, for he was thought to be the householder. Once again I arranged to have Father Everett rescued from his prison of a hiding-place. I advised him to leave London and decided not to use the house again for some time, since it was now known as a Catholic house.

Seeing it was a time for lying quiet, not for working, I determined to take the first chance I got to cross the Channel and come over here.

Commending my friends to different Fathers, I asked them to have a special care of them in my absence. As for my hostess, she had been brought to London when they made that prolonged search for me at her house. Closely examined about me before the Council, she answered all their

[17] April 17, 1606.

questions blamelessly.† In the end they produced a letter
which she had written to one of her relatives, asking him
to procure the release of Father Strange and the other Father
I mentioned earlier. This gentleman was the most important man in the county where they had been captured,[18]
and she thought that through this letter she would be able
to have them released. But this faithless man, who had so
often declared that he was ready to do her any service she
asked, proved once more the truth of the prophet: "A man's
enemies are those of his own household." He forwarded
her letter to the Council.

Holding up this letter for her to see, they said,

"Don't you realize you are wholly at the King's mercy
for life or for death? Your life is yours if you will tell us
where Father Gerard is."

"I don't know," she answered, "and even if I did, I would
not tell you."

Then a lord of the Council[19] who at one time had been
friendly to her on many occasions rose and courteously accompanied her to the door. On the way he said persuasively,

"Have a little pity on yourself and your children and tell
them what they wish to know. If you don't you will have
to die."

In a loud voice she answered:

"Then I would rather die, my lord."

As she spoke, the door was opened, and her servants waiting outside heard her.† They all burst into tears. They had
said this merely to frighten her, for they did not even put
her in prison on that occasion. Instead, they sent her to a

[18] Sir Richard Verney, Sheriff of Warwickshire, was uncle to Sir George
Simeon, who had married Mrs. Vaux's daughter in the previous year.†
[19] Probably the Earl of Northampton.

gentleman's house in the city,† and after some time in custody here they let her free on condition that she stayed in London. One of the leading lords of the Council admitted to a friend that there was nothing against her except the fact that she was a staunch Papist and surpassed others in the evils she instigated.

I was in London still. And as soon as she was released from custody, quite oblivious of herself, she wanted to look after me. Every day she sent me news by letter. She got all I needed for my house, and when she heard that I wanted to go abroad for a time she insisted that I should spare no expense that was necessary to ensure my safety. She would gladly pay for it even if it cost five thousand florins. And in fact she gave me a thousand florins for the journey.

I left her in the care of Father Percy, who had already lived a long time with me in her house. He is still there doing much good, and I am sure he will go on doing good. I went straight to Rome and was then sent back to these parts and was stationed at Louvain. You can hear about what happened to me and about the work of the other Fathers in the *Annual Letters*.†

Twice on the third of May, the day on which Father Garnet went to heaven, I received signal favors, which I believe were due to his intercession. The first was this. When I arrived by arrangement at the port from which I was to pass out of England with certain high officials, they took fright and said they could not stand by their promise. Right up to the time I was due to embark with them they refused to let me come. Then, just at that moment, Father Garnet was received into heaven and did not forget me on earth. Suddenly they changed their minds. The ambassador came personally to fetch me and helped me himself to dress in the livery of his attendants so that I could pass for one of them and escape.† I did escape, and in my own mind I have no doubt that I owed it to Father Garnet's prayers.

The second and greater favor is that three years later, again on the third of May, I was admitted, unworthy as I am, into the body of the Society by the four vows. This I regard as by far the greatest favor I have ever received, and it seemed that God wanted to show me that I owed this also to Father Garnet's prayers, for there was a strange similarity in the circumstances of my profession and of his martyrdom. The day originally fixed for both was the first of May, the feast of the Holy Apostles Saint Philip and Saint James, and in both cases unforeseen delays postponed the event until the third of May.†

God grant that I may always love and dutifully carry the Cross of Christ and walk worthily of the vocation to which I am called. "One thing have I asked of the Lord, and this shall I always ask, that I may live in the house of God all my days." Yes, till I prove myself grateful for the favors I have received. Hitherto I have been a sterile plant. I pray that at last I may begin to bear some fruit by virtue of the olive tree to which I have been grafted.

NOTES

1. EARLY LIFE

PAGE 1 *in Derbyshire.* On the occasion of James I conferring a knighthood on his elder brother, Thomas, at York in 1603, J. G. wrote, "That was to him no advancement whose ancestors had been so for sixteen generations" (Morris, 1). The family came originally from Kingsley, Cheshire, and between 1330 and 1340 entered into the possession of Bryn, J. G.'s ancestral home about five miles south of Wigan, when Joan, heiress of Thomas de Burnull, married William Gerard of Kingsley. A description of Bryn Hall, as it stood in ruins about 150 years ago, is given in Barnes' *History of Lancashire* (3:639). It was probably not here but at Etwall, Derbyshire, the house of his mother, Elizabeth Port, heiress of Sir John Port, that J. G. was born on October 4, 1564. His father, Sir Thomas Gerard, had been knighted in 1553 and was Sheriff of Lancashire in 1558. Like his son John, he appears to have been an adventurous and romantic character. The enterprise to rescue Mary, Queen of Scots, when she was imprisoned at Tutbury, Staffordshire, a few miles from Etwall, and take her to the Isle of Man is the subject of many papers in the Hatfield MSS. The beginnings of the plot can be traced to the year 1569, when J. G. was five years old, though it was not till 1571 that his father was imprisoned in the Tower. On his release in 1573 (Acts of the Privy Council, May 29, 1573) Sir Thomas Gerard took his children back to Bryn (*Hat. Cal.*, 1:595). The price he paid for freedom was the enforced sale of his manor of Bromley to his cousin Sir Gilbert Gerard, the Attorney-General. From August 1586 to October 1588 Sir Thomas was again imprisoned for supposed complicity in the Babington Plot, and on his release he seems to have given up the practice of his faith, though he returned to it before his death in 1601. The family thereafter remained staunchly Catholic and loyal to the Stuart cause. At York James I, on his way to London in 1603, expressed his gratitude to J. G.'s brother, Thomas, for the family's loyalty to his mother. "I am particularly bound", he said, "to love your blood on account of the persecution you have borne for me." For the history of the family, see Morris, passim; *Victoria County History of Lancaster*, vol. 4, 143–46; J. S. Leatherbarrow, *Lancashire Elizabethan Recusants* (Chetham Society, 1947) vol. 110; *Lancashire Register C.R.S.*, vol. 36, passim.

PAGE 1 *as he did before*. Edmund Lewknor, a Chichester man, took his BA from Saint John's, Cambridge, and became a Fellow of Exeter College, Oxford in 1566. He resigned his fellowship on November 26, 1577. Cf. "The Chronology of Gerard's Early Years", Appendix A, 336.

PAGE 2 *sent for by his Superiors*. William Sutton entered the Society in Paris on March 26, 1582. Cobham, Walsingham's agent in Paris, noted his arrival there in a dispatch on March 12. "He is of tall stature, somewhat redfaced, about twenty-five years old [probably he was about thirty at the time], newly apparelled at the cost of the Papists in Paris in a long black cloak faced with velvet, a black 'rashe' doublet, and pair of black 'venetians' with black stockings." *C.S.P. Foreign* (1581–82), 551.

PAGE 2 *then living at Rheims*. This was probably "a noble youth called Lovel". He arrived at Rheims on July 9, 1579, and left to study in Paris on October 9 the same year. T. F. Knox, *Douai Diaries*, 155, 157.

PAGE 3 *Father Thomas Darbyshire.* A nephew of Bishop Bonner, he received rapid ecclesiastical promotion under Mary Tudor and at the time of her death was Dean of Saint Paul's and Chancellor of the diocese of London. On the accession of Elizabeth he was deprived of his benefices and became one of the earliest English Jesuits, entering the Society in Rome on May 1, 1563. Probably he was considered too old to return to England with Persons and Campion. For the most part he was stationed at Paris, where many English Catholics, including Southwell and J. G., came under his influence. His time was divided between teaching poor children their catechism and giving theological lectures at the Sorbonne, where, as Anthony à Wood says, "he taught with great concourse and approbation of the most learned men in that city". He died at Pont-à-Mousson on April 6, 1604. Foley, 3:703ff.

PAGE 3 *the credit for it.* Father Persons was in Rouen in the autumn of 1581. *The Christian Directory* was published in the following year and was Persons' most popular book. It was read by Catholics and Protestants alike and had the largest sale of any English devotional work at that time. In order to counteract its influence a well-known divine, Edmund Bunny, brought out in 1584 a Protestant edition of Persons' treatise purged "of its corruptions and errors". Before 1600 at least twelve Protestant editions had been issued. That to which J. G. refers is Bunny's edition of 1609. *The Christian Directory* remained the favorite book of devotion among English Protestants until the publication of Baxter's *Saints' Everlasting Rest* and Jeremy Taylor's *Holy Dying*. Cf. H. Thurston, "Catholic Writers and Elizabethan Readers", *The Month* (December 1894).

PAGE 3n. *for his journey home.* In the course of a long dispatch dated March 28 Cobham wrote to Walsingham, "They tell me that Sir Thomas Jarret has a son living in the Jesuits' college here. His father's man brought him some relief the other day." *C.S.P. Foreign* (1581–1582), 585.

PAGE 3n. *put in to Dover*. The spy was Thomas Dodwell. In an undated report to the Government he explains how "Raindall, the searcher of Gravesend, receiveth money of passengers, suffering them to pass without searching. I myself escaped twice in this manner [having in company] Hunt, who is now in the Marshalsea, Sir Thomas Gerrat's Kt. second son [J. G.], Berington, Alfield, Pansfoote, son and heir of Mr. Pansfoote of Gloucestershire." Foley, 6:726, quoting *S.P.D.*, vol. 168, no. 35.

PAGE 4 *the previous occasion*. Probably his kinsman, Sir Gilbert Gerard of Bromley, Staffordshire, who was at that time Master of the Rolls. *D.N.B.*, 21: 218.

PAGE 4 *my maternal uncle, a Protestant*. As his mother had no brothers J. G. is probably referring to the husband of one of her sisters. This was most likely George Hastings, who succeeded his brother as fourth Earl of Huntingdon in 1595. He had married Dorothy, sister of Elizabeth Port, J. G.'s mother. His brother, the third Earl, was President of the Council of the North and a fierce persecutor of Catholics.

PAGE 5n. *in the Marshalsea*. This description of the Marshalsea is from a letter of Bishop Aylmer to Burghley dated December 5, 1583 (British Museum, *Lansdowne* MSS 38, no. 87). Aylmer confirms J. G.'s statement about Mass. "Those wretched priests", he writes, ". . . do commonly say Mass in the prison." Seventeen of the prisoners were priests, of whom Hartley, Stephen Rowsham, and John Adams were later executed, while a fourth, Thomas Crowther, died in prison. Morris, 20.

PAGE 6n. *Bartholomew Temple*. In 1585 Richard Shelley, a Catholic layman, presented the Queen with a petition for the relief of Catholics as she was walking one day in her park at Greenwich. He was arrested and examined, and in answer to the question, "Who they be that have been famined in prison", Shelley's reply is recorded in Burghley's hand: "Temple, he said, was famined in Bridewell." British Museum, *Lansdowne* 45, no. 76, fol. 178.

PAGE 6n. *Oxford musician*. Arrested with Edmund Campion at Lydford Grange in July 1581, he was in the Marshalsea when J. G. was sent there in 1583. Later he was transferred to Bridewell. As he cannot be traced after J. G.'s visit, he may have died there from ill treatment. R. Simpson, *Edmund Campion*, 246; *C.R.S.*, vol. 2, 233.

PAGE 6 Agnus Deis. Discs of wax impressed with a cross and the figure of a lamb and blessed by the Pope. The *Agnus Dei* is usually worn like a medal round the neck. In origin it goes back probably to the fifth century and symbolizes Christ, the Lamb of the New Testament. The cross associated with the lamb suggests that its purpose was to protect those who wore it from evil influences as the blood of the paschal lamb protected households of the Jews from the destroying angel. Cf. *Catholic Encyclopedia* (revised edition), 200.

PAGE 6 *pretended to be a Catholic*. This was the same spy, Dodwell. In a report, written probably in February 1594, he refers to the periodic searches mentioned by J. G.: "There are there four seminary priests in one chamber ... and yet notwithstanding their often searching, they have such privy places to hide their Massing trumpery, that hardly it can be found; that they have to themselves often Mass. And now because Sir George Carey [the Knight Marshal] and his servants have so often taken from them their silver chalices, they have provided a chalice of tin." Foley, 6:726, quoting *S.P.D.*, vol. 168, no. 35.

PAGE 7n. *Easter 1585, not 1586.* Cf. deposition of Anne Smith, taken March 12, 1598, but referring to events in 1586, in Samuel Harnett's *A Declaration of Egregious Popish Impostures* (1603), 244. "Upon Wednesday in Whitsunweek [May 25, 1586], whilst she was at Denham [the home of Mrs. Peckham, J. G.'s sister], there came thither maister Salisbury that was executed [Thomas Salisbury executed September 21, 1586] Ma John Gerard and Ma George Peckham." J. G. probably escaped at the end of May or early June. There are records of the sureties to which he refers in the *S.P.D.*, e.g., the fifth renewal. "31st Octob. 1585. John Gerard [*sic*] of Brinne in the county of Lincoln [*sic*], gentleman, to return to the Marshalsea, prisoner, within three months." Morris, 23.

PAGE 7 *Queen of Scots.* Anthony Babington was executed on September 20, 1596, about six weeks after J. G. had arrived in Rome. Father Weston, whom J. G. mentions later in the narrative, describes him as "attractive in face and form, quick in intelligence, agreeable and facetious; he had a turn for literature unusual among men of the world". At the time of his execution he was only twenty-five. J. H. Pollen, *Mary Stuart and the Babington Plot* (Scottish Historical Society, 3rd Series), vol. 3, 106.

PAGE 7 *Father William Holt.* A native of Ashworth, in Lancashire, he was sent to England in 1581 to continue the work begun by Persons and Campion. Like J. G.'s father he was an ardent supporter of Mary Stuart. At the time J. G. met him in Paris, he had just returned from Scotland and was on his way to Rome to take charge of the English College. He died in Spain in 1599. *D.N.B.*, 27:208–9.

PAGE 8 *Father Aquaviva.* One of the most able Generals of the Society. Elected February 19, 1581, he died on January 31, 1615. He showed great interest in England and relied chiefly on Father Persons both in English affairs and in the solution of the Spanish troubles in the Society. Persons, through his influence with Philip II, was able to induce the King to support Aquaviva and not place the Society under the Inquisition. Pastor, *History of the Popes*, vols. 21–24.

2. LANDING

PAGE 10 *had charge of the College.* A school for the sons of English Catholics had been founded at Eu by Father Persons in 1582 and entrusted to a secular priest called Mann or Chambers. "Our Fathers there", in J. G.'s narrative, refers to the Jesuits of the French Province who also had their own school in the town. J. G. makes it clear that Saint Omers, the predecessor of the present Stonyhurst College, was a distinct foundation from Eu. As J. G. stayed at Douai from September 21–26 he probably arrived at Eu at the end of that month. Cf. L. Hicks, *Letters and Memorials of Father Robert Persons*, *C.R.S.*, vol. 39, 1; T. F. Knox, *Douai Diaries*, 220.

PAGE 10 *that same year.* The Earl of Leicester died on September 4, 1588, at his house at Cornbury, Oxon, on the way from London to Kenilworth. Poisoning was suspected.

PAGE 17 *I saw the inn.* Jessop thinks that J. G. crossed the River Yare at Hellesdon and circuited the city until he came to one of the main roads from London; and that, in order to avoid the long street up from Saint Stephen's gates, he rode round the common land outside the walls and entered by the "Brazen Doors". This reconstruction is almost certain. Jessop also gives reasons for thinking that Stalham or Sloley was probably the place where J. G. lodged a night at an inn and Worstead the village where he was arrested. Jessop, 134–36, 148.

PAGE 17 *seven years before.* Robert de Grey of Merton, ancestor of the present Lord Walsingham, was in Norwich Jail at this time. His "relative" would have been John de Grey, who was committed to the Marshalsea in January 1577 and was still there when J. G. was committed in March 1583. His name disappears from the lists after September 1588. Jessop, 149; *C.R.S.*, vol. 2, 232, 283.

PAGE 18 *Catholic gentlemen there.* The names of the principal Catholic prisoners in Norwich Jail are given by Jessop. Shortly before J. G.'s arrival the Council had ordered these men to be removed to Wisbeach because "they do much harm and infect the country by the liberty they enjoy there". However, the order was not carried out until April 1590. Jessop, 148.

PAGE 19 *kept house for them.* Edward Yelverton was the oldest son of William Yelverton of Rougham by his second wife, Jane, daughter of Edmund Cocket of Hempton, Co. Suffolk. At his father's death he had inherited an estate in Grimston, extending between two and three thousand acres. Here, according to the fashion of the time, he kept open house and lived with his own family as well as with his younger brother, a sister who had been left a widow and acted as his housekeeper, and a brother-in-law, who cannot be identified. He was about thirty at the time J. G. met him and a widower. Jessop, 137, 150.

PAGE 19 *as Father Southwell used to complain.* Southwell, however, made frequent use of images drawn from falconry in his writings, e.g., "Yet sith the copies thereof flew so fast, and false abroad, that it was in danger to come corrupted to the print; it seemed a lesse evill to let it flie to common view in the native plume, and with the own wings, than disguised in a coat of bastard feather, or cast off from the fist of such a corrector, as might happily have perished the sound, and stuck in some sick and sorry feathers of his own phansies." *Mary Magdalen's Funerall Teares*, Epistle to the Reader.

3. GRIMSTON

PAGE 21 *Father Edmund Weston.* Born at Maidstone in 1550, he entered the Society in 1575 and arrived in England on September 20, 1584, when there was not a single Jesuit at liberty. He received Philip Howard, Earl of Arundel, into the Church. Captured in August 1586, he remained a prisoner until he was exiled in 1615. His missionary life, written by himself, is printed in *Troubles*, vol. 2, and the continuation in the *C.R.S.*, vol. 1.

PAGE 23n. *the most notorious turncoat of his day.* He was known as "Andrew Ambo", "Old Father Palinode", and it was said that the letters "A.P.A.P." on the weathercock of Saint Peter's church might be interpreted as either Andrew Perne a Papist or Andrew Perne a Protestant or Andrew Perne a Puritan. His name became proverbial so that "if one have a coat or cloak that is turned they say that it is Pearned". Edward Yelverton, Henry and Edward Walpole, and others mentioned in J. G.'s narrative were at Peterhouse while Perne was Master. Cooper, *Athen. Cantab.*, vol. 2, 45–50.

PAGE 24 *profession of the faith*. This sister, Jane Lumner, had been very scantily provided for by her husband, who died in debt. She continued an "obstinate recusant" in the lists of Presentments returned annually to the Bishop of Norwich. The last appearance of her name is in 1615. During this time she changed her residence several times, and it seems that she became steadily poorer as a result of the exactions levied on her. Jessop, 151.

PAGE 25 *the beginning of Elizabeth's reign*. In "A Note of the papists and recusants in the several shires of England" compiled in the year J. G. landed (1588), two "old priests" are named as living in Norfolk, Fisher, and Hall, *alias* Fox. *C.R.S.*, vol. 22, 127.

PAGE 26 *much to suffer for it since*. J. G. leaves it to be inferred that Sir Philip Wodehouse's conversion had not turned out to be as complete as he first thought. He knew that he had given up the faith, but he had not heard that his wife had done so as well. In the statement of his early career which he made on entering the English College, Rome, in 1601, Charles Yelverton says that his aunt, the "wife of Sir Philip Wodehouse ... , on account of the madness of her husband, which very frequently broke out against her, has lately fallen from the Church". Foley, 1:143.

PAGE 26 *same or higher social standing*. Jessop, who made a careful examination of J. G.'s apostolic work in Norfolk, comments that J. G. "has not one whit overstated his remarkable success, and evidently too this was but the beginning of his labours". Jessop, 209.

PAGE 27 *enterprise and ability*. Edward Walpole entered the English College, Rome, on October 23, 1590, some months after his cousin Michael. He was a missioner in England for forty years and died in London on November 3, 1637. For the lives of both these priests, see Jessop, passim.

4. LAWSHALL

PAGE 30 *holds the office*. This was probably William Hanse, brother of Father Everard Hanse, who was executed at Tyburn for his priesthood on July 31, 1581. There is a "Draiton *alias* Hanse in Suffolk" in the list of "papists and recusants in the several shires of England" (1588), who is probably the William Hanse who was one of the Archpriest's Assistants. *C.R.S.*, vol. 22, 127; Camden Society, *Archpriest Controversy*, vol. 1, 206.

PAGE 30n. *the first convent of English Carmelites*. This convent is now at Lanherne, Cornwall. Mary Lady Lovel, the founder, was the daughter of John, first Lord Teynham and widow of Sir Nicholas Lovel. Peter Guilday, *English Catholic Refugees on the Continent*, 360.

PAGE 30n. *Anthony Rowse, the apostate priest*. He arrived at Douai on September 12, 1591, and was ordained there with Father Thomas Everett on May 21, 1592. On his return to England he worked well for several years, but apostatized through fear of persecution in 1605. In 1608 he betrayed Father Henry Garnet's nephew, Father Thomas Garnet, who was executed at Tyburn on June 23, that year. Later he had thoughts of repentance and a Jesuit who was related to him (probably Father Everett) took the risk of visiting him in order to reconcile him to the Church. In 1613 he crossed to Belgium and was given hospitality at the house of the English Jesuits at Louvain, where J. G. was Rector. R. Belvederi, *Bentivoglio Diplomatico*, vol. 2, 282–83.

PAGE 31 *the whole of the first "week".* The Spiritual Exercises are planned to occupy an entire month and the meditations are divided into four "weeks". In the first week the purpose of creation, sin, and hell are considered, in the second the ministry, in the third the Passion, and in the fourth the risen life of Our Lord.

PAGE 32 *beginning to grow in England.* When J. G. first landed in 1588 there were, as he says (21), only four other Jesuits in the country. By 1606, the year he left England, the number had risen to forty-five. In 1614 it reached fifty-nine and in 1620 a hundred and five. In 1632 the number of English Jesuits at home and abroad stood at three hundred and forty-four. Cf. Foley, passim.

PAGE 32 *where his own admirable books were produced.* This "private house", where Southwell had his printing press, probably adjoined Arundel House in the Strand, where the Countess of Arundel lived during the imprisonment of her husband in the Tower. Cf. Christopher Devlin, "Southwell and the Mar-Prelates", *The Month* (February 1948).

PAGE 32n. *labouring under persecution.* Cf. Father Thomas Hunter's MS volume at Stonyhurst, entitled *A Modest Defence of the Clergy and Religious.* The finances of the struggling mission are discussed by Father L. Hicks in a note to *The Letters of Thomas Fitzherbert, 1608–1610 (C.R.S.,* vol. 41, 131–33). In these early days there was a generous spirit of co-operation and both J. G. and Father Garnet assisted all priests who appealed to them for help. In the ten years he had been on the mission, wrote Garnet in a private letter to the General in 1596, there was scarcely one priest entering England whom he had not supported until he could be placed. As the alms received did not cover expenses, Garnet was allowed to spend the patrimony of some of his subjects on the support of the English clergy. At this time Doctor Barrett, President of Douai, declared that he had received more money from Garnet and Southwell than from all the secular priests in England; and Garnet himself, when accused of avarice, offered to exchange what money the Society had in England for that possessed by any single priest chosen by lot from many.

PAGE 33 *all who knew him.* The younger brother, John Wiseman, died as a novice in 1592 at the age of twenty-one; the elder brother, Thomas, died at Saint Omers on August 11, 1596, at the age of twenty-four. Foley, 7, part 2, 853–54.

PAGE 33 *a heavy loss to his country.* Christopher Walpole matriculated as pensioner of Caius College on December 8, 1587, and entered the English College, Rome, on February 2, 1592. He died at Valladolid in 1606. Foley, 6:188.

PAGE 34n. *Saffron Walden, Essex.* Built about 1560 on a half-H plan, facing east. All that remains of it to-day is the north wing, which is now a farmhouse. *Royal Commission Hist. Monuments* (Essex N.W.), 353–54.

PAGE 34 *sought their lives*. The reference is to the Appellant Controversy, which caused dissensions in the recusant body and, as it gathered strength, did more to ruin the Catholic cause than all the persecution. Cf. Father L. Hicks, *The Letters of Thomas Fitzherbert, C.R.S.*, vol. 41.

PAGE 35 De Bono Statu Religiosi. The author, Jerome Platus or Piatti, was novice master at Sant'Andrea when J. G. began his noviceship there in 1588. The book was first published in the following year, and until it was superseded by Alphonso Rodriguez's *Christian Perfection*, it was the standard book for the instruction of novices in the principles of the religious life.

PAGE 36 *leave him at his house*. Henry Drury entered the Society as a Brother and died at Antwerp on September 10, 1593. Arch. S.J., Rome, *Germ*. 171, fol. 273.

PAGE 37n. *Jane and Bridget Wiseman*. Both entered the Flemish convent of Canonesses of Saint Augustine in the "Half-street", Louvain. In 1606 there were twenty-two English nuns in this convent under an English Prioress, Mother Margaret Clement, the daughter of John Clement and Margaret Griggs. In 1609 Jane Wiseman, with J. G.'s assistance, founded an English convent of the Order, Saint Monica's, in Louvain and governed it for twenty-four years. Of all the English convents Saint Monica's was the most intensely loyal to the house of Stuart, and in its list of professed nuns nearly every Catholic family prominent in the Jacobite cause is represented. The church belonging to the convent was said to be one of the finest in the city. When the French invaded the Netherlands in 1794, the community came to England and is now established at Newton Abbot. Peter Guilday, *English Catholic Refugees*, 282–85.

5. BRADDOCKS

PAGE 40n. *Henry Huddlestone of Sawston, near Cambridge.* From J. G.'s time to the present-day Sawston, about five miles south of Cambridge, has remained a Catholic center. Henry Huddlestone married Dorothy, daughter of Robert, first Lord Dormer. Her cousinship with the Duke of Feria was by affinity and half-blood. Morris, 97.

PAGE 40n. *Richard Rookwood of Coldham, near Bury Saint Edmunds.* Coldham, five and a half miles south-east of Bury Saint Edmunds, was another Catholic center established by J. G., which continued through penal times. The Rookwoods were among the first boys at Saint Omers school. Henry Walpole, who passed through Saint Omers on November 13, 1593, stated in his examination that "at Saint Omers there . . . be also three or four Rookwood, brethren and four Mallets, *alias* Ilesleys, which were lately come over". *C.R.S.*, vol. 5, 262.

PAGE 41 *would never have confided in me.* She was two years in Belgium before she entered religion, for she was professed at the Flemish convent of Saint Ursula's, Louvain, with Bridget Wiseman and Margaret Garnet, Father Garnet's sister, on June 5, 1595. She died in 1607 "very sweetly as she had lived, for she was a mild and virtuous soul, sweet and affable in her conversation, and beloved of all the sisters". Adam Hamilton, *Chronicle of Saint Monica's Convent,* vol. 1, 23.

PAGE 41n. *Ambrose Rookwood.* He was executed at the time of the Gunpowder Plot. "But that which moved them [the

conspirators] specially to make choice of Mr. Rooke-
wood", writes J. G. in his *Narrative of the Gunpowder Plot*,
"was, I suppose, not so much to have his help by his living
as by his person, and some provision of horses, of which he
had divers of the best: but for himself, he was known to be
of great virtue and no less valour and very secret. He was
also of very good parts otherwise as for wit and learning,
having spent [much] of his youth in study. He was at this
time [1606], as I take it, not past twenty-six or twenty-
seven years old and had married a gentlewoman of a great
family, a virtuous Catholic also, by whom he had divers
young children." He was executed in the Old Palace Yard,
Westminster, on January 31, 1606. *Narrative*, 85–86.

PAGE 41 *a great friend of our Fathers.* He is described by the
spy Gee in 1624 as "a little black fellow, very compt and
gallant, lodging about the midst of Drury Lane, acquainted
with collapsed ladies". Foley, 1:676.

PAGE 41n. *the most celebrated beauty of her day.* Penelope was
the daughter of Walter Devereux, first Earl of Essex, and
was forcibly and unhappily married to Robert, third Lord
Rich, later Earl of Warwick. Sir Philip Sidney, in one of
his sonnets addressed to his "Stella", refers to the marriage
in a play on her married name—she had "no misfortune
but that *Rich* she is". She was a neighbor of the Wisemans,
and the families were connected by marriage. When Mrs.
Wiseman's house at Northend, Essex, was raided, the widow
rode over to Lord Rich's house at Leighs, in the same county.
Penelope Rich became Lord Mountjoy's mistress shortly
before J. G. met her and had three daughters and two sons
by him. She died about twelve months after Mountjoy.
D.N.B., 58:120.

PAGE 42n. *Charles Blount, eighth Lord Mountjoy*. In 1603 he was created Earl of Devonshire, and on December 25, 1605, he married Lady Rich after the divorce and in the lifetime of her husband. He died of pneumonia, not, as J. G. says, of a broken heart, a few months later, on April 3, 1606. As the marriage was in defiance of the recently enacted canons of 1604, it gave great offense to the King and retarded the promotion of William Laud, who, as the Earl's chaplain, performed the marriage in his home at Wanstead. Fynes Moryson, Mountjoy's secretary (1600–1602), described Mountjoy as a man "of stature tall, and of very comely proportion; his hair was of colour blackish. His forehead was broad and high; his eyes great, black and lovely; his nose something low and short and a little blunt in the end; his cheeks full, round and ruddy; his countenance cheerful". *The Complete Peerage*, vol. 9, 346.

6. BADDESLEY CLINTON

PAGE 49 *where she is living now*. "The Lady Mary Percy, daughter to the great earl of Northumberland, with many other persons of quality, leaving their own country retired into Flanders, living there at Brussells in much retreat and devotion; they began to think of leading a religious life, and erecting a monastery. And conferring these their good desires with very reverend Father Holt of the Society of Jesus, and by his advice, they soon resolved upon this great work; and to undertake Saint Benedict his Rule and holy Order, which, of all others, had heretofore most flourished in that now heretical kingdom, confiding it might happily in future times be again a fit reception for them." *Annals of the English Benedictine Nuns* (*C.R.S.*, vol. 6, 2). This was the first English convent founded after the Reformation. In 1794 the community was transferred to Winchester, thence in 1857 to East Bergholt, and finally in 1863 to Teignmouth.

PAGE 49 *a great help to the others.* In a letter of March 8, 1590, Father Southwell describes an earlier meeting of this kind. "We have altogether, with much comfort, renewed the vows.... *Aperuimus ora et attraximus spiritum.* It seems to me that I see the beginnings of a religious life set foot in England, of which we now sow the seeds with tears that others here- after may with joy carry in the sheaves to the heavenly granaries. We have sung the canticles of the Lord in a strange land and in the desert we have sucked honey from the rock and oil from the hard stones. But these our joys ended in sorrow, and sudden fears dispersed us into different places; but in fine, we were more afraid than hurt, for we all escaped." R. Challoner, *Memoirs of Missionary Priests*, 213–14.

PAGE 52n. *account of this search.* Father Garnet gives a more detailed account of this search in a long Latin letter to the General, Father Aquaviva, dated November 19, 1594. He tells how at the moment the pursuivants arrived everything was being got ready for the departure of the priests. "The horses were being cared for ... the men servants and maids were busy in various ways ... some getting breakfast ready, others cleaning the boots, others putting out our cloaks and requirements for our journey." Then a youth going out of the house caught sight of a person unknown to him and, hastily locking the door behind him, took to his heels. Mean- while two Catholic servants got wind of what was up and came running down from the stables armed with farm imple- ments. They threatened the officers, who now politely asked admittance. Meanwhile from inside the door, already locked, was barred. When everything was hidden away, the officers were admitted. With great skill Miss Vaux kept the search party from looking in the stable where they would have found all the horses ready for the priests' departure. At the end of the search the priests came out of hiding and all said Mass. The account occupies some twenty-five hundred words, about a quarter of the whole letter. Stonyhurst MSS, *Anglia*, vol. I, no. 73.

7. FATHER OLDCORNE

PAGE 53n. *Thomas Habington of Hinlip House, Worcestershire.* At the time of the Babington Plot (1586) his brother was executed and he was imprisoned in the Tower. In 1593 he was allowed to return to his house at Hinlip, and in his forced retirement he devoted himself to antiquarianism and became a pioneer in scientific county history. His son, William Habington, attained distinction as a poet in the reign of Charles I. Thomas died on October 8, 1647, at the age of eighty-seven. There are portraits of him and his wife [see 53] in Nash's *History of Worcestershire*, vol. 1, which is largely based on the MS materials collected by him. Wood, *Athen. Ox.*, vol. 3, 222–25, *D.N.B.*, 23:414–15.

PAGE 53 *perfect as a Catholic center.* The position of Hinlip House on a hill three miles north-east of Worcester and commanding a wide extent of country made it an ideal refuge for priests. The house, which no longer stands, was said to have had eleven secret chambers, hidden behind the wainscots of rooms and built in the form of false chimneys. It was here that Father Garnet and Father Oldcorne were captured after being forced out of their hiding-places by bad air.

PAGE 54 *Father Thomas Lister.* He took a doctorate at Pont-à-Mousson in 1592 and came to England in 1596. Arrested at the time of the Gunpowder Plot and banished in 1606, he returned to England a short time later and died there about 1626. Foley, 7, part 1, 462.

PAGE 56 *when it is plucked.* Thomas Pennant comments on this moss. "Some eminent botanists of my acquaintance have reduced the sweet moss, and the bloodly stains to mere vegetable productions, far from being peculiar to our fountain. The first is that kind of moss called *Jungermannia asplenioides*, Fl. Angl. 509, imperfectly described and figured by Dillenius in his history of mosses. This species is also found in another holy well in Caernarvonshire, called *Ffynnon Llanddeinioen*, in a parish of the same name. The other is a Byssus, likewise odoriferous: common to *Lapland*, and to other countries beside our own. Linnaeus ... says the stone to which it adheres easily betrays itself by the color, being as if smeared with blood; and if rubbed, yields a smell like violets." Thomas Pennant, *Tour in Wales* (1810), 53–54.

PAGE 58 *Mr. John Lee.* His name occurs frequently in the letters of J. G., written after his escape from England. J. G. entrusted him with much financial business connected with the English mission. Stonyhurst MSS *Anglia*, passim.

PAGE 59 *Father John Bolt.* He was born about 1563 and quickly won a high reputation for musical talent and was summoned to court. When he left court in order to become a Catholic, Elizabeth was so displeased that she soundly rated her Master of Music and threatened to throw "her pantoufle at his head for looking no better unto him". She even went to the length of offering to overlook his conversion and allow him to remain a Catholic if he would return to court. Bolt, however, preferred to live by teaching music in Catholic families where he could practice his religion. In this way he resided with Sir John Petre at Thorndon in Essex, with Richard Verney at Compton in Warwickshire and with others, finally being domiciled with the Wisemans at Braddocks. When he was arrested in March 1594, Topcliffe threatened to torture him, but through the intercession of Lady Penelope Rich, who had known him at court, he was released and withdrew to the Continent. After some years at the English School at Saint Omers he went to the Convent of English Benedictine nuns at Brussels "to help their music which hath been so famous". He tried his vocation as a Benedictine monk, but finding that this life was not suitable for him he went to Douai College, where he was ordained priest in 1605. Some years after, he resided in the diocese of Cambrai. On a visit to Louvain in 1613 he was persuaded by Jane Wiseman, then Prioress of Saint Monica's Convent, to accept the post of Organist and Chaplain to the Convent. There he passed the remainder of his life, dying on August 3, 1640. *C.R.S.*, vol. 3, 31; Grove, *Dictionary of Music and Musicians*, vol. 1, 359.

PAGE 60 *with the forefinger.* The relics mentioned thus far are all preserved at Stonyhurst; the rest have been lost. With the reliquary containing Robert Sutton's thumb (not, as J. G. thought, his forefinger) is a paper in J. G.'s hand giving the same account of the relic. In a list of martyrs which he drew up in 1594 J. G. repeats these details and adds, "Of this man it is constantly reported that he was seen by his keepers to pray in the midst of a light within the prison the night before he suffered." *C.R.S.*, vol. 5, 291.

8. "PEINE FORTE ET DURE"

PAGE 62 *by one of their own household.* This was John Frank. His deposition taken before Young on May 12, 1594, is in the Public Records Office. It was at his house that Jane and Bridget Wiseman, and others whom J. G. sent across to the Continent, stayed on their way through London. *S.P.D.*, vol. 248, no. 103.

PAGE 62 *at his house.* It was "a white house in Lincoln's Inn Fields". On May 3, 1594, after J. G. had been seized, Henry Walpole, his fellow-Jesuit, was examined in the Tower about this house, "but he utterly denieth to disclose the name of the owner of the said house or of the gent, to whom he was directed that lodged in the same house". From a later passage in the same report it is clear that the "gent. to whom he was directed" was J. G. *C.R.S.*, vol. 5, 249–50.

PAGE 63 *to go to London.* J. G.'s memory is at fault. Mrs. Wiseman was not arrested on this occasion. She rode over to the house of her neighbor Lord Rich and was presumably arrested later. *C.S.P.D.* (1595–1597), 504, no. 103.

PAGE 64 *for the same reasons.* Margaret Clitherow, who was crushed to death at York March 26, 1586. Her fame had spread through a life written by her confessor, John Mush, one of the priests she had been condemned to death for sheltering.

PAGE 65 *they would take from her.* Her children, Bridget and Jane, who were nuns at Saint Monica's convent in Louvain, gave the compiler of Saint Monica's Chronicle further information about their mother's life in prison. The story is told there how Topcliffe made her "for a space to lie with a witch in the same room, who was put in prison for her wicked deeds, [but] she never had the power to exercise her necromancy in the room where Mrs. Wiseman was, but was forced to go away into another place". It is also stated there that the Queen on hearing how "for so small a matter she should have been put to death, rebuked the justices of cruelty and said she should not die". Adam Hamilton, *Chronicle of Saint Monica's*, vol. 1, 83.

PAGE 66n. *Golding Lane, Holborn.* An old lane in the parish of Saint Andrew's, Holborn, dating from the thirteenth century. From a survey of the manor of Finsbury made in 1567 and printed in Strype (vol. 4, 120) it appears to have contained good tenements with gardens. It was outside the city boundaries and, like all the houses taken by J. G., with easy access to the open fields. H. A. Harben, *Dictionary of London*, 263.

PAGE 66 *four or five miles from London.* In a letter of March 17, 1594, Father Garnet gives a long description of the house, but apart from saying that it was "outside the walls" he gives no indication of its locality. It was here that he received priests coming from abroad, until the place became known to the authorities. In the garden there was a three-roomed cottage, where he retired "when there was need to write or read something of great importance" or to confer with others, since it was "not allowable to speak in a natural voice inside the house for fear of being heard in the road hard by". Stonyhurst MSS *Anglia*, vol. i, no. 73.

PAGE 67n. *on March 15, 1594.* It was a general and carefully planned search covering the whole of London, and the excuse was the recently discovered plot of the Irishman Cahill to kill the Queen. "Before that tumult of Golden Lane", wrote Father Garnet in an account of this incident, ". . . they had laid a plot of these great stirs, and prepared people's minds by a Proclamation, wherein they commanded straight watches to be made, certain days, in a week, everywhere, for priests and Irishmen", and he adds that there "was such a hurly-burly in London as never was seen in man's memory; no, not when Wyatt was at the gates. . . . That very night there had been there Long John with the little beard [i.e., J. G.] . . . if I had not more importunately stayed him than ever before." Garnet to Persons, September 6, 1594. Stonyhurst MSS Grene's *Collectanea* P., vol. 2, 550.

PAGE 68 *for such a fine work.* Cf. "The examination of William Wiseman", dated March 19, 1594. "He confesseth that a book entitled 'Hieronymi Plati de Societate Jesu de Bono Statu Religiosi' is his own . . . and saith that the said book containeth nothing but true doctrine and that he translated it with his own hand." He was further asked to identify the owner of a breviary which had been seized by the searchers and which presumably belonged to J. G. *S.P.D.*, vol. 248, no. 36.

9. SEARCH AT BRADDOCKS

[*No notes*]

10. ARREST

PAGE 79 *landlord's own house*. As appears from the deposition of the traitor, Frank, it was a house called "Middleton's" in Holborn. This man may have been a sea captain of that name who had a brother "with the enemy" at Antwerp. He was detained for examination by Young in the following August. *C.S.P.D.* (1595–1597), 544.

PAGE 79 *knew me well*. Probably this pursuivant knew J. G. when he was confined in the Marshalsea ten years previously. It was perhaps Newell. About a year later he searched the house of J. G.'s sister, Mrs. Jenison, in Derbyshire. Morris, 2.

PAGE 82 *Fathers sent on this mission*. These instructions were given to Persons and Campion by the General, Father Aquaviva, when they set out from Rome in 1580, and are quoted in part by Richard Simpson in his *Edmund Campion*, 99–100. "They were not to mix themselves up with affairs of state, nor to write to Rome about political matters, nor speak nor allow others to speak in their presence against the Queen, except perhaps in the company of those whose fidelity has been long and steadfast, and even then not without very strong reasons." From 1586, in the instructions given to Father Garnet and all the Jesuit priests, including J. G. who subsequently entered England, the last clause, *except perhaps*, etc., was omitted.

PAGE 83n. *the Counter in the Poultry*. Father Garnet calls this "a very evil prison without comfort". It was made up of "some four houses west of the parish church of Saint

Mildred's", in Bread Street. Stow, *Survey of London* (ed. Thoms), 99, 131.

PAGE 84 *for the blood of Catholics*. In his *Narrative of the Gunpowder Plot* J. G. expresses his admiration for Southwell, who "was delivered over by God's ordinance to encounter hand to hand the cruellest tyrant of all England, Topcliffe, a man most infamous and hateful to all the realm for his bloody and butcherly mind". *Narrative*, 18.

PAGE 84 *deliberately rude to him*. Father Southwell treated Topcliffe in the same way. "Though he readily answered the questions of others, yet if Topcliffe interposed he never deigned him a reply; and when asked the cause of this, he answered: 'Because I have found by experience that the man is not open to reason.'" Henry More, *Historia Provinciae Anglicanae*, lib. 5, no. 15.

11. THE COUNTER IN THE POULTRY

PAGE 88 *who had met or protected us*. The examination of Richard Fulwood, taken from the *S.P.D.*, vol. 248, no. 40, is printed in Morris, 159.

PAGE 89 *His good and best Spirit*. Speaking in particular of "Little John", J. G. in his *Narrative of the Gunpowder Plot* again explains how much priests relied on their servants: "Yea, he might have made it almost an impossible thing for Priests to escape, knowing the residences of most Priests in England, and of all those of the Society, whom he might have taken as partridges in a net, knowing all their secret places which himself had made.... So that as no one did more good than he in assisting the labours of all the Priests that were workmen in that vineyard, so no ten men could have done so much harm as he alone might if he had been so disposed; by which he well knew he might have made himself great in the world, not only by their rewards for so great and extraordinary service, but also by the spoil of Catholics' goods, being so many and so great." *Narrative*, 187.

PAGE 89 *as a priest*. Michael Walpole entered the Society on September 8, 1593, and returned to England at the end of Elizabeth's reign. He became one of the most conspicuous English Jesuits, and was twice imprisoned and twice exiled. In 1609 he published in London an English translation of Boethius' *De Consolatione Philosophiae*, and in the following year, when James I wrote his apology for the new oath of allegiance, he answered it with an *Admonition to English Catholics*. He died in Seville, probably in 1624. Jessop, 299.

PAGE 90 *the best man in the course*. This was probably Edward Lusher. In his letter of September 6, 1594, to Father Persons (Stonyhurst MSS, *Anglia*, vol. 1, no. 81), Father Garnet speaks of "Edward, John's companion who was taken in a garden in the country: but he showed himself nimble, escaped into the house, shut the door and escaped away". There is an Edward Lusher who entered the seminary at Valladolid on September 26, 1608, after two years' study at the school at Saint Omers. He died attending the plague-stricken in London on September 27, 1665. *C.R.S.*, vol. 30, 99.

PAGE 91n. *for harboring priests*. This suit was found at Braddocks. The report on the search notes that "there was a seminary priest [J. G.] in the house which escaped from the Justices, leaving his apparel behind". *C.S.P.D.* (1591–1594), 484.

12. THE CLINK

PAGE 95 *Catholics confined there.* "A Table of Catholic Prisoners", printed in the *C.R.S.*, vol. 2, 286, notes that J. G. was transferred to the Clink in July 1594. From the same source it is possible to compile a list of some of J. G.'s fellow-prisoners, who included for a short time Robert Wiseman. The Clink was so called "from being the prison of the Clink liberty or manor of Southwark, belonging to the bishops of Winchester". E. Brayley, *History of Surrey*, vol. 5, 348.

PAGE 95 *as I have written above.* By September, if not earlier, J. G. was apparently in touch with Father Garnet. In his letter of September 6, 1594, to Father Persons, Garnet wrote, "He [J. G.] hath been very close; but now is removed from the Compter to the Clink, where he may, in time, do much good." And later, on November 19, "The arraignment of the three Jesuits, Southwell, Walpole and Gerard is stayed. Gerard is in the Clink, somewhat free; the other two so close in the Tower that none can hear from them." Stonyhurst MSS, *Anglia*, vol. 1, nos. 81, 82.

PAGE 96 *stood by him.* Ralph Emerson landed in England with Edmund Campion on June 25, 1580. He had been ten years in prison when J. G. met him in the Clink and is described by a spy as "a very slender, brown, little fellow". He died at Saint Omers on March 12, 1604. *S.P.D.*, vol. 173, no. 64.

PAGE 100n. *Old Kent and Peckham Park Roads.* Rigby's fine physique, which the Earl of Rutland commented on, was the cause of intense suffering when he came to be executed.

After he had been cut down by the hangman "he stood upright on his feet like a man a little amazed, till the butchers threw him down. Then coming perfectly to himself, he said aloud and distinctly: 'God forgive you. Jesus, receive my soul.' And immediately another cruel fellow standing by, who was no officer, but a common porter, set his foot upon Mr. Rigby's throat, and so held him that he could speak no more. Others held his arms and legs while the executioner dismembered and bowelled him, and when he felt them pulling out his heart, he was yet so strong that he thrust the men from him who held his arms. At last they cut off his head and quartered him. . . . The people going away complained very much of the barbarity of the execution; and generally all sorts bewailed his death." Challoner, *Memoirs of Missionary Priests*, 244–45.

PAGE 102 *the priest who lodged with him*. He was imprisoned first in the Counter in Wood Street, and probably later transferred to Bridewell, where J. G. would have seen him at the time he visited John Jacob there (cf. p. 6). "William Heigham and Roger Line, gent., they were taken without Bishopsgate at Mass with Blackburn, *alias* Tomson that was hanged. They are in execution for 100 marks apiece." (Recusants in the Counter in Wood Street, *S.P.D.*, vol. 190, no. 3). They were both committed by Sir Francis Walsingham, Roger Line on February 3, 1585, William Heigham on July 30, the same year. (*S.P.D.*, vol. 195, no. 51). The Lines were well-known recusants from Ringwood, Hampshire. *C.R.S.*, vol. 43, 88.

PAGE 102 *went to his younger brother*. When Roger Line was in the Counter in Wood Street, his uncle, Richard Line of Ringwood, was dying. The "property" referred to by J. G. was probably the manor of Laybrook, which passed into the hands of Roger's younger brother, another Richard Line, who died seized of this manor in 1599. *Victoria County History of Hampshire*, vol. 4, 610.

PAGE 106 *when he came to be martyred.* Father Jones was executed at Saint Thomas Waterings on July 12, 1598. In the course of his speech on the scaffold he exculpated Mrs. Wiseman, denying he had received money from her or had said Mass in her cell.

PAGE 107 *Father Curry.* A native of Cornwall, he was ordained March 23, 1577, and arrived in England in January 1590. After working in Kent and Sussex, he came to London about Michaelmas 1593. From his association with Ralph Sherwin, John Cornelius, and others, he became known as "the friend of martyrs". Foley, 1:397.

PAGE 107 *would confess anything.* J. G.'s tribute is confirmed by a letter of Mr. Richard Young, an Essex magistrate, to the Privy Council. Young gives the names of seven of William Wiseman's servants in Colchester Jail who have refused to take the oath or inform on their master. *C.S.P.D.* (1591–1594), 484.

PAGE 109 *damning the book.* The priest was John Mush, and his letter to William Wiseman is printed in *The Archpriest's Controversy*, vol. 1 (Camden Society, *New Series*, 56:53–62). From this letter it is clear that Mush did not know Wiseman. Mush, however, had a fine record of priestly work, and he was rightly sensitive to any suggestion that he and his fellow priests were unequal to their responsibilities. But he was evidently unaware that the Wisemans were great benefactors to all the clergy and had been particularly generous to the priests confined in Wisbeach Jail. There are several captured letters from these priests to Mrs. Wiseman, thanking her for her many gifts to the clergy in this prison. *C.S.P.D.* (1591–94), 484.

PAGE 110 *lay-folk than to religious.* As this book was written on odd scraps of paper and without ink J. G. was not in the best position to reflect on its doctrine. He seems to have satisfied himself with the essential duty of a censor, and assured the author that it contained nothing against faith or morals. As William Wiseman expected that J. G. would be executed, he was anxious to put on record for the sake of himself and his family some summary of his spiritual teaching and have it approved by him before his death. In these circumstances J. G. would not have felt called upon to check the exuberant and extravagant affection shown in a work which was expressly intended for the family and was more in the nature of a father's testimony, for as Garnet points out in a letter to the General dated January 28, 1598, it was "a book which he made in his extremity to his wife". Stonyhurst MSS *Anglia A*, vol. 2, no. 33.

13. THE DEAN'S SYLLOGISM

PAGE 112 Memoriale *by Father Granada.* "The Memorial of a Christian Life" has remained one of the most popular ascetical treatises up to the present time. For beauty of expression combined with solidity of doctrine the author, Louis of Granada, O.P., is probably unsurpassed even among the Spanish ascetical writers.

PAGE 112 *two months later he was dead.* This may have been a gentleman called James Linacre. Watson in his *Quodlibets*, a book written against the Society to which J. G. refers later, says: "He dealt so in like manner with James Linacre, his fellow prisoner in the Clink, from whom he drew there 400 pounds. And afterwards got a promise of him of all his lands; but was prevented thereof by the said Linacre's death." Jessop, 220.

PAGE 113 *Father Coffin*. He was admitted to the English College, Rome, in July 1588, just before J. G. left for England. He arrived in England in 1594, and later he joined the Society. Foley, 6:178.

PAGE 114 *why they were caught*. It seems that the ordinary route was from Gravesend to Dunkirk and was organized by Richard Fulwood. It was probably owing to Fulwood's imprisonment that J. G. was forced to send these boys via Ostend. Fulwood's system is described in a report of the spy Healy to Lord Salisbury (April 1606): "The priests of the country command such youths as they make choice of unto him, who placeth them in some blind alley near the water, until wind serves for passage, which fitting, the vessel (which is some old hoy or such like, to avoid suspicion) goeth down empty towards Gravesend, and he provideth a pair of oars and boats, the passengers and carriage, and so ships them into the bark, commonly beyond Greenwich, and conveys the money which belongs unto them afterwards himself. They ship them to Gravelines or Calais and take forty shillings for the passage." *S.P.D., James I*, vol. 20, no. 47.

PAGE 114 *contracted consumption, and died*. The Latin phrase is *morbus regius*. Consumption is a form of scrofula, or King's evil, and seems to be the disease most likely to be brought on by the causes J. G. describes. However, in classical Latin *morbus regius* would be jaundice, and this may be the meaning here.

PAGE 117n. *Gabriel Goodman, Dean of Westminster, 1561–1601*. He is described as "a sad grave man". He had previously been chaplain to Sir William Cecil and was always on intimate terms with him. J. G. calls him a "good old man". He was nearly seventy at the time J. G. was examined by him and died a few years later, leaving many charitable bequests to the poor and sick. *D.N.B.*, 22:130.

14. THE BLOODY QUESTION

PAGE 122n. *disloyalty to the Crown*. Cardinal Allen made a strong protest against this procedure in his *True, Sincere and Modest Defence* (1584), which answered Burghley's *Execution of Justice in England*. Burghley's attempt to justify this novelty in legal procedure had profoundly disturbed public opinion both at home and on the Continent. *Lives of the English Martyrs*, vol. 1, 2nd series, 19–21.

PAGE 122 *no such mercy in me*. Robert Southwell, executed at Tyburn on February 21, 1594, and Henry Walpole on April 7, at York in the following year, were special victims of Topcliffe, who had them in his hands for several years.

PAGE 123 *Queen's Bench was sitting*. A survey-book of the year 1616 among the Moore MSS at Cambridge, in the course of an account of some of the Topcliffe lands, gives this information about the younger Topcliffe that confirms J. G.'s statement. "He committed a felonie, and was thereof convicted, and in the lifetime of his father had his pardon, and after committed a second felonie, his father livinge, by killing the Sherife of Middlesex in Westminster Hall, and fled; and after that his father dyed, and the son procured a second pardon." *Athenaeum*, October 5, 1878.

PAGE 123 *about to be hanged on his own gibbet.* The comparison of Aman and Mardocheus in the Book of Esther readily occurred to persecuted priests. Cf. Robert Southwell's poem *Scorn Not the Least*:

> *In Amans pompe poore Mardocheus wept;*
> *Yet God did turne his fate upon his foe.*

PAGE 126n. *William Atkinson, who later apostatized.* In 1595 Atkinson told Robert Cecil that he had "lost millions of Catholic friends who maintained me before" and offered his services to murder the Earl of Tyrone. "I could easily poison [him]" he wrote, "through a poisoned host ... and pretending to wish to be a Franciscan friar under Bishop Macraith, who is one, and is daily with Tyrone and his ghostly fathers." (*C.S.P.D.* (1595–1597), 14, no. 49.) Apostate or mad priests were always a great menace to their former brethren. "These naughty priests afflict us much," wrote a Jesuit in December 1606, "for besides Skydmore, the Bishop of Canterbury's man, Rowse, Atkinson, Gravener and other relapsed, which openly profess to betray their brethren, others are no less dangerous which persuade a lawfulness of going to sermons and to service." (Morris, 305.) Atkinson was responsible for the death of at least one priest, Father Thomas Tichbourne, who suffered at Tyburn on April 20, 1602.

PAGE 128 *pull it off me by force.* On February 28, 1594, Benjamin Beard, a prisoner for debt in the Fleet prison, offered to inform on priests in return for his release. In the course of his letter to one of the Council he speaks of "two Jesuits lately arrived, the parties being apparelled in silk, wearing shirts of hair underneath, by which only mark I judge them to be Jesuits". *S.P.D.*, vol. 247, no. 104.

15. TOWER AND TORTURE

PAGE 130 *Greek, and Hebrew characters*. For the fullest account of the inscriptions described by J. G. see Morris, 290–97. There is in J. G.'s cell a simple and rough carving of a large heart pierced by an arrow with the initials "J. G." below. This is noticed as "I. G." among the inscriptions listed in the account of the Salt Tower in the survey of the Royal Commission of Historical Monuments, vol. 4, *East London*, 82. As the first letter is unmistakably a "J" the design may have been carved by Gerard.

PAGE 130 *barely form the letters*. The modern reader can make the same comparison from the two pages of MS reproduced in the *C.R.S.*, vol. 5, 190, 259, in the section devoted to Henry Walpole's letters and examinations. J. G.'s testimony is confirmed by the Jesuit Father Holtby, who was sent some verses written by Walpole while he was awaiting execution in York Jail: "My friend", he says, "hath his own copy in Yorkshire, which is so ill writ (by defect of his thumbs) that he hath very much ado to read it, though I think acquainted with his hand." Jessop, 253.

PAGE 130 *way of Christ's counsels*. This is the poem beginning *Why Do I Use Paper, Pen and Ink*. The stanza lingering in J. G.'s mind was probably the following:

> *We cannot fear a mortal torment, we;*
>   *This martyr's blood hath moistened all our hearts;*
> *Those parted quarters when we chance to see:*
>   *We learn to play the constant Christian's parts.*

> *His head doth speak and heavenly precepts give,*
> *How we the like should frame ourselves to live.*

There are thirty stanzas. The poem is printed in part in L. I. Guiney's *Recusant Poets*, 178–80, and in full in *The Month* (January–February 1872).

PAGE 137 *Her Majesty's Secretary.* Robert Cecil, the second son of Lord Burghley. After considerable delay caused by the rivalry of the Essex faction he had been appointed Secretary of State in the previous year.

PAGE 143 *be it done.* On June 11 Garnet wrote to Father Persons: "We have also lately heard for certain that the Earl of Essex praised his [J. G.'s] constancy, declaring that he could not help honouring and admiring the man. A secretary of the Royal Council denies that the Queen wished to have him executed. To John this will be a great trouble." Stonyhurst MSS, Grene's *Collectanea* P., vol. 2, 548.

16. CLANDESTINE CORRESPONDENCE

PAGE 153 *have me tried and condemned.* As early as May 1595 Charles Paget, an English exile, wrote from Brussels to Thomas Throgmorton at Rome that "executions are out for Fathers Edmondes [William Weston], Walpole, and Gerard, and Mr. Pound".

PAGE 158 *occur to me at the moment.* The reference is to the famous verses of Colossians 2:3, 9. This cavalier touch seems to show that J. G. never expected his artless narrative to fall under the eyes of any but his intimate friends.

PAGE 158 *when I came up for trial.* This document was sent to Doctor Abbot, Master of University College, Oxford, and later Archbishop of Canterbury. He made it the subject of his first lecture in the School of Divinity in the following Michaelmas Term. From this lecture further details of J. G.'s interrogation can be gathered. "At first sight what they [the examiners] had heard appeared damnable and blasphemous", he writes. "They were insistent, therefore, in asking and urgently beseeching that he [J. G.] should write out his view of the matter in his own hand and put it in his own words. Were it to be merely reported, an inaccurate or infelicitous construction might be put on the report. But the Jesuit began to hedge considerably. He had no intention whatever of committing himself to writing—not because what he had said turned out any the less true, but because he was unwilling to broadcast that sort of thing. But the Royal Commissioners pressed him to agree at least to add a note, in writing, to a report of his statement made by witnesses, so that it would be plain that this was in fact his own and his companion's [Southwell's] defense. But he refused to do this either. What nattily sophisticated men they are! They do their best with frivolous restrictions of meaning, or rather with disgraceful and shocking evasions, to bury the truth in a cloud of darkness. 'I did not see' means 'I did not see with the purpose of telling you about it'. 'The Son of Man did not know the Day of Judgement' means that 'He did not know with the purpose of intention of declaring or revealing it'." (Trans. from Latin.)

The amusing encounter between J. G. and Abbot narrated later seems to show that this book never came into J. G.'s hands, though he had heard it described in general terms.

In Strype's *Annals IV* (ed. 1824), 427–29, Coke's letter to Burghley is printed with an extract from the official report which confirms the accuracy of Abbot's statement. Coke refers to "this strange opinion of these boy priests and devilish good Fathers" and states that "he [J. G.] was requested to set down his own opinion therein lest he should be mistaken. But he denied the same; not because it was untrue but because he would not publish it. Then being requested to subscribe the same he denied the same, also."

PAGE 159 *a stricter and more secluded prison.* Much remains to be learned about the recusants in this period, and it is impossible at present to explain the postponement of J. G.'s execution, which was clearly intended at one time. From February 21, 1595, when Father Southwell was martyred, no priest was executed in London until July 12, 1598, when the victim was J. G.'s friend John Jones. Possibly as a result of the popular disapproval at Southwell's execution, the Queen, six weeks later, expressed her "intention to banish the seminary priests that are in divers prisons in the realm" (Acts of the Privy Council, vol. 27, 21). This may be an indication that bloody persecution was being steadily fought to a standstill by the resolute behavior of Catholic priests and laymen.

17. ESCAPE

PAGE 160n. *the Queen's Privy Garden.* John Arden was a Northants gentleman, belonging to a well-known family at Evenley. He had been condemned in 1587 for alleged complicity in the Babington Plot. Northants Record Society, *Finch-Hatton* MSS 124, fol. 32.

PAGE 171n. *At Uxbridge*. Father Tesimond, who landed in England in 1597, says that Father Garnet was living at the time at a house called Morecroftes. "It was about twelve or thirteen miles from London, near a village called Uxbridge, and the name of the house was Morecroftes. I and my companion walked thither, and arrived there an hour or two before sunset. We were received with the warmest welcome and the greatest imaginable charity. I found with Father Henry two or three other Fathers of the Society who had come to confer with him on their affairs. Thus they were accustomed to do, one at one time and another at another." Father Tesimond's Narrative of his landing in England, in *Troubles*, 1:177.

18. LONDON AND HARROWDEN

PAGE 175n. *that any age or nation produced*. In 1596 Alabaster was chaplain to the Earl of Essex's famous expedition to Cadiz. On his conversion to Catholicism in 1597 he wrote *Roxana*, "a tragedy against the Church of England", which is highly praised by Doctor Johnson in his discussion of Latin verse in England. "If we produced", he wrote, "anything worthy of notice before the elegies of Milton, it was perhaps Alabaster's *Roxana*." His conversion caused great concern to the Government, and his own account of it, entitled *Seven Reasons*, was rigorously suppressed. Alabaster was imprisoned several times for his faith. After twice returning to Protestantism and twice again renouncing it, he ended his days as parson of Saint Dunstan's-in-the-West in 1640. His English sonnets are inedited; they number about eighty-five, and run in groups or sequences. They portray some profound spiritual experiences and were written in 1597 while he was in the Clink prison and was conscious (as he himself says) of unwonted inspiration. Of his Latin epic, *Elisaeis*, Edmund Spenser wrote enthusiastically:

> *Nor all the brood of Greece: so highly praised:*
> *Can match that Muse when it with bayes is crowned*
> *And to the pitch of her perfection raised.*

L. I. Guiney, *Recusant Poets*, 335–49, *D.N.B.* i, p. 1:211.

PAGE 176 *for his expenses.* Under the examination on July 22, 1600, William Alabaster confessed that "after Gerard the priest's escape out of the Tower he had conference with him and this examinate received in Brussels thirty pounds by order and credit of Gerard and that from thence he went to Father Persons in Rome". *S.P.D.*, vol. 275, no. 32.

PAGE 178n. *Mr. and Mrs. Heywood. Cf. S.P.D.*, vol. 271, no. 107. Mr. Heywood is noted as a recusant in London in Burghley's list of recusants, 1588. *C.R.S.*, vol. 22, 123.

PAGE 179n. *Lincoln's Inn Fields.* A short time before this the first houses were built on the Fields. Agas' map of London (c. 1591) shows three houses in a position approximating to the present Sardinia Street. Between there and Holborn is another row of three houses on the north side. By 1641 nearly all the south and west sides were covered with houses. William Kent (ed.), *An Encyclopedia of London*, 440–41.

PAGE 179n. *George Blackwell.* One of the most experienced priests on the English mission. He was nominated Archpriest in 1598. As the violent persecution made the appointment of a bishop impossible, in the estimation of both the Roman authorities and the majority of English priests and laymen, the office of Archpriest was created with the object of promoting discipline and organization among the secular clergy. His appointment occasioned the formation of a small faction among the clergy at home and abroad (known as the Appellants), which was to do incalculable damage to the recusant cause. The Government, working through this body, fomented dissension among the recusants for many generations. At the time of the incident recorded by J. G., Blackwell had been out of prison only a few months. In a spy's report of the time he is described as a man "of comely stature, not very low, grey-haired and about the age of fifty-eight or sixty. His beard grey, and in his upper lip a red spot of hair differing in colour from grey. He is lean-faced, a little hollow-eyed, fair and well spoken." *S.P.D.*, vol. 261, no. 97.

PAGE 179 *escape into a hiding-place*. A detailed account of this search is given in *The Lives of Philip Howard, Earl of Arundel and of Anne Dacres, his wife* (ed. 1857), 216. The Countess of Arundel rescued him by bribing the officer in charge of the search, and in gratitude "besides a good sum of money given at that time, she sent him every year as long as he lived a venison pasty to make merry with his friends at Christmas".

PAGE 180 *much more than usual*. About this time Father Garnet, afraid that J. G. might be recaptured and handled more severely than before, thought of sending him back to the Continent. "Father Gerard is much dismayed this day", wrote Father Garnet to Father Persons on March 31, 1598, "when I wrote to him to prepare himself to go. He came to me of purpose. Indeed he is very profitable to me, and his going would be wondered at. I hope he will walk warily enough. . . . You know my mind; if you think it good, I desire his stay. All the rest are well." (Stonyhurst MSS, Grene's *Collectanea P.*, vol. 2, 551.) About eighteen months later, on July 17, 1599, a search was made "for one Jarrett escaped from the Tower" at Ufton Court, Berkshire, the home of a Catholic, Francis Perkins, about six miles from Reading. A. Mary Sharpe, *A History of Ufton Court,* 157–60.

PAGE 181n. *Elizabeth Vaux.* She was the daughter of Sir John Roper, who was raised to the peerage in 1616 as Lord Teynham. In 1590 she married George, the second son of William, Lord Vaux, in whose favor the eldest son, Henry, had renounced his inheritance to the barony. When her father-in-law died she was left in charge of her infant son, Edward, fourth Baron Vaux.

PAGE 183 *to give me Father John Percy.* This was Father John Percy, *alias* Fisher, famous for his controversies with Archbishop Laud. This incident is narrated by Henry More (*Historia Provinciae,* lib. 8, c. 23): "He was sent to Tournay for his noviceship in 1594, and towards the end of the second year over application had so injured his head that he had to be forbidden to use any kind of prayer. Sent to recruit in his native air, he passed through Holland on his way to England. At Flushing he was taken by some English soldiers. As the letter he was carrying showed who he was, they threatened him with torture unless he revealed who had brought him over from Rotterdam. He was ready to confess anything about himself, but he would say nothing of anyone else. They hung him up by the hands to a pulley, and then tortured him by twisting a sailor's cord round his head. During the torture he fixed his mind on the eternity of either pain or joy, and uttered nothing but 'O eternity!'. The harm the soldiers tried to do him turned out a remedy, for the headache and singing in the head, from which he had suffered in the noviceship, diminished from that time and gradually ceased. He was taken to London in custody and committed to Bridewell, where his cell was an utterly unfurnished turret. His bed was the brick floor and a little straw, till he was helped by the care and charity of his Catholic fellow prisoners, and of our Father Gerard. The latter, who was in the Clink, kept up a secret correspondence with him, and came to his help both with his advice and money. After about seven months he succeeded in making his escape through the tiling, together with two other priests and seven laymen."

PAGE 187n. *March 24 and April 1, 1599.* I am grateful to Father Godfrey Anstruther, O.P., for confirming my conjecture that Kirby Hall is the mansion referred to by J. G. and for calling my attention to the two leases of Kirby Hall in the Finch-Hatton collection in the custody of the Northamptonshire Record Society. When the Hatton peerage was created in 1643 the title was taken from Kirby.

19. JOHN THE PRIEST

PAGE 193n. *in July 1599.* A letter written in London on July 22, 1599, helps to date this incident. The writer says: "I wrote to you of one of Mr. Heywood's house searched and a man there taken. I have learnt his name since to be John Lillie. He is sent to the Tower upon suspicion of helping Gerard the Jesuit out of the same place." *S.P.D.*, vol. 271, no. 107.

PAGE 197 *as before he had saved me.* The same incident is narrated by Father Oswald Tesimond, *alias* Greenway, in the Narrative of his landing in England: "To put my recollections of it down briefly. One day the Lieutenant of the Tower, a man of great cruelty towards Catholics, but above measure hostile to our Society, asked him whether he knew Father Garnet's house, which was that of Anne Vaux and her sister, Mrs. Brooksby, and he saying 'No', the Lieutenant said: 'That is right: if you do not know it, we do, and we are so certain about it that we expect soon to have him in our hands. I would never have told you this if I were not sure that you are a close prisoner, and that you cannot possibly let Garnet know or anybody else.' He then named the place and the house, being unable to contain himself for joy at the expectation of his speedy capture." (*Troubles*, 1:179–80.) Father Tesimond goes on to tell of how he himself was saved by a similar warning which J. G.'s friend Father Roger Filcock sent to him from his prison.

PAGE 197 *suffering from consumption*. This statement indicates the date of this narrative. John Lillie left Rome for England on May 15, 1609. J. G., therefore, wrote the above in the second half of that year. Earlier he refers to Drury's martyrdom "two years ago". Drury was executed on February 26, 1607.

PAGE 201 *quiet in that house*. Northamptonshire was strongly Puritan. Their leader was Edmond Snape, curate of Saint Peter's, Northampton, who caused frequent disturbances in the county. Some time before this incident Burghley had visited the county in order to settle the religious disputes. *The Puritans in Northamptonshire*, a tract in the British Museum, *Lansdowne* MSS 64, fol. 51.

PAGE 202n. *Chancellor of the Exchequer*. Sir John Fortescue was the son of Adrian Fortescue, executed under Henry VIII for refusing the oath of supremacy. His son, Sir Francis, was first cousin to Roger Lee, their mothers, Cecily and Amelia, being daughters and co-heiresses of Sir Edmund

Ashfield of Ewelme. (*Visitations of Oxford*, Harleian Society, vol. 5, 168.) What remains of the great Elizabethan mansion at Salden, now a farmhouse, is described in the *Victoria County History of Buckinghamshire*.

PAGE 204 *once they had met him*. During these years Father Anthony Hoskins, *alias* Rivers, wrote a series of important newsletters which show how well posted he was in the news of the day affecting Catholics. With the exception of a few which were intercepted and are now in the Public Records Office, these letters are in the Westminster Archives and are printed in part in Foley, 1:1ff.

20. WITH SIR EVERARD AT CARDS

PAGE 206n. *Sir Everard Digby*. He came from an ancient Rutlandshire family associated with Stoke Dry, a small village on the west side of the road from Kettering to Uppingham. Nothing now remains of his house. In his *Narrative of the Gunpowder Plot*, J. G. says he was "as complete a man in all things that deserved estimation, as one should see in a kingdom". In 1596, when he was only sixteen, he married Mary Mulshaw, then a girl of fifteen, whose father had built the great mansion Gothurst (now Gayhurst) in north Bucks., which still stands as one of the finest examples of late sixteenth-century domestic architecture.

PAGE 206 *Gentlemen Pensioners*. "He confesseth that he was a pencon to Quene Elizabeth about six yeres, and tooke the othe belonging to the place of a penciner and no other." Examination of Sir E. Digby. *C.S.P.D.*, *James I*, Gunpowder Plot Book, part 2, no. 135.

PAGE 207 *match for his sister.* This sister entered the Benedictine convent at Brussels on July 5, 1608. She died in 1659. *C.R.S.*, vol. 14, 180.

PAGE 208 *for he was alive then?* William Mulshaw died in 1602. *Victoria County History of Bucks.*, vol. 4, 346.

PAGE 209 *and still does to this day.* Owing to her husband's part in the Gunpowder Plot, Lady Digby was deprived of the education of her two sons, the future Sir Kenelm and Sir John Digby. She survived for a widowhood of nearly fifty years. Holy Oaks, her husband's house at Stoke Dry, demised by her in 1645, was still under sequestration for her recusancy in 1653, the year of her death. *Victoria County History of Rutland*, vol. 2, 223.

PAGE 209n. *reports to Cecil.* About 1602 Atkinson wrote to Cecil: "It is credibly reported that Mr. John Gerard, Fisher [Father Percy] and Litstar [Father Lister] are to be at a hunting in Beskwood Park, for not long since they were with Mrs. Griffin of Dingley, and they were determined to go to the Lady Markham, Sir Griffin Markham's wife, and likewise Francis Tresham, young Vaux and Mr. Griffin's son and heir was to accompany them." Beskwood Park was a royal hunting-ground, where Sir Griffin Markham was keeper of the lodge. *Hat. Cal.*, 12:229.

PAGE 210 *gives him his due.* In his *Narrative of the Gunpowder Plot*, J. G. wrote a long appraisement of Sir Everard Digby's character. "He was so much and so generally lamented", J. G. concludes, "and is so much esteemed and praised by all sorts in England, both Catholics and others, although neither side do or can approve this last outrageous and exorbitant attempt against our King and country, wherein a man otherwise so worthy, was so unworthily lost and cast away to the great grief of all that knew him and especially of all that loved him." *Narrative*, 90.

PAGE 211 *abandoned by physicians.* A man who corresponds to this description is the famous physician George Turner. He had studied at Cambridge and Padua, and although he was well known as a Catholic he was elected a Member of the College of Physicians on August 12, 1602, on the recommendation of Sir Robert Cecil, who wrote from court at Oatlands to the President declaring that he was unexceptionable except for "his backwardness in religion in which he is in no way tainted for malice or practice against the State, and therefore may receive this favor, seeing he is for his knowledge and practice so well esteemed by diverse noble men and others in this place and her Majesty herself". He died on March 1, 1610. Cooper, *Athen. Cantab.*, vol. 2, 526–27.

PAGE 211 *or spoke to one another.* In the letters which Sir Everard Digby wrote to his wife during his captivity in the Tower there are many messages for J. G., to whom he always refers as "Brother", e.g., "Give my Brother many thanks for his sweet comforts, and assure him that now I desire death". Philip Sidney, *A History of the Gunpowder Plot*, 127.

PAGE 212 *in my defense before the court.* There is no full report of Sir Everard Digby's speech at his trial, but from the letters he sent to his wife there is no doubt about his intention to speak in defense of J. G., e.g., "Whatsoever I could do for him [J. G.] or any of his, I would do it though it cost me never so much; but I have been sparing in that, because I may do more in public which will, I think, be best." Philip Sidney, *A History of the Gunpowder Plot*, 130.

PAGE 212 *with reverence and respect*. J. G. is not here thinking about the personal comfort of the priest. Behind his concise statement is evidently the idea that the success of the missionary effort depended on the heroic co-operation of the laity who were prepared to give priority to the needs of a priest in the arrangement of their household. In this scheme their house was regarded primarily as a base from which the priest could operate. First consideration, therefore, was to be given to the siting of the chapel and the priest's quarters. An elaborate system of hiding-holes had to be arranged throughout the house irrespective of the convenience or the privacy of the occupants. Also, there had to be easy access to the open country in the event of a sudden raid. The laity were also expected to introduce priests into the society of the neighborhood, and altogether it called for their most intimate co-operation with the priestly ministry.

PAGE 213n. *twelve miles east of Oxford*. Agnes Wenman was the daughter of George Fermor, of East Neston, Northants. She was distantly related to the Vaux family, as her grandmother was Maud, daughter of Nicholas, Lord Vaux. She seems to have been an intimate friend of Elizabeth Vaux, and at the time of the Gunpowder Plot both she and her husband, Sir Richard Wenman, were suspected of complicity. Sir Richard was knighted in 1596 for his conduct at Cadiz, and long after J. G. wrote his *Autobiography* he attained his ambition, when he was made a peer of Ireland in 1628 as Baron and Viscount Wenman. Thame Park was an old Cistercian property. In the chapel, built by Robert King, the last Cistercian Abbot of Thame, are the family tombs, and among them lies Father Bernard Stafford (d. June 11, 1788) the last Jesuit to serve as chaplain to the family. Stapleton, *Oxfordshire Missions*, 251.

PAGE 213 *His name was Abbot.* This was George Abbot, later Archbishop of Canterbury. He was the son of a clothmaker of Guildford and had suffered persecution under Mary Tudor for his staunch Protestantism. This might explain why he was "a persecutor of Catholics". "They [recusants] may expect little mercy when the metropolitan is mediator", wrote the Earl of Northampton in 1612 of some Catholic prisoners. At the time of his encounter with J. G. at Thame Park, Abbot was Master of University College and lecturer in Scripture at Oxford. "He was 'stiffly principled' in Puritan doctrines, and his views, cast in a dangerously narrow mould, took from his habitually gloomy and morose temperament a fanatical coloring." (*D.N.B.*, 1:6.) Later he became Dean of Winchester (1599), Bishop of Lichfield (1609), London (1610), and finally, Archbishop of Canterbury (1611). In 1621 he had the misfortune to kill a beater when shooting at a buck with a crossbow in a Hampshire hunt. The canon law declared that a prelate who had committed homicide incurred an "irregularity" and was incapable of exercising jurisdiction; three bishops-elect refused to be consecrated by him, and his "theological question" became, as he said himself, the talk of laymen "to the rejoicing of the papist and the insulting of the puritan". *D.N.B.*, 1:5; David Mathew, *The Jacobean Age*, 111–13.

PAGE 216 *his room to his company.* J. G.'s deep affection for Southwell and Garnet probably put an edge on his remarks. At the time of this conversation Abbot was associated in J. G.'s mind with an attack on Southwell and at the time of writing (1609) with an attack on the memory of Garnet, whom he had described as "a drunken sot". Neither then nor afterward does he seem to have taken the trouble to find out what Abbot had said about him in a lecture given at Oxford in the autumn of 1597 and published the following year. See note to chap. 16, p. 303.

21. FRIENDS AT COURT

PAGE 218 *for the noviceship*. Roger Lee entered the novitiate at Rome on October 27 1600. Foley, 7:446.

PAGE 219 *a free man*. Father Strange entered the Society at Sant'Andrea in 1601, and returning to England two years later he was stationed with J. G. at Harrowden. In a letter of August or September 1606 Father Blount refers to Father Strange's imprisonment: "Thomas Strange remaineth in the Tower, still most resolute and constant, notwithstanding his often racking and torturing, insomuch as his very enemies do highly commend him." (Stonyhurst MSS, *Anglia*, vol. 2, no. 64.) Mrs. Vaux in a letter mentioned by J. G. later in the narrative (238) speaks of Father Strange's property. "His estate", she says, "is and shall be after the death of his mother 800 li. a year, and the very report that he were stayed in this fashion [i.e., arrested] would kill his Mother, whose only child he is." *C.S.P.D.*, *James I*, vol. 16, no. 43.

PAGE 219 *Father Hart*. A native of Kennington, Kent. He studied at Westminster School, at Oxford and London, where J. G. met him. He says himself that his parents were "of the higher class and were able to spend £200 a year". On his admission to the English College on October 31, 1599, he wrote an account of his early career in which he describes his first meeting with J. G. "Mr. Strange", he writes, "promised to acquaint me with Father Garret [J. G.] . . . and presently, so soon as he was named, because I had heard such great fame of his great resolution with which he suffered the torture in the Tower of London, I was inflamed with an earnest desire to see him". And he describes how after "many lets and hindrances before I could see him" he was "greatly comforted through his most sweet counsel". (Foley, 1:169–70.) In 1611 he was seized at Harrowden when the house was raided on a report that J. G. had slipped back to England. He died in South Wales on July 26, 1650, at the age of seventy-three.

PAGE 219 *my hostess' son*. As Elizabeth Vaux had to notify the Council of how her son was being educated, it was a measure of prudence to have a "schismatic" tutor. Smith was succeeded by another schismatic, Tutfield, who later became tutor to Lord Mordaunt's children. *Hat. Cal.*, 17:528.

PAGE 220n. *October 24 the following year*. Cf. Foley, 6:217. Thomas Smith was a native of Staffordshire. He later became a Jesuit and evidently continued his teaching career at Saint Omers.

PAGE 220n. *around recusant houses*. I am indebted to Father Godfrey Anstruther, O.P., for the names of the three boys educated with the baron. They were John Mulshaw, son of Thomas Mulshaw of Finedon, who was five years here before he went abroad and became a Jesuit; John Sweetman, who also became a Jesuit—the son of Elizabeth Vaux's baker; and Henry Killinghall, who, unlike the other two, was not a local boy. He was born in York Jail, where his mother was imprisoned for the faith. He, too, became a priest.

PAGE 221n. *the winter of 1598–1599.* Sir Henry Norris, son of Henry, Baron Norris of Rycot, near Thame was wounded at Finniterston in June 1599 and died after the amputation of his leg. In a discussion of family settlements a Lady Susan Chamberlain mentions that his sister-in-law, Lady Bridget Norris (née Kingsmill and niece of Sir Robert Cecil), the wife of his brother Thomas, is "become a great Catholique and takes great paines to convert her sisters" (*Hat. Cal.,* 8:160). Henry was in England in passage for the Irish war in November 1598 (ibid., 436) and apparently doubtfully enthusiastic for the war. His brothers William (d. 1579), John (d. 1597), and Thomas (d. 1599 about the same time as Henry) were deeply involved in Irish politics and unlikely to have such scruples as J. G. says this knight later experienced.

PAGE 223 *in the Queen's disfavor.* In November 1599 Essex returned from Ireland without leave in order to justify his measures there. He was imprisoned and eventually released. The duel, therefore, would have occurred between his disgrace at the end of 1599 and his execution for high treason on February 25, 1601.

PAGE 224 *Agnus Dei.* See note above on p. 271.

PAGE 225 *as I am told.* Shortly after succeeding his father as fourth Earl of Clanricarde on May 20, 1601, Richard de Burgh distinguished himself at the battle of Kingsale. Later he was created Earl of Saint Albans. His son, the fifth Earl, is described by the historian Lecky (vol. 2, 163) as "a man of the most stainless life and sensitive honor ... at once a sincere Roman Catholic and a devoted servant of the Government". The family remained Catholic until the eighth Earl conformed in or shortly before 1681. *The Complete Peerage,* vol. 3, 230–33.

PAGE 227n. *the fifth Earl.* J. G.'s friend has to be (1) "the son and brother of an earl and himself the heir to an earldom"; (2) the brother-in-law of a knight or married to the sister of a knight whose rank "was below that of a baron"; (3) alive in 1609 when J. G. was writing; (4) in London between 1599 and 1605, in order that J. G. could have met him there.

Francis Manners seems to meet the requirements. After a foreign tour (1598–1600) he was evidently in London in 1600 for he took part in the Essex rising early in 1601. He was the son of John Manners, the fourth Earl of Rutland, who died in 1576, and brother of Roger Manners, the fifth Earl, who married in 1598 Elizabeth, daughter of Sir Philip Sidney and Frances Walsingham. As Roger Manners (d. 1612) had no children, his brother Francis was heir to the earldom. Francis Manners was a Catholic, "he was son and brother to an earl and himself the heir to an earldom". He was, moreover, alive in 1609 and had been in London in 1600–1601.

The only difficulty arises from his marriage. Francis Manners married Frances, daughter of Sir Henry Knyvett of Charlton, Wilts., and widow of Sir William Bevill. As Frances' maiden name was Knyvett, J. G. may have thought that she was the sister, and not, as in fact she was, a connection of Sir Thomas Knyvett who claimed to be *de jure* Lord Berners and might therefore well be the knight whose "rank was below that of a baron". Though Sir Thomas Knyvett obtained from James I the right and title to the barony he died in 1611 (shortly after J. G. wrote) before obtaining confirmation of the grant. It is not known whether he was a Catholic, but he otherwise corresponds with J. G.'s description of his wealth and power. Historical MSS Commission, 12, part 4, *Rutland Papers*, passim.

Another possibility is William Percy (1575–1648), the poet and dramatist. He was the third son of Henry, ninth Earl of

Northumberland, and brother of Henry the tenth Earl, and his heir until the birth of Algernon Percy, later the eleventh Earl, who was baptized on October 13, 1602. In this case the "brother-in-law" would be Sir William Herbert, who married William Percy's sister, Eleanor, and claimed to be the sixteenth feudal Lord of Powis, a title which had fallen into abeyance in 1551. In 1629 Sir William Herbert was created Baron Powis. At the time of the Oates Plot his grandson was imprisoned for the faith, and the house remained staunchly Jacobite.

PAGE 236n. *on April 5, 1611.* Oliver Manners was ordained priest after J. G. wrote his *Autobiography.* When he died in 1618 Bellarmine, who had ordained him, wrote to J. G. "The memory of that excellent Mr. Oliver has brought me no little sadness or rather grief, not on his account, who is now translated from this world to the joys of paradise, but for the sake of many whom without doubt he would have converted to a good life, if divine providence had permitted him to live longer." (Stonyhurst MSS, *Anglia A*, vol. 8, no. 107.) His early death probably saved him from becoming a man of mystery. Well-connected converts, such as Oliver Manners, George Gage, and Toby Mathew, were compelled by the persecution to maintain close secrecy if they became priests. Otherwise they would have to give up all hope of returning to England and serving their countrymen. James I, in fact, made great use of both Toby Mathew and George Gage during the negotiations for the Spanish match. But as these men were on friendly terms with the Jesuits they became the objects of suspicion and hostility in certain Catholic quarters. It was perhaps failure to penetrate their reserve which gave rise to the legend of the lay-Jesuit and the Jesuit in disguise.

22. LAST DAYS OF WORK

PAGE 243n. *second Earl of Huntingdon.* As Henry Hastings' mother was Jocosa, sister of the first Lord Teynham, Henry Hastings was first cousin to Elizabeth Vaux. He afterward became Sir Henry Hastings of Kirby, and then of Braunston. At the time of the Gunpowder Plot he became suspect but was not molested. H. N. Bell, *The Huntingdon Peerage*, 61; *Hat. Cal.*, 18:5.

PAGE 243n. *nine ways at once.* In his book *A Decacordon of Ten Quodlibetical Questions* (1601), William Watson had published the names of a large number of Catholics who were J. G.'s converts or hosts. The harm he did the Catholic cause through this book was immense, but he was probably partly mad. At this time he was busy delating J. G. to Cecil for imaginary political intrigues, and in the following year (1603) he was himself executed for indubitable plotting. On the scaffold he repented and begged pardon for all the harm he had done to his fellow Catholics. *D.N.B.*, 60:42.

PAGE 244 *at Brussels.* This was perhaps Helen Dolman, daughter of Sir Robert Dolman of Pocklington, Yorks., who was professed at Brussels on April 29, 1608. *Register of Benedictine Convent at Brussels, C.R.S.*, vol. 14, 179.

PAGE 245n. *at Valladolid.* Cf. *Diary of the English College*, Foley, 6; *Valladolid Registers, C.R.S.*, vol. 30. Apart from the students at the two colleges account must also be taken of several young men, like Woodward, who were sent to Douai, and others, like the two Wisemans, who entered directly the Jesuit novitiate.

PAGE 245n. *in November 1587*. In his MS of the life of Campion at Stonyhurst, Father Persons speaks of him as "that blessed gentleman and saint, Mr. Henry Vaux, whose life was a rare mirror of religion and holiness unto all that knew him and conversed with him. He died most sweetly and comfortably in England, having resigned long before his death and in his perfect health his inheritance to the Barony to his younger brother, reserving only a small annuity to himself whereby to live in study and prayer all the days of his life." He was the author of a long poem on the Passion of Christ, which is apparently lost.

PAGE 247 *in trust for the Society*. In 1611 there was a rumor that J. G. had returned to England, and in the hope of catching him Salisbury ordered another raid on Harrowden. On the vigil of All Saints, 1611, the walls were scaled at night, and the pursuivants broke into the Fathers' rooms before warning could be given. All the altar furniture, plate, and vestments mentioned by J. G. were seized, along with the two Fathers, Percy and Hart. The inventory of these ornaments made out by the Government confirms the details of J. G.'s description. P.R.O. Transcripts 9, no. 89; Foley, 7:1028.

23. THE POWDER PLOT

PAGE 248 *that we would have to suffer*. In her examination Elizabeth Vaux stated "she heard not of the broils at London till Wednesday [6th November] after the attempt had been done. And then Sir George Fermor and his lady coming thither by accident told her of it." (*C.S.P.D.*, *James I*, vol. 16, no. 88.) Father Strange in his examination (ibid., 19, no. 43) stated that news reached Harrowden on

November 4, but this is clearly a mistake. Catesby and Percy were slain and the two Wrights, Rookwood and Grant, captured at Holbeach House, near Stourbridge, when their party was overtaken there on November 9. If J. G. is referring to this incident, and not to the capture of Fawkes and others in London, he would have received news of it before Harrowden had been invested.

PAGE 249 *four or five days*. The search began on November 12. "I have used all possible expedition for my repair to Mrs. Vaux, her house at Harrowden, whither I came with as much secrecy as could be on Tuesday, the 12th of this instant month, between twelve and one of the clock of the same day." William Tate to Salisbury, November 13, 1606. *C.S.P.D.*, *James I*, 216, no. 92. In his *Narrative* (138) J. G. gives a more detailed account of this search.

PAGE 249 *working in England*. Father Thomas Laithwaite died in England on June 10, 1655, forty-nine years after his admission to the Society. For his examination see Morris, 404–5.

PAGE 251 *grievous than the last*. On February 22, 1604, a proclamation was issued ordering all Jesuits and seminary priests to leave the country before March 19, and the fine of £20 a month for recusancy was again put into force, and made retrospective, so as to cancel any relief that had so far been granted in the new reign. On April 24 a bill was introduced into the Commons re-enacting all the Elizabethan measures against Catholics, with additional penalties for those who sent their children abroad for a Catholic education. A fresh wave of executions began in July the same year. The effect of these laws on the Catholics who entertained priests is referred to in Father Garnet's letter to Persons on October 4 the following year: "if any hostess be not quite undone she speedeth better than many of her neighbors".

PAGE 252n. *January 27, 1606.* Cf. *C.S.P.D., James I*, 19, no. 11. In the same letter Father Garnet gives a vivid description of the conditions in the hiding-place. "After we had been in the hole seven days and seven nights, and some odd hours, every man may well think we were well wearied, and indeed so it was, save that sometimes we could half stretch ourselves, the place being not high enough, and we had our legs so straightened that we could not sitting find place for them, so that we both were in continual pain of our legs, and both our legs, especially mine, were so much swollen, and mine continued so till I came to the Tower. If we had had but one half-day's liberty to come forth, we had eased the place from books and furniture, that having with us a close stool [commode] we could have abidden a quarter of a year. For that all my friends will wonder at, especially in me, that neither of us went to the stoole all the while, though we had means to do *servitii piccoli* whereof also were at a nonplus the day of our taking. We were very merry and content within, and heard the searchers every day most curious over us, which made me indeed think the place would be found. And if I had known in time of the proclamation against me, I would have come forth and offered myself to Mr. Abington, whether he would or no, to have been his prisoner."

PAGE 253 *in such good company.* After serving as cook at the seminary at Douai, Ralph Ashly entered the Society as a Brother and came to England with Father Greenway in March 1598. For eight years he acted as Father Oldcorne's servant and was captured with Nicholas Owen ("Little John") at Hinlip House on January 23, 1606. After severe torture in the Tower he was executed in company with Father Old-corne at Worcester on April 7 the same year. Foley, 4:267ff.

PAGE 253 *break his constancy*. There is no record of Nicholas Owen's parentage, place and date of birth, or entrance into the Society. Probably he was a carpenter or builder by trade and became a Jesuit before 1580. Arrested on January 23, 1606, he was taken to the Marshalsea and then to the Tower. He was hung up with enormous weights attached to his feet until, in J. G.'s words, "his bowels gushed out with his life". J. G., *Narrative of the Gunpowder Plot*. He died on March 2, 1606. Godfrey Anstruther, O.P., "Notes on the English Martyrs", *The Ransomer*, vol. 12, nos. 5, 11.

PAGE 253n. *five consecutive days*. Cf. *Narrative*, 181, 271.

PAGE 253 *saintly martyr's death*. Father Oldcorne and Brother Ralph Ashly were executed at Worcester on April 7, 1606.

PAGE 253 *the calumnies against him*. Garnet was tried at the Guildhall on March 27. The King was present "privately" during the proceedings, which lasted from eight in the morning till seven in the evening. Morris (390) quotes a contemporary report that the King stated that "the Jesuit had not had fair play", but I have been unable to trace the authority for this.

PAGE 254n. *with his life*. This account is from a report written by North, the Spanish Ambassador's Secretary, and is cited by Cornwallis in this letter as an instance of the "trouble" taken "to make Garnet innocent". *Hat. Cal.*, 18:265.

PAGE 255 *Father North*. He is probably Robert Jones, a native of Chirk, Denbighshire, who worked for several years with Father Oldcorne. In a report on recusancy from the Sheriff of Herefordshire to the Privy Council in 1605 his name occurs several times and he is called "the firebrand of all" the priests in that part of the country. Foley, 4:368–92.

PAGE 256n. *of their order*. The Proclamation is listed in the *C.S.P.D.*, *James I* (1603–1610), 280, and is followed by a description of J. G. (see Appendix J), Garnet, and Greenway. This presumably was sent to the post offices throughout the country.

PAGE 256 *it convinced him*. The letter cannot now be traced, but a copy fell into the hands of Father Michael Walpole. "Touching Gerard's letter," he writes (January 29, 1606), "which I have seen, I can only say this much, that it seemed to be so effectual that nothing can be more; so that I am fully persuaded that the King's Majesty himself and the whole Council remain satisfied of him in their own hearts, and his Majesty is reported for certain to have declared so in words upon sight of his letter." Bartoli, *Inghilterra*, lib. 6, c. 6, 510.

PAGE 256 *principal plotters*. Cf. Salisbury's letter to Sir Thomas Edmunds, January 22, 1606. "And although in his Majesty's book there is not any mention made of them [the three Jesuits named in the Proclamation], yet it is but a frivolous inference that thereby the Jesuits seek to serve their turn in excusing of their Order." *Hat. Cal.*, 18:28. It is significant that although Fathers Garnet and Oldcorne were captured on January 27, Salisbury was not officially informed until January 30. As he must have known earlier, it seems probable that he withheld official intimation of their capture until he had eliminated all the witnesses in Garnet's favor, for the conspirators, who were tried on January 27, were hastily executed on January 30 and 31.

PAGE 257 *from the attempt.* No full report of Digby's speech is extant, but from the messages to J. G. contained in the letters which he wrote to his wife there is no doubt about Digby's intention to clear J. G. (see above the note for p. 212 on p. 313). In one of these letters he states that in his examination "before all the Lords, I cleared all the priests in it for anything that I know, but now let me tell you, what a grief it hath been to me to hear that so much condemned which I did believe would have been otherwise thought on by Catholic ... when I heard how Catholics and priests thought of the matter, and that it should be a great sin that should be the cause of my end, it called my conscience in doubt of my very best actions ... only this caused me to wish life till I might meet with a ghostly father". Philip Sidney, *A History of the Gunpowder Plot*, 123–24.

PAGE 257 *still alive.* It is typical of J. G.'s methods that he wrote three letters in order to make sure that his statement of innocence reached the Council. Only two of the three letters are extant, addressed to Lennox and Salisbury, and both dated January 23, 1603. In the first he suggests that "all the principal conspirators ... may be asked at their death, as they will answer at the dreadful tribunal unto which they are going, whether they did impart the matter to me, or I practice the same with them in the least degree, or whether they can say of their knowledge that I did know of it. And I know that it will then appear that no one of them will accuse me, if it be not apparent they do it in hope of life, but do give signs that they die in the fear of God and hope of their salvation." *C.S.P.D., James I*, vol. 18, no. 35.

PAGE 258 *the whole English mission.* It is one of the strongest arguments for J. G.'s innocence that he is not mentioned in any of the twenty-two interrogatories to which Father Garnet was submitted. Nor is there any indication that Garnet, who was very candid in his answers, considered it at all necessary to cover J. G.

PAGE 258n. *appearance in their house. C.S.P.D., James I*, vol. 16, no. 88. The four spies whose offer of services Salisbury accepted are:

1. George Southwicke, a bankrupt ex-Catholic (*Hat. Cal.*, 18:47), who had been watching and reporting the movements of English Jesuits overseas. In a curious letter to Salisbury on November 5, 1605, he asserts that for the *last eight days* he has been riding day and night to discover the plotters (*G. Plot Book*, no. 16) and asks for a warrant to apprehend J. G., which was granted and was renewed on November 19.

2. William Udall, who had been imprisoned at the time of the Watson Plot (1603). In June 1606 he was still confident that J. G. was "about London" and as late as August tells Salisbury he has special information about J. G.'s whereabouts and promises to deliver both him and Greenway shortly *(Hat. Cal.*, 18:173, 181, 242). In July 1608 he stakes his claim to payment for discovering "5 presses for seditious books and a Jesuit". *C.S.P.D., James I* (1603–1610), 449.

3. W.N., whose identity is uncertain. He was living at the *Sign of the White Rose* at Calais, waiting to arrest J. G. on his landing. He was well-informed and apparently got wind of J. G.'s plan for escape (*Hat. Cal.*, 18:103–4). In June 1606 he crossed to England to "spend a few weeks here to see if I can meet Jarret [J. G.], who is still in England, although the common report beyond the seas is that he is on that side, and Father Baldwin [at Saint Omers] told me he had come over". *Hat. Cal.*, 18:84, 103, 176.

4. Lady Markham, perhaps the most dangerous of them all. Her husband had been imprisoned at the time of the Bye Plot (1604) and later exiled. Salisbury accepted her offer to betray J. G. in return for the re-establishment of the family fortunes. In November she was at Harrowden during the search. After looking for J. G. in Northamptonshire she came to London in January, where she "hopes soon to see Gerard". Salisbury gave her a blank warrant for J. G.'s arrest. *C.S.P.D., James I* (1603–1610), 259, 278, 280.

Two other Catholics made offers to Salisbury to catch the "chief Jesuits" but it is uncertain whether he accepted them. The spy called Radcliff seems to have been too well known to Catholics to be of use to the Government (*Hat. Cal.*, 18:41, 43); the other, Alexander Bradshaw, formerly a student for the priesthood at Rome, became deeply involved in attempts to betray J. G. and Greenway, claiming he was particularly suited to the work because "the Jesuits of all men have embraced me", but he was too late in the field. Ibid., 8–9, 18, 382; Westminster Archives, 8, no. 23.

PAGE 258 *no one knew about.* From a reference in Wadsworth's *English Spanish Pilgrim* (1629), 25, this can be identified as the house of Doctor Taylor. In gratitude for this service "he had done for their Society in protecting in his chamber that Jesuit Father Gerat", Father Richard Blount gave his son, Mr. Henry Taylor, an introduction to Count Gondomar, the Spanish Ambassador, which obtained for him the post of Secretary in the London Embassy.

PAGE 259 *used to keep for him.* On April 4, Garnet wrote two letters to Anne Vaux which were intercepted by Wade, Governor of the Tower, and forwarded to Salisbury, and apparently mentioned certain books at the Vaux household at Erith in Kent and at the other house referred to by J. G.

This was the cause of the raid (*Hat. Cal.*, 18:97). In another letter to Anne Vaux on April 21 Garnet states that Erith and "the other house" have been ransacked. *C.S.P.D., James I* (1603–1610), 312.

PAGE 262 *answered all their questions blamelessly.* Elizabeth Vaux was brought to London on November 16. (Postscript of Tate's letter to Salisbury, G. *Plot Book*, no. 21). She reached London on the evening of November 18 and was examined the same night (*Hat. Cal.*, 17:496). For her examination see *C.S.P.D., James I*, vol. 16, no. 88.

PAGE 262n. *in the previous year.* This letter is dated November 12, the fourth day of the search at Harrowden, and was written probably with the help of J. G., when he came out of his hiding-place at night (cf. p. 210). "Your niece Mary", Mrs. Vaux writes, "will rather give you her portion than have him [Father Strange] come in question" (*C.S.P.D., James I*, 216, no. 227). Sir Richard Verney received it on the next day and forwarded it to Salisbury the same evening. *Hat. Cal.*, 17:484.

PAGE 262 *heard her.* "There were also divers of her servants committed to several prisons, and often and strictly examined with many menacings if they would not confess Father Gerard to have been at Lord Vaux his house, but nothing could be wrung out of them." *Narrative*, 141. For their examinations see Morris, 455n.

PAGE 263 *in the city.* The house of Sir John Swinnerton, who had charge of the impost on wines (*Hat. Cal.*, 17:168). In an undated letter addressed to Salisbury and written from this house (ibid., 645) Elizabeth Vaux states that the reason of her detention is "to draw from me the discovery of that

party [J. G.]" and protests that "it is not in my power to
do it, but I pray Jesus will deliver him into your hands if
he be guilty, which I have very strong reasons to make
doubt of".

PAGE 263 Annual Letters. Letters written every year to the
General of the Society in Rome, giving an account of the
principal events in each Jesuit house during the previous
twelve months. Some of the *Annual Letters* to which J. G.
refers are published in Foley, 7:2.

PAGE 264 *and escape.* J. G. crossed in the suite of Marquis of
Saint Germain, the Spanish Ambassador, and Baron Hobach,
the Ambassador of the Netherlands, who landed at Dover
on April 21, 1606, on a short visit to England (*Hat. Cal.*,
18:117). His escape may have been arranged from abroad,
for the spy N. W. seems to have gotten to hear of the plan.
On May 20 Father Baldwin, then at Brussels, wrote to Father
Persons in Rome: "Since my last, five days ago, arrived at
Saint Omers Father Gerard, where also is one Richard Fulwood, whom Father Garnet was wont to use in all his chief
business of passage, receiving and retaining all things. I take
it he be a Jesuit also. They are yet secret and so it is req-
uisite for a time, especially in that the Marquis Ambassador
brought them, and by his dexterous and courteous manner
had great care of them." From another letter of Father Baldwin, dated July 3, it is clear that J. G. was more than "tired".
"Here [Brussels] now is Richard Fulwood, who telleth me
that Father Gerard is very sick at Saint Omers; that said
you would have him come to Rome. I fear that journey
will kill him." Stonyhurst MSS *Anglia A*, vol. 6.

PAGE 264 *until the third of May.* Cf. the letter of Sir Dudley
Carleton to John Chamberlain, May 2, 1606: "It was looked

yesterday that Garnet should have come a-maying to the gallows, which was set up for him in Saint Paul's church-yard on Wednesday, but upon better advice for fear of dis-order among the prentices and others in a day of such misrule." *C.S.P.D., James I*, vol. 21, no. 4.

Appendix A

THE CHRONOLOGY OF GERARD'S EARLY YEARS

The chronology of J. G.'s early career, as it is given in the transcript of his *Autobiography*, is impossible to reconcile with the dates established by other records. It has been assumed, therefore, that J. G.'s memory was at fault, and that while his accuracy in recording the events of his missionary life is almost uncanny, his recollection of his early years is confused.

However, it seems more probable that mistakes were made by the copyist. Two statements in the *Autobiography* suggest this. J. G. says that he was given a dispensation for ordination because he was "a few months short of the canonical age" (i.e., twenty-five). As he was ordained in the summer of 1588, "when the Spanish fleet was approaching England", this would place his birth in the last months of 1564. This agrees with the statement of Father Nathaniel Southwell that he was born on October 4, 1564. And yet if he were nineteen (as the MS reads) when he first went to France, then on his own record of the intervening time he would have been over twenty-five when he *started* his course in Rome. The error is glaring. However, as the MS reads "I was nineteen ... *and still a boy*", there can, I think, be little doubt about an error in transcription, for it is very unlikely that an Elizabethan in his twentieth year would describe himself as "still a boy".

A further reason for thinking that the copyist has made a mistake is an independent statement made by J. G. to which Father Godfrey Anstruther, O.P., has kindly called my attention. In January 1628, nearly twenty years after writing his *Autobiography*, J. G., in a deposition concerning the life of Edmund Campion, says, "I never saw the blessed Father Campion, for I was in France while he was laboring hard in England in the vineyard of Christ." (Westminster Archives 2, no. 39.) This testimony is accurate and shows that in his own mind there was no confusion about the dates of his early life.

As Gerard's original MS appears to have been lost, we have no means of knowing whether he used Roman or Arabic numerals in giving his age or whether he wrote out his age in words. If he used Roman numerals a mistake in transcription is easily explained. In view of his accuracy in all other places where his statements can be checked, it is improbable that J. G. wrote that he was fifteen when he went to Oxford and nineteen when he first left England. I have therefore amended the transcript and substituted for figures there given the figures most probably written by J. G. As reconstructed from records independent of the *Autobiography*, his early career was as follows:

1564   October 4. Born. Nathaniel Southwell, *Catalogus Primorum Patrum*. Stonyhurst MSS.

1575   December. Matriculated at Oxford. A. Clark, *Register of the University of Oxford*, vol. 2, part 2, 63.

1577   August 29. Arrived at Douai. F. T. Knox, *Douai Diaries*, 129. (In March 1578 the College migrated to Rheims.)

1580–1581	Autumn to summer. At Cleremont, Paris.
1581	Autumn. Went to meet Father Persons at Rouen. L. Hicks, *Letters and Memorials of Father Persons*, C.R.S., vol. 39, 42–43.
1582	Spring. Returned to England. (A spy reported that he was at Cleremont in March 1582, *C.S.P. Foreign* [1582], 585.)
1583	March 5. Committed to the Marshalsea. *Prison Lists*, C.R.S., vol. 2, 233.
1584	Easter. Released.
	(Sureties given at intervals 1585–1586. Morris, 23.)
1586	c. end of May. Left England and met Father Holt at Paris. See note for p. 7 on pp. 272–73; L. Hicks, op. cit., 303.
1586	August 5. At English College, Rome. *Pilgrim Book:* Foley, 6:559.
1588	c. July. Ordained.
1588	August 15. Entered the Society and then left for England.

These dates are certain and correspond exactly with the sequence of events in the *Autobiography* and with the periods of time allotted to each. J. G. says he was at Oxford "less than a year", at Rheims "about three years", at Cleremont "one year", when he fell seriously ill, and "about a year" in England before he attempted to return to the Continent. He also says that after his release from prison it was some time before he could free himself from the

obligation to report there at stated times. All these statements are confirmed by the records cited in the table. He
must have been in England, therefore, nearly two years
after his release from the Marshalsea. Presumably it was at
this time—no other time is possible—that he became an
expert at hawking.

The only apparent difficulty comes from his statements about Mr. Lewknor and Father William Sutton. Sutton first came back to England as a priest in July 1577
(F. T. Knox, *Douai Diaries*, 126), just before J. G. crossed
to Douai, and it was some time in the same year, 1577,
that Lewknor resigned his fellowship at Oxford (C. W.
Boase, *Register of the University of Oxford*, vol. 1, 263).
But J. G. does not say that he had Lewknor and Sutton
as tutors after leaving Oxford, but, simply, that they
were tutors living in his father's house. Following the
method he is going to adopt throughout the narrative,
J. G., while talking about Bryn, gathers together all that
he had to say on the subject of his home and records
as a point of interest that these two men lived at Bryn
as tutors under the protection of his father. While
J. G. was at Rheims and Paris, Lewknor, who did not
leave England till May or June 1579 (*Douai Diaries*, 153),
was at Bryn teaching Latin to J. G.'s brother, who as
heir did not go abroad for his education. On J. G.'s
return from Paris in March 1582 Sutton, who had been
on a visit to the Continent, returned to Bryn in company
with J. G. and there taught him and his brother Greek (*Catalogus Primorum Patrum*). It is, of course, possible that J. G.
had Lewknor to teach him for a year at Bryn before going
to Rheims if, like some other Fellows of Oxford Colleges,
Lewknor left the University sometime before resigning his
Fellowship.

Appendix B

FATHER GARNET'S COUNTRY RESIDENCE

Father Garnet's headquarters in the country cannot be identified with complete certainty. John Gerard says it was in Warwickshire about a hundred miles from London. Alan Fea (*Rooms of Mystery and Romance*) claims that it was Coughton Court, rather more than a hundred miles, but Granville Squiers (*Secret Hiding-Places*, 28–34) argues (I think conclusively) for Baddesley Clinton, a beautiful and perfectly preserved mansion just ninety-nine miles from London. It is secluded and difficult to find, and this would account for difficulty of the Government spy in describing the exact position of the house (*S.P.D.*, vol. 229, no. 78). It is eighteen miles from Hinlip Hall, the residence of Father Oldcorne in Worcestershire, which Gerard says was "not far off"; and the tradition that Guy Fawkes lived there could easily be explained by the confusion of the names Vaux and Fawkes, for Garnet's country home was with the two Vaux sisters. On investigating the hiding-places at both places, Squiers discovered that those at Baddesley Clinton corresponded exactly with the description given by Gerard. In the base of the west wing at Baddesley there is a tunnel running its entire length. Originally the house sewer, it was converted into a hiding-place (probably) by Nicholas Owen, who diverted the sewage by building on a garderobe turret projecting from the walls. The main entrance was down a shaft from the sacristy, and there was another entrance from the priest's room. Near the exit of the tunnel was a heavy stone slab, fitted into vertical grooves in the walls, and round the slab water would have seeped into the tunnel from the moat. Gerard says he was standing up to his ankles in water. Squiers (33) quotes the accounts of other priests in hiding with Gerard and shows that they fit in exactly with the construction of the hiding-place at Baddesley Clinton.

Appendix C

SAINT WINEFRID'S WELL

Holywell, as a place of pilgrimage, has an unbroken history from pre-Reformation days to the present time. In the sixteenth and seventeenth centuries the Government seemed unable to check the flow of pilgrims. Writing in 1624 the informer Gee reported that "every year about midsummer many superstitious Papists of Lancashire, Staffordshire and other more remote places go in pilgrimage, expecially [*sic*] those of the feminine and softer sex, who keep there their rendezvous, meeting with divers priests, their acquaintance, who make it their chief synod or convention for consultation and promoting the Catholic cause, as they call it.... Let me add that they were so bold, about midsummer last year (1623) that they intruded themselves divers times into the church or public chapel at Holywell and there said Mass without contradiction. It is not unlike they will easily presume to the same liberty here in England." (John Gee, *Foot out of the Snare*, in Somer's Collection of Tracts, vol. 3, 64–65.)

Gee's account is confirmed by an official report to the Council dated October 28, 1626, from the Mayor of Poole, Montgomery (*S.P.D., Charles I*, vol. 38, no. 73): "According to your Lordships' commandment ... I have taken the best course I could for restraint of the resort of persons ill-affected in religion to Saint Winefrid's well in Flintshire, both by binding the lodgers or strangers there to discover the names of their guests to the next Justices of the Peace, and by a watch there kept, which course ... has taken such good effect, that where heretofore there was for all the summer time usual resort thither of people in troops both men and women, many of them being of note, by way of pilgrimage ... there hath not been any such repairs thither this last summer."

However, the same measures to stop pilgrimages were repeated ten years later (cf. *S.P.D.*, *Charles I* [1636], vol. ccvlxi, no. 25). In 1629 the names of notable persons who visited the well on Saint Winefrid's day were sent to the Council (ibid., vol. 151, no. 13); the list includes Lord William Howard, Lord Shrewsbury, Sir Thomas Gerard, Mr. Blundell of Crosby, Sir John Talbot of Bashaw, Lady Falkland, etc., "with divers other knights, ladies, gentlemen and gentlewomen of divers counties to the number of fourteen or fifteen hundred; and the general estimation about a hundred and fifty or more priests, the most of them well known what they were".

The record of some of the miracles that occurred at Saint Winefrid's well can be read in Foley, 4:536–37.

Appendix D

BRADDOCKS

Braddocks is now a farmhouse. Two-thirds of the original mansion which stood in a fine deer park has been pulled down, but the remaining portion, the right wing of the old house, contains the hiding-place which Gerard describes. In the chapel Nicholas Owen removed the tiles from the fireplace and constructed a false hearth. "Beneath this", writes Granville Squiers (*Secret Hiding-Places*, ch. 23), "he burrowed downwards into the solid brickwork. The place he made adjoins the large living-room below and is located high up and slightly to the side of the Renaissance fireplace. It was separated from this room only by the lath and plaster covered with a panelled wainscot."

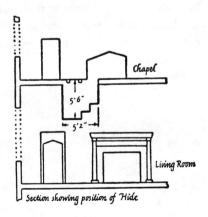

Section showing position of Hide

The big living-room is much altered and restored; the stone fireplace, however, is still there, though the heavy overmantel has gone. "The chapel above", continues Mr. Squiers, "is unfurnished, but in good condition. When I saw it first the Tudor arch of the fireplace had been blocked up for longer than the oldest inhabitant could remember, but when we broke into it the chimney was piled high with generations of birds' nests. Beneath this we found the hearth had been solidly replaced. It took two or three days to get it uncovered, but we were finally rewarded by being able to examine the hole, the brickwork of which looked as fresh as if Nicholas Owen had quarried it out only the week before.... Searching carefully beneath the considerable debris of the bottom of the hide I discovered a few tiny fragments of wood ash, which I believe to be some of those which rained upon the unfortunate Gerard in the last awful night of search. When the remains of the false hearth were removed the few ashes below would have passed unnoticed, and since the story was apparently not brought to light until long after the hide had been closed again these fragments should be authentic.... It will be remembered that Mrs. Wiseman thrust a small pot of quince jelly in Gerard's hands as he went into the hiding-place and it is interesting to note that an old quince tree still stands in the garden."

Appendix E

FATHER SOUTHWELL'S DEFENSE
OF EQUIVOCATION

A contemporary account of Father Southwell's defense of equivocation is printed in Janelle's *Robert Southwell*, 81–82.

"The Attorney [Sir Edward Coke] ... particularly accused Mr. Southwell of a dangerous point of most wicked and horrible doctrine, saying that he did teach a gentlewoman that if she were examined whether Robert Southwell were at her father's house, she might swear no, with the intention to herself not to tell them of it. For proof thereof they brought forth Anne the said daughter of Mr. Bellamy. She being sworn said that he had told her that if upon her oath she were asked whether she had seen a priest or not she might lawfully say no, though she had seen one, keeping this meaning in her mind that she did not see any with intent to betray him.

"Mr. Southwell answered that that which he had said in such manner as he spake it (if they would give him leave to interpret his own meaning) he would prove was agreeable to the Word of God, to the laws both canon and civil, and was not his own opinion only, but the opinion of the Doctors and Fathers of the Church, and according to the policies and proceedings of all ages, and in all Christian nations; and that if they should not admit that, they should take away the government of all states, both ecclesiastical and temporal, yea, and the secrecy of man; and that without it, neither this state, nor any other state, government or policy could possibly stand. And then going about to show what he said, and to prove it, they continually interrupted him, exclaiming still of the barbarous doctrine, seeking to persuade the people that they [the Jesuits] taught that it was lawful to commit wilful perjury; wherewith he began to be somewhat earnest in expelling so horrible a crime, and told Mr. Attorney that he must confess as much, 'or else I will prove you no good subject nor friend of the Queen.' 'Yea,' saith Mr. Attorney, 'let me hear that.' 'Suppose,' saith Mr. Southwell, 'that the French King should invade Her Majesty, and that she (which God defend) should by her enemies be enforced to fly to some private house for her safety, where none knew her being but Mr. Attorney; and that Mr. Attorney's refusal to swear, being hereunto urged, should be a confession of her being in the house (for I suppose that also); if Mr. Attorney in this case should be examined and should refuse to swear that he knoweth that Her Majesty is not there, with this intention, not to tell them: I say, Mr. Attorney were neither Her Majesty's good subject nor friend.'

"The Chief Justice said he should refuse to swear. Mr. Southwell answered, that were by silence to betray his sovereign. The Attorney said that the case was not like, and being moved in choler did often call Mr. Southwell boy-priest, and told him that he had not read the Doctors. 'I have read those that have read them, and you, Mr. Attorney, in the study of your laws, do not presently go to the grounds and principles of the law, but take other men's reports.' 'Ay,' saith the Attorney, 'you have studied Doctor Allen, Doctor Parsons, Doctor Hold, Doctor Traytor, etc.' 'Then', said the Lord Chief Justice, 'if this doctrine should be allowed, it would supplant all Justice, for we are men, and no Gods, and can judge but according to their outward actions and speeches, and not according to their secret and inward intentions.' Mr. Southwell said that in this case, two things are to be presupposed, that the refusing to swear is a confessing the thing, and that the oath be ministered by such as have no lawful authority, and that every oath ought to contain judgement, justice and truth, and that no man is bound to answer every man that asketh him, unless he were a competent judge; and here gave an instance of a thief urging a true man to swear by the highway; and as he was going forward to explain his meaning, he was continually interrupted, so as they would be no means permit him to say any more. Then he desired them to bear with him, saying they would not suffer him to prove what he had said, always denying that even if he had said any such thing, in such sort, as they objected. Here again Topcliffe began to be earnest in most railing manner, as is always usual with him ... but he was soon willed to surcease. And something concerning the indictment only being said to the jury, they were sent into a house apart, to consult of their verdict."

Appendix F

FATHER GARNET'S KNOWLEDGE OF THE GUNPOWDER PLOT

Garnet was examined twenty-two times concerning his knowledge of the Gunpowder Plot before any matter for an indictment could be found. Eventually the Government laid a snare in which he was successfully trapped.

Garnet's jailer, feigning friendship, offered to show him a way in which he might converse secretly with Father Oldcorne through a cleft in the wall of his fellow-prisoner's cell. However, as J. G. says in his *Narrative*, the place was "purposely so contrived as that the sound of their words must needs be carried to another place, not far off, where this keeper would stand and some other with him, to have a double witness in their double hearing". After the two priests had heard each other's confession, Oldcorne asked Garnet how he had fared in his examinations, and Garnet in his reply was overheard to say, "No man living can touch me in that matter [the plot] but one". As J. G. continues, "This was the word that afterwards bred him so much trouble."

When the conversation was reported to the Government, Garnet was examined under torture; and in order to save his fellow-priests and other friends from further persecution—for he saw that the Government was determined to discover the person who could incriminate him—Garnet, when he was taken down, decided "to deal plainly with them in all things", and, in justice to his fellow-Catholics, to make a straightforward statement of all he knew and suffer the consequences. Garnet therefore revealed that the man was Greenway (then safe on the Continent), and admitted that he himself had both "simple knowledge" of the conspiracy and a fuller and more precise knowledge "in so secret a manner that it was never lawful for me to utter it, being in confession".

By "simple knowledge" Garnet meant that he had been aware that Catesby and his friends were planning some kind of disturbance, for, as he was acquainted with them, he could not help observing their restlessness in the summer of 1605. After he had formed these vague fears—for they were no more than this—Garnet had been told of the plot, four months before it broke, under the seal of confession. In July 1605, Catesby had spoken of it to Father Greenway in confession; and Father Greenway, failing to dissuade his penitent from the enterprise, asked Catesby's permission to mention the matter to his Superior, Father Garnet, under the seal of the sacrament. He hoped that if Catesby knew that Father Garnet also condemned the plot there might be some chance that it would be abandoned. At the same time Father Greenway sought and obtained Catesby's leave for both himself and Father Garnet to reveal what he had told them in confession about the plot to save themselves from torture, "but not in any other case."

In this dilemma Father Garnet acted in the manner any prudent priest would have acted. He said nothing. His vague fear that something was afoot was both prior to and quite independent of anything he knew in the confessional, and theoretically he was free to report this fear to the Government. But in practice no priest, either then or now, with knowledge of a thing in two distinct ways, viz., under the most inviolable secrecy and from his own observation, would venture to use his "simple knowledge" at the risk of seeming to violate the sacramental seal. And in any case all that Garnet knew from his "simple knowledge" was (as he was well aware) already known to the Government. Since the beginning of the new reign Catholics had been restive. For at least two years before the plot Garnet had done all he could to hold men like Catesby in check on the grounds that armed resistance of any kind would be disastrous to the Catholic body; and at the same time in his letters to Rome he had done his utmost to get papal support for his counsels of patience. Indeed Garnet did secure from Rome condemnation of violent action, and showed the Pope's letter to Catesby. In fact he did all that was possible, without endangering the secrecy of the confessional, to stop any foolhardy attempt at a *coup*.

S. R. Gardiner, however, severely censures Garnet's conduct after the plot had been disclosed to him in confession. "There was all the more reason [now]", he writes (*What Gunpowder Plot Was*, 193), "why he [Garnet] should take every opportunity that occurred to him to learn the secret out of confession, and so to do his utmost to prevent the atrocious design from being carried into execution." But after Garnet had learnt of the plot in the confessional he was tied. Catesby was not his penitent and in no circumstances could he bring the subject up in conversation with Catesby himself, either in or out of the confessional, much less could he seek him out, as Gardiner suggests that he should have done, and remonstrated with him more vehemently than he had done before. It is a violation of the seal for a priest to act in any way whatsoever that betrays the knowledge he has gained in the confessional, whether this knowledge be used to reinforce a protest based on "simple knowledge" or as an incentive to discover the thing known in the confessional from non-confessional sources.

Garnet, however, was too modest a man to claim that he acted the part of the prudent priest to the extent of being beyond all possible criticism, and he was too humble a man to claim that he was placed in the position of a martyr. Instead, he submitted his dilemma to the court and left God to judge whether or not he had acted rightly.

Appendix G

FATHER GARNET'S STRAW

Foley (4:129–31) transcribes from a paper in the British Museum (Papers relating to the English Jesuits, Add. MSS 21, 203 *Plut.*, 152, F.) *A relation of the figure which appeareth in the ear of a straw in the chaff or husk thereof.*

"After that Father Henry Garnet, Superior of the Society of Jesus in England, was executed by commandment of James now King of that realm, the third day of May, being the feast of the Invention of the Cross, in the year 1606, his head appeared in that lively colour as it seemed to retain the same hue and shew of life which it had before it was cut off, so as both heretics and Catholics were astonished thereat, and so much the more, in that according to custom being cast into hot water it received no alteration at all; as neither it did after it was placed upon London Bridge, and set up there upon a pole. Whereupon there was such resort of people for the space of six weeks as that was admirable, the citizens flocking thither by hundreds to see so strange and wonderful a spectacle, as the head of this glorious martyr did exhibit, whose face continued without any change, retaining a graceful and lively countenance, and never waxed black, as usually all heads cut from the bodies do. Whereupon the magistrates of the city, and Council confounded with the miracle, and displeased with the continual resort of people to behold the unexpected event, gave order that the head should be put so as the face should be turned upwards, and the people thereby not able to view the face as they had been accustomed. There have been so many to see it at once sometimes, what from the bridge, what from places near thereunto, as from the water and houses, as divers there present have thought them to have been to the number of 400 or 500 persons.

"When, as his face was thus turned, he then appeared miraculously in the ear of corn which was stained with his blood and taken up by one who purposely came to the place where he was executed, intending to dip some handkerchief and other linen in his blood, and to that end hastened to the place, and placed himself as near the scaffold as he could, and feigned at the time of quartering this glorious martyr to be forced by reason of the throng of people pressing to see, to put himself under the scaffold, where he received the blood which streamed down through the chinks of the boards, upon his hat and apparel, and dipped such linen as he had prepared in the same. The multitude withdrawing themselves (the martyr being quartered) he came forth amongst them, and standing by the side of the scaffold, he saw the hangman cast the quarters into a great basket near the same side, upon one of which the ear stood, and when he threw the quarter in, the straw flew off and fell into his bosom, which he took and kept, for that he saw it was sprinkled with blood, and afterwards presented it to a Catholic woman, a tailor's wife in London, who placed it in her reliquary, with other relics, turning the ear in form of a ring round. This woman retained it devoutly until upon occasion of speech of this martyr, she began to tell him with whom she spake, that she had some of his blood upon an ear of corn; he requested to see it, and she delivering him her reliquary wherein it was, he viewed it, and through the crystals discovered the face of a man, whereat stricken with admiration he acquainted the woman with what he saw; all of which happened in his presence that took up the straw first, and so those three persons saw distinctly a face of a man in glorious manner, having with all proportion most exactly beard, mouth, eyes, forehead, and upon his head a crown, a cross in the forehead and a star, and in the lower part of his face, as the chin of a cherub. This admirable thing they shewed to some other friends, and so by degrees the report was spread throughout the whole city, and that time chiefly when as the Lord of Northampton had divulged the contents of a speech of his which he had against the Pope, Jesuits, and particularly Father Garnet at his arraignment. The miracle being divulged and hundreds having seen it, many in merriment said: 'A straw for my Lord of Northampton's book.' And to make the thing more public which God had so admirably wrought, the matter was so handled that even the heretics themselves should be eye-witnesses of this wonder, so that in the Spanish Ambassador's and others' hands, many, yea, and those also of the Council of the King, might see it. To the Spanish Ambassador's house for many days there was such public resort of nobility and gentlemen, not only Catholics, but also schismatics and heretics to view it, that there wanted not those which continually entered for that purpose, and having seen it departed so confounded, edified, and comforted therewith, as with one accord they acknowledged it to be supernatural. And for more confusion of the enemies of the Catholic Church, sundry heretical painters being sent for and demanded whether they could by their art express the like face, they denied it to be possible. The face appeareth little one way, and turned another way, or removed farther off, much greater, and always in that perfection and glory, as it worketh that effect in the earnest beholders as the sun doth in those that fix their eyes upon his brightness, and with all the whole ear hath the natural colour, that only part where the face is, being brighter, and the face in the ear of husks wherein the corn grew as it were incised (?), although all proportions be made with his own blood: all which cannot be expressed by any art, tongue, or pen as the thing is in itself.

"The heretics, especially bishops and ministers, do attribute this work of God to witchcraft, or to some special water, or such like secret invention; and for that they know the wonder thereof was divulged over all the realm, they have caused divers inventions to be made to express the face, nothing at all like the true representation, to the end to take away or at least obscure the worth of the miracle. The Bishop also of Canterbury hath laboured with painters purposely to practice the imitation, which such as have seen it refused, for that they knew it was impossible for them to represent by any art of theirs."

[Then the writer goes on to describe the incident concerning Father Oldcorne which John Gerard relates on p. 253.]

"There have other wonders happened by which it seemeth that God would manifest the glory of this holy saint, and of his companion, Father Edward Oldcorne, priest, also of the Society of Jesus, condemned to death about the same time the other was, and executed in Worcester in the marches of Wales. Before the house in which they were apprehended, there grew a crown in the grass a foot and a half resembling a sea rush, and the crown formed a most perfect figure or fashion, and very green, to the great admiration of all such as came to see it, who were many, and so much the more that no beast eating the grass near could ever touch that part where the crown grew. Also when Father Oldcorne's bowels were cast into the fire, with those of two others executed with him, the fire continued for fourteen days together to the astonishment of all, so as huge numbers came to see it; and although there fell sometimes in this space as great rain as usually hath been seen, yet was not the fire quenched but continued burning as it did the first day and hour it was kindled, until such time as by public order the sticks and bands were scattered and cast the one from the other, which was the fourteenth day after the execution."

Appendix H

FATHER GERARD'S LIFE AFTER HIS ESCAPE FROM ENGLAND

Father Gerard crossed to Belgium on May 3, 1606, in company with the Ambassadors of Spain and Flanders. After six weeks at Saint Omers he went on to Tivoli for a rest. Early in 1607 he was appointed English Penitentiary at Saint Peter's, and two years later was sent to Flanders to help in the foundation of the first novitiate of the English Province at Louvain. In 1614 a Jesuit house of philosophy and theology was established at Liége and Father Gerard became its first Rector. "He built it from the foundations in a fine style with alms collected from all quarters." (Nathaniel Southwell, *Catalogus Primorum Patrum*, 32.) In 1622 he visited Rome to get papal support for the new Institute of Religious Women founded by Mary Ward; and on his return to Belgium he was made Rector of the house of the English Jesuits at Ghent, where the newly ordained priests made their "third year" of probation under his direction. From 1627 to 1637, the last ten years of his life, he was confessor to the English College at Rome. He died there at the age of seventy-three on July 27, 1637.

Appendix I

CONTEMPORARY DESCRIPTIONS
OF FATHER GERARD

There are three contemporary descriptions of John Gerard's appearance. The earliest is Topcliffe's and was drawn up some time after J. G.'s escape from the Tower. It runs thus in his own abominable spelling:

"Jhon Gerrarde ye Jhezewt is about 30 years oulde Of a good stature sumwhat higher then Sr Tho Layton and upright in his paysse and countenance, sum what stayring in his look or Eyes, Currilde heire by Nature & blackyshe & apt not to have much heire of his bearde. I thincke his noase sum what wide and turning Upp, Blubarde Lipps turnings outward, Especially the over Lipps most Uppwards towards the Noase Kewryoos in speetche If he do now contynewe his custome And in his speetche he flourrethe & smyles much and a falteringe or Lispinge, or doublinge of his Tonge in his speeche." [1]

The second is from the spy William Byrd and is addressed to Robert Cecil, August 27, 1601. "Gerard's discovery may the better be, by observing this description of him and his habit. To be of stature tall, high shouldered, especially when his cope is on his back, black haired, and of complexion swarth, hawk nosed, high templed, and for the most part attired costly and defencibly in buff leather garnished with gold or silver lace, satin doublet, and velvet hose of all colours

[1] *S.P.D.*, vol. 165, no. 21.

with clocks corresponding, and rapiers and daggers gilt or silvered." [2]

The third was circulated at the time of the Gunpowder Plot: "John Gerard, *alias* Brooke, of stature tall, and according thereunto well set; his complexion swart or blackish: his face large; his cheeks sticking out, and somewhat hollow underneath the cheeks; the hair of his head long, if it be not cut off; his beard close, saving little mustachoes, and a little tuft under his lower lip; about forty years old." [3]

[2] *Hat. Cal.*, 11:365.
[3] *P.R.O.* Proclamation Book, 121.

INDEX